STRATEGIC PLANNING AND MANAGEMENT IN PUBLIC ORGANIZATIONS

Behavior in Organizations

Meshack M. Sagini

University Press of America,® Inc.
Lanham · Boulder · New York · Toronto · Plymouth, UK

Copyright © 2007 by
University Press of America,® Inc.
4501 Forbes Boulevard
Suite 200
Lanham, Maryland 20706
UPA Acquisitions Department (301) 459-3366

Estover Road
Plymouth PL6 7PY
United Kingdom

Library of Congress Control Number: 2005927675
ISBN-13: 978-0-7618-3239-3 (paperback : alk. paper)
ISBN-10: 0-7618-3239-4 (paperback : alk. paper)

Dedication

I unreservedly dedicate this scholarly work to my wife, Rachael Nyabate and my children – Paul Mairura, Dennis Onkoba, Eileen Moraa, and Kathy Bosibori. I also thank them wholeheartedly for their love, patience, and support during my many, long and lonely hours away from them, my intentional and frustrating disregard for attending to their needs, and for providing me with the warmth and strong family ties which were a source of strength for my literary accomplishments. I also thank Rachael for supporting me financially in order to complete this study, which originally was my doctoral dissertation at Michigan State University.

Contents

List of Figures

List of Tables

Preface

This empirical and theoretical research sought to establish the extent to which planning techniques, planning participants, planning parameters, and planning products were used by planners to make decisions concerning effective allocation of resources at four community colleges in Michigan. The researcher used the strategic planning theory of management in the light of organizational theory and the rational planning model. The research viewed planning to include leading, directing, evaluating, controlling, budgeting, decision-making and programming. It was intended that data would be collected and analyzed to judge not only the relationship between means and ends, but also how this relationship brought to bear on major environmental trends which influenced decision making approaches that determine the direction of each institution and vision of its leadership.

Data were collected on the basis of informed opinion, interviewing and tape recording. It was analyzed with the use of non-parametric statistics and interpretive commentary. Having been a product of data analyses and interpretation, the findings of the study addressed planning and management concerns in the areas of demographics, formal planning, strategic planning, decision-making, and the degree of success or failure of goal implementation. One paramount finding was based on the understanding that urban institutions used different planning models as compared to those used by rural institutions.

In conclusion, and for the purpose of maintaining anonymity, the colleges were categorized as A, B, C, and D. Based on the analysis, it was evidently clear that the rational model was perceived as a good planning technique by planners of college D only. The planners of college A, B, and C used the consensus or democratic approach in decision-making. Overall, this experiment on the implementation and evaluation of institutional policy showed that planners who neither used the rational nor the consensus did not decisively use other planning models (anarchy, compromise, bureaucratic, and political). This behavior was displayed based on the understanding that organizations are structural institutions that are politically, consciously, and superstitiously engineered as they evolve and revolve on their socially, naturally, and ecologically constructed cultural orbits. Their orbital behavior has become the niche of management scholars who specialize in their analysis for the purpose of constructing and reconstructing their empirical viability. Policy makers who rationalize their raison detre, form the community which they ritualistically and politically inspire, empower and change. Graduate students, scholars, policy makers, and the intelligentsia searching for planning models will find this book to be theoretically and conceptually enriching and excellent, particularly in implementation evaluation as a major element of effective managerial behavior.

The book has five chapters. Chapter 1 deals with colleges as organizations that are structured to function through a variety of processes for which the problem and purpose of the study were investigatively designed. Chapter 2 concerns the review of the literature. Chapter 3 is about the methodology and instrumentation. Chapter 4 presents the data analysis. Finally, Chapter 5 is a conclusion that comprises the summary, implications, recommendations and an interpretive commentary.

Meshack M. Sagini, Ph.D.
Oklahoma City, Oklahoma
Spring 2004

Acknowledgements

A dissertation is a product of immense personal indebtedness. This one could not have been produced and published without differential and genuine support and encouragement from: Bernard Lall, Sage Foundation, Kabede Daka, Denford Musvovsi, D. Chongo Mundende, Mogaka Mogambi, Patrick Wavomba, James Obegi, Mona Lisa, Stephen Bina, Ando Johnson, Norwegian Publishing House, Anthony LaPena, Marinus Swets, Pat Oldt, Dick Bezile, Patricia Pulliam, Till Peters, Richard Calkins, Cornelius Eringaard, Darrel Welles, Jean Calvert, Robert Deaver, Sharon Heydlauf, Clyde LaTarte, Robert Carlton, Allaire George, Lee Howser, David Ingall, Ray Moore, Wallace Ollika, Michael Walreven, Paul Wreford, Daniel Blitz, Jean K. Christensen, Anne C. Erdman, Patricia Hall, Inja Kim, Greg Koroch, David Mayick, Anne E. Mulder, Milton Richter, Robert VanArkel, Michael Walsh, William Weirick, Rachel Sagini, Paul Sagini, Jim Lantz, John Carlson, Sally Mathiesen, March Forist, Dan Hrmon, Jesse Fox, Dennis Mulder, Lon Hulton, Richard Conrath, Dr. Burns, Samuel Harris, Douglas Campbell, Kenneth Neff, Harry T. McKinney, Peggy Riethmiller, Kennedy Harding, Philip Cusick, James Costar, and Bouldor Pfeiffer. In addition, special thanks goes to Professor Howard Hickey, my mentor at Michigan State University.

Introduction

Professor Sagini's book is an interesting and original contribution to the vast literature on strategic planning and management in the public sector. What is especially noteworthy is the book's topical focus on community colleges, important public institutions that deserve close scientific investigation.

Strategic Planning and Management in Public Organizations is a complete, revised, expanded and updated version of the author's doctoral dissertation on comparative perceptions of planning in four community colleges in the state of Michigan in the United States of America. One obvious strength of the volume for the intelligent lay person, as well as the scholar unfamiliar or new to the subject, is the author's literature review that pays some needed attention to the history, evolution and the crucial role played by community colleges across the country in the American system of higher education. The case study of four Michigan community colleges presents a rare detailed analysis of the character and structural dynamics of community colleges. What is more to this readable work forms part of an expanding body of new scholarship on policy, management and operation of post-secondary public higher educational institutions. The book assumes correctly that an objective understanding of the issues of strategic planning and management of formal organizations in the public sector that focuses on the perceptions of key actors, requires the integration of the theoretical and methodological insights of the disciplines of sociology, psychology, economics, education and anthropology, privileging the rational actor model.

Too often policy and management issues are analyzed as if the areas of sociology or economics can be isolated from one another. The multidisciplinary orientation of Professor Sagini's book is thus commendable, and should provide a model for similar studies. The book's analytical interest in community colleges also has clear implications for the special contribution community collages across the United States can make toward sustainable, long term economic development both at the state (Michigan) and national levels.

It is worth mentioning in this respect that both President Bush (Republican) – in his second term State of the Union address to the U.S. Congress – and Governor Jennifer Granholm (Democrat) of Michigan – in her third annual State of the State address before the Michigan State Legislature – paid some well-deserved attention to the urgent need to strengthen and improve both the quality and quantity of the products of American higher education noting the vital and strategic role community and four-year colleges can play in the growth and prosperity of the American economy.

In her address Governor Granholm stressed the importance of a well-trained workforce in fostering renewed economic growth. She observed that in order to attract high technology driven enterprises that offer high paying and secure jobs, the State of Michigan must ensure that a large proportion of its high school graduates attend at least two-year community colleges or some other form of post-secondary education. She made it clear that a high school diploma was no longer enough for the skills required of Michigan residents for the 21st century economy (see the Editorial, *The Michigan Daily,* Wednesday, February 9, 2005: 4).

The new pressure likely to be put on community colleges, not only to double or triple enrollments but to improve the quality and range of the curricula and instruction, will no doubt, demand cutting edge approach to strategic planning and management of community colleges, now called upon to serve as an essential link, in the emergent supply-chain of America's educational products, the scientific study of which, Professor Sagini's welcome and timely publication could prove to be indispensable.

Professor Maxwell Owusu
University of Michigan, Ann Arbor
Spring 2005

Chapter 1

Organization Structure and Processes

The structure and processes of organizations are empirical paradigms and the critical models that explain how organizations evolve, prosper and recreate themselves in the midst of environmental turbulence. The twentieth century was characterized in part by the development and pervasiveness of large-scale organizations in the realms of corporations, academia, labor, Government and the military industrial complex.

Organizational structures and processes affect the behavior of organizations, their employees, and those who interact with them. Contemporary organization theory is a diverse body of thoughts that is intensely interested in and largely modeled on the bureaucracy. Max Weber believed that bureaucracies, because of their structural and procedural attributes, behaved in predictable ways. He maintained that the bureaucracy is highly efficient, powerful, and ever-expanding. American society and all other societies are still very dependent on the principles of bureaucratic organization.

"Scientific Management," popularized by Fredrick Taylor, became the core approach of orthodox public administration to the design of organizations and work processes at the beginning of the 20th century. The "Human Relations" approach claims that Scientific Management is inadequate because it fails to meet the social and psychological needs of workers as human beings. The Human Relations approach grew as a result of the Hawthorne experiments from 1927 to 1932 in Chicago. Leadership is viewed as extremely important to organizations, but it remains inadequately understood. Leadership has many definitions, but at the most basic level, it is the consistent ability to influence people, to motivate them to serve a common purpose, and to fulfill the functions necessary for successful group action. A continuing controversy is whether leadership is primarily the result of situational factors, personality traits, or specific combinations of both. Irrespective of the controversial nature of leadership theory the literature suggests that leaders must: (1) believe that success is possible, (2) communicate well, (3) be empathic with other individuals in the organization or its environment, (4) be energetic, (5) exercise sound judgment, (6) act in reasoned, consistent ways, and (7) be aware of their own strengths and weaknesses. Recently, organization theorists have begun to study "public entrepreneurship." An important observation is that such entrepreneurs view public organization as powerful instruments for political, social, and economic change. They also view these organizations as tools for achieving their own goals. This new public management theory is rooted in the capitalistic corporate culture. Leadership styles vary from authoritarian to laissez faire. These styles are decision making models.

Organization theory seeks to understand what motivates human beings in organizational settings. Abraham Maslow's theory of a hierarchy of human needs and "expectancy theory" are discussed. According to expectancy theory, the key to motivation is the capacity to afford workers the opportunity to achieve their goals, while keeping them informed of what activities or efforts will lead to the attainment of their goals. Organization theory currently relies heavily upon systems theory—both "open" and "closed" models—to advance understanding of how organizations and individuals interacting with them behave. Open system models emphasize the importance of the organizational environment, while closed system models emphasize stability, control mechanisms, and predictable responses.

The ecological model of organizations emphasizes variation in behavior, selection, and retention of "positively selected variations." This model articulates the organization's evolutionary roots. The organizational culture perspective contends that basic beliefs, assumptions, norms and values exist within an organization and affect individual behavior and decisions. These cultural forces of behavior modification are symbolic artifacts that continuously help to restructure the architecture of the organization (Sagini 2001). The evolutionary approach rejects the view that organizational survival is attributable to rationality. It supports the view that organizational survival is largely a matter of luck because organizations can usually change only marginally in the face of volatile environmental changes.

Classical organization theory in public administration was developed largely by Luther Gulick and Lyndall Urwick in the 1930s. The acronym, POSDCORB, still describes much of the public administration approach to organization and education. The meaning of POSDCORB=planning, organizing, staffing, directing, coordinating, reporting, budgeting. To overemphasize

POSDCORB is to limit organizational creativity. The classical (orthodox) public administration approach relied heavily upon organizing based on the following criteria: purpose, process, place, or clientele/material. However, during the 1940s, Herbert Simon and Dwight Waldo showed the serious weaknesses of the classical approach. Simon demonstrated conclusively that the purpose, process, place, and clientele-material scheme was self-contradictory and very difficult to apply. He also developed the idea that administrative behavior was "intendedly rational," rather than actually rational in all cases. Waldo exposed the implicit value structure of the classical approach, which was at odds with values deeply rooted in the U.S. political culture. Despite the devastating intellectual critiques of the classical approach, it has become so ingrained in administrative culture that it is still relied upon in practice to a considerable extent.

Contemporary managerial perspectives of organization theory are results-oriented. They tend to emphasize clear objectives and flexible processes for achieving them. These perspectives emphasize operations management for effectiveness. Management by Objectives (MBO), Total Quality Management (TQM), and Performance-Based Organizations (PBOs) are other managerial means for promoting the effective organization. "Organization humanism" argues that effective management is promoted by satisfying workers' needs and developing their human potential.

The political approach to public administrative organizations focuses on their public nature and the nature of their political support, power, responsiveness, representativeness, and political accountability. According to the political approach, (1) the organization of public agencies should be pluralistic, (2) a high degree of autonomy should exist to enable agencies to focus on serving their clientele, (3) agencies should maintain a close connection with their corresponding legislative committees and subcommittees, and (4) agencies should be decentralized in order to facilitate representation, participation and inclusion. However, the legal approach to public organization promotes an adjudicatory structure in which an adversarial process can take place. This process is presided over by an administrative law judge (ALJ) or hearing examiner. Procedures are trial-like, but more flexible than those used in courts. The legal approach maintains that it is important for agencies that exercise adjudicatory functions to (1) maintain independence from the rest of the government, (2) protect themselves from the idiosyncrasies of a single director or commissioner, and (3) be insulated from expert influences.

Alternative Dispute Resolution (ADR) is strongly supported by the New Public Management because it offers much greater flexibility than traditional adjudication. ADR emphasizes negotiated rulemaking and greater administrative responsiveness. It appears that in the future, public organizations will be more anticipatory, both in terms of allowing workers to play a greater role in organizational decisions and in providing the general public, or segments of it, a formal opportunity to take part in organizational decision-making.

Two models of administrative organizations of the future are democratic organizations and market-based organizations. Democratic organizations promote employee participation, advocacy administration, and citizen participation. Market-based organizations are strongly advocated by the NPM and NPR. They promote employee empowerment, flatter organizational structures, a customer-driven focus, and privatization. Above all, these organizational theories help to explain the validity and viability of the complex and marvelous purpose or raison de tre of organizations.

In a global economy, high performance in the new work culture requires individual and institutional cooperation because of the complexity of our times and the explosion of information. Whether in nations, regions, organizations, or teams, this necessitates the cultivation of a synergistic culture. With the globalization of knowledge, economies, and markets, cross-cultural competence becomes essential. Such skills help us in coping with changing transnational corporate and work environments, with environmental scanning and forecasting, with understanding of foreign and emerging markets, especially in the Third World.

Global managers can exercise a synergistic role in this process and improve their international performance through greater effectiveness with cultural differences. Manifold opportunities to apply such insight exist with ethnic and minority groups at home, especially in management and marketing; with the selection, preparation, support and evaluation of expatriate personnel; with a cosmopolitan approach to business development abroad. In an interdependent world, metaindustrial executives are expected to exercise such collaborative leadership not only in improving the human condition, but the performance of the planet's citizens.

World trade is both a learning laboratory and a mechanism for doing this. Peaceful and cooperative free enterprise on an international basis contributes not only to global economic development, but can reduce the North/South gap in terms of poverty and population. The export/import exchange, particularly of information and new technologies can foster political and social stability, as well as human resource development. Among the healthy related trends in this regard is the growth of multinational corporations, joint ventures, and entrepreneurial activities.

Tomorrow's market frontiers, both global and interplanetary, are being probed today by innovators. One such market is the Pacific Basin. Another is the emerging market of space industrialization (Harris 1992). Observing the 500th anniversary of Columbus' voyage in 1992, we too are exploring another New World. Open, creative risk-takers and top performers are needed now to confront the new market and cultural challenges. Opportunities in this new market and cultural setting can be imported if academic leadership in all institutions, especially in community and junior colleges, can plan more strategically (Harris and Moran 1991).

In the light of the discussed theories, this study concerns comparative perceptions of planners in four public institutions of higher learning in Michigan. The strategic factors of institutional environments of the 1970's and early 1980's caused a far-reaching impact on national life and indirectly on the four and many of America's colleges and universities. Externally, there were economic recessions, oil embargoes, tax limitation initiatives, and the erosion of constitutional legitimacy—Watergate scandal and Cold War Politics. Evidently, these economic and political conditions made their environment to be extremely confusing. The oil embargo and the fuel crisis of the 1970's produced a painful blow to the American economy. "With the geometric increase in fuel prices, the relationships that served as the bond of the entrepreneurial system were shattered" (Hoverland, McInturff, and Rohn, Jr. 1986, 2). The result of these conditions was chaos, bankruptcies, and a terrible recession. The loss of business life eroded the tax base and forced the taxpayers to resist taxation formuli. Local, state, and federal legislatures cut budgets, reviewed them, and restructured them.

The impact of budgetary cuts on socioeconomic life including educational institutions was severe. First, all governmental units reduced their expenditures. Second, the budget cuts or reductions limited initiatory possibilities for future growth and long-term projections and budgeting plans.

Internally, since taxpayers resisted taxation measures, governments imposed unit budget cuts, and the total situation looked chaotic, growthless, and hopeless; enrollments cripplingly declined, tensions increased and made decision making a nebulous endeavor; and finally, the struggle for institutional survival and maintaining open door policy was not only further challenged by the disruptive internal and external forces, but these forces caused the death of some institutions whose resurrection has remained uncertain. The forces caused organizational structures to experience conflicts.

The external and internal conditions which created problems in national and educational life were or are trends of the environment which impact(ed) on institutions and influenced institutional managers (planners) and policymakers to react perceptively, rationally, or irrationally in order to maintain the status quo or change it. Such reactions became the genesis of polemical or controversial debates geared to making the right choices as they sought for answers. Since these debates were and are based on differential perceptions of planning reality by community leaders, legislatures, administrators (planners), faculty, students, and board members, these groups tried to articulate the issues for purposes of seeking better solutions.

The continuous attempt by institutional planners to seek strategic, tactical, and operational measures of institutional effectiveness has necessitated for many, the use of the rational planning model to delve into and intellectually to probe institutional mechanisms for administrative (planning) efficiency, and effectiveness.

In other words, as Moore (1983, 75-76) points out:

> any reasonably alert educator knows, critical and fundamental shifts are occurring in the American society and economy, and colleges are being pressed to cope with their ramifications, acceleration of technology, shifts in values, economic uncertainties, blurring of sex roles, tightening of resources, changes in demographics—all these factors are altering the fabric of American life. The inexorable change in society creates an imperative need for change in education. That imperative may be strongest for community colleges, precisely because they are—and should be—both in and of their communities. That being the case, they have a dual responsibility: to shape their environment and to be shaped by it.

In the process of making attempts to fulfill the dual responsibility, the organizational structure (see Figure 1.1) and the strategic forces (main external and internal factors which contribute to the formation of viable strategic policy) (Myran 1983) generate organizational conflicts which by themselves are essential for contributing to change.

Problem

The study sought to establish whether or not planning models existed in four different Michigan community colleges as perceived by college planners. In other words, whether the colleges' planning models existed or not was scientifically an unverified fact subject to investigation. Secondly, if the colleges had planning model(s), the study sought to identify and verify the model(s), and examine or analyze them in light of a formal, rational planning model, and strategic management theories.

The study examined and assessed the relationship between planning by the officials of the four colleges in Michigan and execution of plans and the extent to which the colleges were held accountable for carrying out their stated goals and objectives. Data were collected, analyzed, and assessed to judge the relationship between perceptions of planning and actual outcomes of the planning process at these colleges.

In these colleges, and perhaps in many other colleges and universities around the world, the planning function is an everyday activity of institutional management. However, oftentimes little attention is given to the rational planning model as a major element of institutional management. Careful and systematic investigation of this process was the purpose of this inquiry.

Table 2.1
A Comparison of Cultural Differences and Need Formulation

East Asian Countries	United States of America
1. Equity is more important than wealth.	Wealth is more important than equity.
2. Saving and conserving resources is highly valued.	Consumption is highly valued, awareness for conservation is growing.
3. Group is the most important part of society and is emphasized for motivation.	Individual is most important part of society and the person is emphasized for motivation, although team emphasis is growing.
4. Cohesive and strong families and ties often extend to distant relatives–even the nation and its leaders. Relationship transcends society with strong network of social ties.	Nuclear and mobile family. Experimentation with new home/housing/commune living communities of non-relatives. Fluid society that de-emphasizes strong, social ties.
5. Highly disciplined and motivated workforce/societies. hierarchy.	Decline in the "protestant work ethnic" and
6. Education is an investment in the prestige and economic wellbeing of the family.	Education is an investment in personal development/success.
7. Protocol, rank, and status are important.	Informality and competence are important.
8. Personal conflicts are to be avoided–e.g., few lawyers.	Conflict is energy, to be managed– many lawyers.
9. Public service is a moral responsibility.	Distrust of big government and bureaucracy.

Source: Harris, P.R. and Moran, R.T. (1991) *Managing Cultural Differences: High-Performance Strategies for a New World of Business* (Houston: Gulf Publishing Company): 394.

Purpose of the Study

The purpose of the study was fourfold:

1. To determine whether goals and objectives of the colleges were clearly identified and effectively implemented in consonant with their institutional missions
2. To determine whether programs were developed to achieve institutional goals and objectives
3. To observe, analyze, and reflect on the role of institutional research to the planning process
4. To determine whether goals, objectives, and research were articulated in the context of formal planning model and rational ways.

Rationale for the Study

The questions which this study intends to answer are:

1. How do planning techniques used by college planners help them to solve their urgent problems?
2. What characteristics of the planning techniques, planning, and the decision setting contribute to the outcomes as perceived by the planning team?
3. Does the rational model of decision-making have any relevance to their planning?
4. Are there generalizations that can be drawn from their experiences that are reasonable hypotheses for use in other colleges and universities?
5. Is the planning process of each institution formal, rational or strategic?

Research Assertions

The major theme underlying the study is that institutions formally use planning models to improve their institutional management and operations. Based on this assumption, institutions will tend to use planning models which enable them to operate more efficiently and effectively. Efficiency is the process of producing the desired result with minimum effort and expense in a given time. Effectiveness is the realization of organizational mission, which the goals and objectives address.

Assertion 1: Planners who display authoritarian decision-making styles in their colleges are more likely to use rational planning than other planning models.

Assertion 2: Planners who successfully use any one of the other commonly known decision-making styles are less likely to use the rational planning model in their colleges.

Assertion 3: Planners who neither use the rational or any one of the more commonly known planning models tend to use more than two of them.

Theoretical Framework

Formalized planning is the degree to which a system or an institution is pre-specified in terms of its membership, responsibilities, authority, and discretion in decision-making. In the context of strategic management, the degree of formalized planning is effective because it correlates with cost, comprehensiveness, accuracy, and successful planning (Johnson 1975).

The three basic organizational structures of formalization which graphically display different distributions of authority are the classical pyramid, the matrix, and the team. Although it is found in most organizations, the pyramidal structural form is a product of classical organization theory in which both the team and the matrix are inextricably intertwined. The team theory, which is commonly used in Asia (Japan) places emphasis on participatory management in which leaders and followers have authority to contribute to decision-making. This collective decision-making approach motivates personnel to be productive because they professionally and psychologically get satisfaction. Because participants experience satisfaction, the team approach evokes feelings of belonging and ownership. Both belonging and ownership are manifestations of group solidarity, unity and security.

The formal planning model is attractive because it is believed that it prevents ad hoc and random decision-making which unnecessarily and inexpensively narrows choices for the future. Formalized planning gives the institution a structural framework of objectives, goals, and the strategies for decision-making. Such a formal planning structure provides a two-way channel of communication whose actions help to maintain interactive, iterative, and hierarchical consistency (Johnson 1975). Communication is the process through which the organization informs and clarifies goals internally and externally. Internally, it provides a social medium for organizational coordination and control. Externally, its vitality is essential for political responsiveness, accountability, coordination and promotion of external support. Above all, to communicate is to exercise power.

Methodology

To articulate the empirical and theoretical purpose of the study, this research was pedagogically conducted as follows:

1.   The researcher conducted an extensive literature review (Chapter 2) on planning in two-year colleges and other institutions of which colleges and

universities, business, public administration, military, and industry are organizations which utilize similar management planning techniques, theories, and models. Those which were relevant and applicable to higher education management were emphasized in the study. The review of the
literature is found in Chapter 2.

2.   With advice of a higher education professor and research director, two rural
and two urban colleges were selected for comparative analysis. A group of
42 top and middle-level college administrators (planners) from each of the
four colleges were identified and selected on the basis of informed opinion.
In other words, all the planners were selected for the study not only due to
their planning experience, position, and acceptance, but because the chief
planning official of each college recommended them to inform the study.

3.   Measurable responses from the survey sample (college planners, who included members of the presidents' cabinets or administrative councils,
presidents, vice presidents, deans, directors, controllers, and recorders) were
collected. The researcher examined available and accessible planning
documents too. These documents included past master plans, official institutional facts, and minutes or agenda, college history documents, calendars
(bulletins), missions, goals, objectives, and management reports.

4.   Three techniques were used to analyze data and display results. First, the
researcher interviewed all potential respondents from the colleges and selectively tape recorded responses which were used for analytic induction
and interpretative commentary. Second, cross-tables (histograms) containing tabulated sets of numbers and their percentages were displayed. In addition, the researcher used the scientific calculator and computer for the purpose of data reduction and more accurate computational analysis. The
attempt to use these analytical methods was not only an introduction to the
researcher's methodological eclecticism, but it was also an appropriate way
of trying to approximate the truth more accurately.

5.   Finally, comparative analysis on the intra- and inter- institutional management theory and model was reflected on the colleges' planning theories and
model(s). Such an analytic comparison enabled the researcher to identify a
suitable planning model, or models for the colleges. The evolutionary dis-
covery of the model(s) was a product of comparative analysis of the long-
range traditional and the strategic management models.

Through such analytical comparisons, contrasts and observation of similarities and differences, clarifications were made.

Limitations of the Study

Although the sample survey was designed to allow comparisons that yield statistical reliability, the size of the sampled colleges and the economic and logistical capability of the researcher had a considerable influence on the study.

Limitations were a function of the lack of internal validity. They were considered when the researcher drew conclusions about the validity of the study. The major sources of the limitations included the imperfections in the measuring instrument itself, interpretations arising from reading or scoring of the instrumented information, and inconsistency arising from the subjects who were interviewed. For example, the respondents may not have used or known the concept of the model as the researcher's.

The sample survey used in this study was limited to four of the 29 public community colleges in Michigan. The study is an illustrative example of the planning styles and strategies of these four higher education institutions. The institutions should not necessarily be viewed as classic models for emulation; however, each college's planning style is a product of its own unique evolutionary development. Although it might be expected that an analysis of the comparative planning approaches of the four colleges may be beneficial to other institutional planners, not all planning styles of these colleges may be suitable and emulative in other more complex planning institutional environments both at home and abroad.

Overview

The entire study has five chapters. Chapter 1 is composed of the problem, purpose, and a brief summary of theoretical and methodological underpinnings of the study. Chapter 2 contains a review of literature on conventional and strategic perceptions of planning. Chapter 3 presents the methodology which formed the basis for data collection and analysis. Chapter 4 is based on data analysis and histogrammic display of results. Finally, Chapter 5 gives summary, implications, conclusions, and recommendations.

Chapter 2

Review of Literature

Chapter two is based on the review of the literature on community colleges and universities and on strategic planning and decision making in many organizations. The central themes articulated include: (a) history, philosophy, governance, and planing structures of community colleges; (b) planning and strategic planning; and (c) consensual rationality. The six major areas of this chapter include but are not limited to:

1. Historical development of the community college
2. Philosophical bases of the community college
3. Governance of community colleges
4. The theory of strategic planning
5. Perceptions of strategic decision making
6. The rational model

The major economic, technological and global challenges that affect higher education institutions are problems of which retrenchment, inflation, recession, and apparent difficulty to strategically adjust to new high technology demands. These problems have not reached a paralyzing phase. Creative and innovative attempts for reassessing and modifying their missions and goals can be sensed on campuses, in the press, in scholarly and professional literature, and in legislative fora across the nation and, perhaps, around the world. The articulation of such problems will not necessarily be fruitless in addressing synergistic change in the community colleges.

In Michigan, these problems have not only been publicly articulated, but such an articulation has raised issues related to compensation of full and part-time faculty, open-door policy, definitions of quality in the face of retrenchment, mileage politics, matching institutional goals, business and community needs, community college relations, and whether or not colleges should collaborate with business, government, industry, labor, and the press in providing resources for training and retraining of workers who need relevant and marketable skills. Economically, a well-trained labor force will revitalize the productive capacity or the "economic engine" (LeTarte, January 29, 1987) of society. On the other hand, a strong economy helps to promote people's standard of living, health, education, ability to pay taxes and credits, and strong communities within the state, nation, and indirectly around the world.

The public articulation and justifiable rationalization of these issues, according to Wing (1982), does not only create avenues for the exploration of further and more complex issues and alternatives, but the emergent complexity of issues and alternatives becomes the springboard for identifying opportunities and constraints and weaknesses and strengths. Through this dialectical process of sensitizing and articulating reality, missions, and goals emanate from the interaction of institutional and community dynamics. Such dynamics in structure and content impact on institutional planners to plan for institutional change. The nature, character, and theories of change will be discussed in this chapter. Table 2.1 shows the relationship between needs and specific issues. Normally, needs are translated into institutional goals.

A. Historical Development of the Community College

The public community college received its evolutionary roots from the elementary and secondary school system during the late 19th and early 20th centuries. The principles and traditions upon which the public schools were built guided public community colleges. Of the classical traditions, three have been outstanding as they have been applied in the past, and as they apply at present (Monroe 1976):

1. Universal opportunity for a free public education without distinction based on social class, family income, ethnic, racial, or religious background.
2. Originally, local control and support of free, nontuition educational systems; however, today local control remains to be true, but students pay a relatively low tuition in most community colleges all over the country
3. A relevant curriculum designed to meet both the needs of the individual and those of the community, state, and nation.

In Michigan, the First Community College (Grand Rapids Junior College) started in 1914; Jackson 1928; Lake Michigan 1946; and Montcalm 1965.

Table 2.1

A Comparison of Cultural Differences and Need Formulation

East Asian Countries	United States of America
1. Equity is more important than wealth.	Wealth is more important than equity.
2. Saving and conserving resources is highly valued.	Consumption is highly valued, awareness for conservation is growing.
3. Group is the most important part of society and is emphasized for motivation.	Individual is most important part of society and the person is emphasized for motivation, although team emphasis is growing.
4. Cohesive and strong families and ties often extend to distant relatives-even the nation and its leaders. Relationship transcends society with strong network of social ties.	Nuclear and mobile family. Experimentation with new home/housing/commune living communities of non-relatives. Fluid society that de-emphasizes strong, social ties.
5. Highly disciplined and motivated workforce/societies. hierarchy.	Decline in the "protestant work ethnic" and
6. Education is an investment in the prestige and economic wellbeing of the family.	Education is an investment in personal development/success.
7. Protocol, rank, and status are important.	Informality and competence are important.
8. Personal conflicts are to be avoided-e.g., few lawyers.	Conflict is energy, to be managed- many lawyers.
9. Public service is a moral responsibility.	Distrust of big government and bureaucracy.

Source: Harris, P.R. and Moran, R.T. (1991) *Managing Cultural Differences: High-Performance Strategies for a New World of Business* (Houston: Gulf Publishing Company): 394.

In 1945, the state had eight community colleges. In 1960, Michigan had sixteen. As of 1987 there were 29 (*Research committee: The Impact of Community Colleges on Michigan and Its Economy 1984*, 8). In 1922, there were 207 community colleges in the country. The growth and expansion of these institutions is a recent development of post-secondary education in Michigan and the United States. In 1990, the whole country had 1,224 community, technical, and junior colleges in which more than 5 million students attend. These statistical estimates show that the community college movement plays a significant role in the higher education system of the United States (Parnell 1987). Specifically, the current number of these colleges is 1036 (Marlow-Ferguson 2001).

In the first place, as Monroe (1976) argues, it is apparently clear that the rapid expansion of the colleges in question started after 1945. This phenomenon of growth was attributed to:

1. Growing demands of business and industry for technically trained employees,
2. The existence of local communities which had and have both sufficient taxable wealth and population willing to support community colleges,
3. Most important, a body of parents and citizens who aspired to have their children enjoy fulfillment of a dream for a college education, but who were financially unable to afford the luxury of an education at a private college or a state university, where tuition, room and board, and other expenses were and are beyond the reach of even the most animated parents.

Secondly, parents, local and civic leaders, governmental commissions, and educational organizations popularized the community college movement by making recommendations supporting legislation for the colleges. The arguments of these public and private groups, according to Monroe (1976), articulated three claims which were popular with the 19th century elementary and high school evolutionary transition.

The claims suggested that:

1. national income increases in proportion to the increase in educational investments;
2. the national security is made more secure from the ravages of illiterate, uneducated citizens who might be inclined to be disruptive to public welfare; and
3. the pursuit of freedom for the individual and the promise of the good life for all could be best secured by extending secondary educational opportunities.

"These three arguments are the ones used in support of free elementary schools in the 1830's and 1840's and for the public high school in the period from 1870-1900" (Monroe 1976, 14).

It is noteworthy to say that the development of the colleges became more and more complex with the increase and expansion of higher education, industry, and automation. This development changed the role of the community colleges from being merely academic and literary institutions to ones which also provide service, vocational/technical, remedial, and transfer functions.

During the first half of the 20th century, community colleges were, in reality, junior colleges whose values evolved from 19th and early 20th century middle and high school educational values. Unlike the modern community college, the junior college was in essence, "a transfer-oriented institution, offering liberal arts courses to freshmen and sophomores, to a multi-purpose community college" (Brint and Karabel 1989; Neufeldt 1991, 61). Obviously, by the 1920s, the junior college movement had established the academic, political and curricula parameters by which it would be judged. However, lacking the traditions of elitist notions of intellectual excellence and competitiveness, this lack became a barrier to their students whose entry into elitist schools like Michigan, Columbia, Stanford, Chicago, and etc. was viewed as burdensome and unwarranted.

After World War II, the functional role of government expanded greatly. America became economically, politically, militarily, and diplomatically the most powerful nation on earth. While the challenges of greatness were enormous, they opened opportunities and potentialities in every avenue of its growth. Government labor, industry, corporations, and business needed technically trained labor force. The great demand for skilled and semi-skilled professionals influenced national and state legislatures, educational engineers, planners, and economists to envision the creation of multi-purpose institutions that "provided everything" to cater for local student needs. This vision of a multi-purpose local institution evolved first in California during the Great Depression. During the 1950s and 1960s, the community college movement was popularized by state legislatures, the media, community college presidents, local agents, and community decision leaders, The demands of the Civil Rights Movement in terms of opportunity, equality and liberation reinforced the idea of the need for educational expansion in terms of "Democratization, equality of opportunity, vocational and continuing education, open door college, guidance, nontraditional student" (Neufeldt 1991, 60) and community adult education (Brookfield 1985). Evidently, it was during the 1950s and 1960s when the community college movement attained a high degree of distinctiveness in its "historical development, liberal philosophy, diverse student body, faculty, organization, facilities, finances, community relations, programs, services and delivery systems" (Hankins 1989, 11). According to Hankins, this was their mission. This new mission transformed the junior college into the community college. The transformation was not only a shift in emphasis from a transfer-oriented to a vocational non-transfer institution, but this new institutional mission articulated the needs of both the traditional and non-traditional student in education. Both traditionalism and non-traditionalism were offered a new choice which rationalized the needs of corporate America rather than those of intellectual elitism and the selectivity of elitist universities.

Sociologically speaking, it might be argued that while the desire to produce skilled but powerless individuals was good in a capitalistic corporate economy, their "transformation" was a revisionist but naturally evolutionary dialectic. The dialectic serves both the "consumer choice" and "business" models of the capitalist society. This transformation took place between 1930s and 1970s. During the 1980s, 70%-80% of community college students were enrolled in vocational and "non-transfer" programs rather than being in 4 year colleges and universities. The gradual and well-calculated vocationalization of the community college had been completed. This form of gradual, uninterrupted, and transformative completion is called "the diverted dream" (Brint and Karabel 1989). Since community college students who transfer to four-year colleges and universities fulfill general education requirements, the colleges fit well in the structure of American higher education in which 7-20% transfer to 4 year colleges (Richardson and Bender 1987).

However, the dream of transfer-oriented liberal arts students was shifted to vocational and non-transfer non-status. The inculcation of a vocational rather than an elitist intellectual ideology became dominant on community college campuses. Since these campuses have their own organizational self-interests, and given the fact that these organizations are apathetic rather than pragmatic to business practice, it is interesting that they cultivated their own niche within the corporate society which is reminiscent of their unevolutionary exceptionalism (Brint and Karabel 1989). This form of exceptionalism which is essentially a form of American ingenuity, is characterized by "the avoidance of early selection, the lack of sharp segmentation between different types of institutions, relative freedom of movement both among and within institutions, openness to new fields of study, high levels of enrollment, and the provision of opportunities for educational mobility well into adulthood" (719) - life-long education.

These institutions are organizations whose identity of self-interest is identical to self-presentation, self-preservation, and self-perpetuation. To validate their continual survival and productivity, they inadvertently use a meritocratic ideology to legitimate inequality thereby, perceptually creating the idea of classlessness in American higher education and society in general. As academic, service, vocational, and technical institutions, community colleges have become a sanctuary in which constrained intellectual refugees operate (Sassower 2000). These colleges are working class environments for strangers in paradise (Ryan and Sackrey 1984). They are populated with working class women who labor in the factory of knowledge (Tokarczyk and Fay 1993) without exception, where they discuss with "the faculty in the new millennium" (*The Journal of Higher*

Education 2002, 1). The most important societal changes which will affect these academic institutions and faculty performance in higher education in general, will be the issues of "diversity, technology, and globalization" (1).

Although scholars such as McGrath and Spear (1991) and Brint and Karabel (1987, 1989) have asserted that the "crisis" of the community college movement is its non-traditional and weak and disordered academic culture that is rooted in ineffective and unintelligible hopes and dreams, given the remedial and developmental practices that characterize the activist nature of their curricula and instructional schemes, legislatures, college boards, and policy researchers continue to support them by emphasizing their contributions to individual rather than group mobility in American society. Individuals who can pay for it (education), benefit from it and be rewarded through it gratifies the system's criticism and cynicism of specific and general institutional academic culture(s). Therefore, in spite of their intellectual and socio-economic marginalization, their contribution to individual and societal edification is not without some merits. That is why, in a majority of states, legal mandates and historical precedents are used by state coordinating councils and governing boards to "plan and set goals and objectives, allocate resources for programs and institutions, approve capital projects and new instructional programs, monitor institutional performance, review programs, and provide information and guidelines for institutional and campus planners" (Wing 1982, 51).

These colleges, particularly the historically black colleges and universities, HBCUs, have a strong community college component within their structure and curricula. These institutions act as the springboards for mobility in society and as gatekeepers that doubly separate "wheat from chaff". For instance,

> the customized contract training arrangements between the colleges and corporations have contradictory side effects which reinforce the gatekeeping phenomenon. In this case, corporations receive economic benefits because contracting with community colleges is often cheaper than providing in-house training for employees. Community colleges receive increased revenue and increased political support from corporations. However, the training emphasis is likely to hurt the colleges by detracting from their already weakened liberal arts and transfer programs. The overall effect of customized contract training is to push these institutions further in the direction of becoming primarily vocational, rather than educational institutions. This in turn, will provide even fewer opportunities for upward mobility for poor and minority students (Pincus 1989, 77).

As this situation persists, operational and structural reformers have continued to use intellectual polemics to support the status quo, or challenge it with new and largely unattainable visions respectively. In other words while operational reformers see nothing wrong with the traditionally established values upon which the colleges are rooted, structural reformers feel that these institutions of "hope and promise" need to be equipped and modernized to run like universities that provide for transfer credits and award baccalaureate, masters, and doctoral degrees (Dougherty 1992). Neither argument will hold much water unless the needs of society and its organizations are critically analyzed to determine the very essence of the community college movement and its historic and conservative role in providing service to society.

In spite of its inherent academic, political, and social weaknesses, and like the differential and dissimilar weaknesses characteristic of baccalaureate, graduate, and post graduate institutions of higher education, community colleges promote social solidarity when its members believe that they have a substantial common ground of interest that they gain more than they lose by sticking together and maintaining intact their political and social cohesion in a class-structured society. The possibility of rising in the social scale in order to secure a larger share of the privileges of the society makes people willing to stick together and play the game as long as they believe it gives them a fair deal (Brint and Karabel 1989, 730; and Warner et al. 1944, 157) which they perceive to be a form of the dream.

Philosophical Bases of the Community College

In the light of the educational thoughts of the founding fathers, the needs of the individual and nation, America was forced to democratize education and eliminate barriers based on class, poverty, race, and cultural deprivation. President Truman's 1947 Commission on Higher Education expressed similar concerns, but in a more emphatic manner. The Commission stated that:

> Equal educational opportunity for all persons, to the maximum of their individual abilities and without regard to economic status, race, creed, color, sex, national origin, or ancestry is a major goal of American democracy. Only an informed, thoughtful, tolerant people can maintain and develop a free society. Equal opportunity for education does not mean equal or identical education for all individuals. It means, rather, that education at all levels shall be available equally to every qualified person. ... The commission does not subscribe to the belief that higher education should be confined to an intellectual elite, much less a small elite drawn largely from families in the higher income brackets, nor does it believe that a broadening of opportunity means a dilution of standards either of admission or of scholarly attainment in college work. ... The danger is not that individuals may have too much education. It is rather that it may be either the wrong kind for the particular individual, or education, dominated by inadequate purposes (*Community, Technical, and Junior College Journal* 1987, 3)

The commission's document on higher education and Monroe's monographs may be paraphrased to clarify that:

1. Democratic society cannot exist wholesomely without a well-educated citizenry.
2. Universal availability of public education through the 14th year was essential.
3. Since the social purpose of education is also an individual purpose, higher education should allow those with potential abilities, who desire it, can afford it, and can profit from it, to develop their talents for social and self-service.
4. The admission policy was or is "open door." Its purpose is to make sure that every person is granted the opportunity to succeed or to fail by his or her own efforts.
5. A diversified curriculum (comprehensive) which has four main aspects:
   a. development of techniques of introducing students to the life of intellect;
   b. education for transfer to senior colleges and universities;
   c. the curriculum has diversity occupationally or vocationally;
   d. the educational needs of the part-time adult student are taken care of;
   e. colleges must adjust their missions to meet the high tech needs of business, industry, state, labor and government.

In short, what these authors imply is that community college education is excellent education because it is designed to meet the needs of the students and their individual communities. Secondly, the teaching approach is eclectic, and it makes higher education available and attractive to students of all ages, all social classes, and all varieties of ability. To make the curriculum more relevant and manageable, colleges provide counseling and guidance and encourage students to become higher achievers. To the extent that the community college will make these principles realities, it will justify its growing importance in the structure of American higher education.

Governance of Community Colleges

The governance of a community college is both internal and external. Those who exercise governance over the community college are persons who are legally responsible for the management tasks of the institution. Faculty governance (internal governance) is not part of this type of management. However, external governance agencies, such as the state legislature, governor, State Board for Higher Education, Association of American Community and Junior Colleges, AAUP, AFT, NEA, SCUP, ACCT, and the Board of Trustees are external management agencies which contribute to decision-making mechanisms, policies, laws, and procedures which enhance the smooth functioning of the community college movement.

Internally, the chief executive (president), his vice presidents, deans, and department chairpersons who individually and collectively the managers of their areas of responsibility in the institution. Their chief functions include planning (programming, organizing, staffing, leading, coordinating, controlling, and evaluating).

It should be made clear, however, that in a public setting, internal governance activities are delegated from the external section of management. Since boards are either elected or appointed from the external sphere, they cannot be an internal management agency for institutions. They are external management agencies.

In the case of Michigan, for instance, the state has three major legal responsibilities in regard to community and junior colleges. These include:

1. to provide leadership and supervision through the Superintendent of State Education;
2. to generally plan and coordinate education; and
3. to advise the legislature on the financial requirements for the colleges (*Constitution of the State of Michigan* 1963, 65, 67).

In brief, both internal and external governance structures for the community college carry out their tasks in the light of the law. Each of the 50 states has its own unique governance structure, laws, policies, and procedures. No two of them are alike in every respect; however, similarities and differences between and among them exist and such are not the subject of this book.

B. The Theory of Strategic Planning

One of the ways this topic and research problem could be related to its purpose and objectives is to attempt to define "planning" as a term, frequently used in higher education management. In this regard, it may be said that planning is a campaign to move an institution toward its image of the future, on a timetable that is both desirable and feasible. Planning ideas emanate from "individuals, institutions, and society" (Jedamus and Peterson 1981, 114). At the institutional level, planning may be viewed as a separate and analytically oriented institutional function, as an integral part of the decision-making and control function, or as a more politically oriented policy making function. The planning function identifies possible future states of the college, and develops relevant strategies, policies, and procedures for selecting and getting to one or some or all of them.

Planning is a broad topic in organizational management. It has many definitions and meanings reflected in those organizations and their individuals. "To some, planning is synonymous with perspective on management and decision making that emphasizes rationality, utilization of information and control of influence of future events" (Lee 1979, 2). Executives in business and military organizations call planning strategic planning. Government officials call it "policy analysis." It may refer to a set of techniques used for organizing and analyzing information. Examples of such techniques include Management Information systems, MBO, Simulation Modeling, and Resource and Expenditure Forecasting. Planning may imply an organizational model, an ideal state of the organization, a blueprint for the future condition of an institution or organization. The notions may or may not be stated in a master plan, an institutional mission statement or a document of organizational goals and assumptions.

Planning is associated with people working in an office of planning and/or institutional research and with the organized process conducted by these offices, such as incremental budgeting, program planning, and budgeting and program evaluation.

Planning is "a process which establishes objectives; defines strategies, policies and sequences of events to achieve objectives; defines the organization for implementing the planning process; and assures a review and evaluation of performance as feedback in recycling and process" (Johnson 1975, 51).

Planning may be considered as a philosophy of "projective thought" (looking ahead). In this sense, planning is an attitude or state of mind, a way of thinking, or process of making plans.

> Planning may be viewed in terms of structure. Long-range planning refers to the development of a comprehensive and reasonably uniform program of plans for the organization, reaching out over a long period of time. It is an integrating framework within which each of the functional plans may be tied together and an overall plan developed for the entire institution (Johnson 1975, 51).

Technically, "planning determines the objectives of administrative effort and devises the means to achieve them" (Halstead 1974, 2). The planning strategy enables administrators to react perceptibly to probable and possible future events and changes which affect the institution. Because it is a cyclical and continuous process, it increases the opportunity to identify issues and alternatives which are consistent with established goals. The identification of issues and alternatives increases the chances of securing maximum returns with minimum cost.

The planning process is different from a plan. "A plan is a document which outlines a complete program of action to follow in attaining goals and objectives" (*Planning Universities* 1974, 18). It is possible, but not desirable, to have a document which has the appearance of a plan without reflecting the planning process. A master plan, proposal, or a goal, are examples of plans. By itself, or without being used, reviewed, and continually evaluated, a plan is a static, rather than a dynamic document. Figure 2.1 shows one example of how to strategically formulate a master plan goal or objective and determine policy.

Figure 2:1. Objectives Determination and Master Strategy Formulation

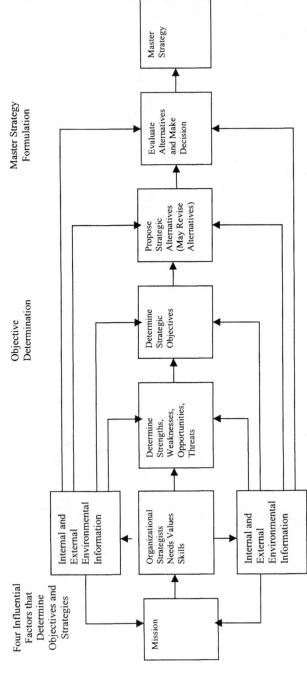

Source: Higgins, M. James and Vincze, W. Jullian. *Strategic Management and Organizational Policy: Test and Cases.* (Chicago: The Dryden Press, 1986): 5.

On the other hand, regardless of its depth and comprehensiveness, a plan is a temporary guide, not a final solution. To be effective, the plan has to be responsive to the needs of the institution, individuals, private and public institutions, and the general public which, morally and materialistically supports the institution. In spite of its limitations, and strengths, the uniqueness of the master plan (plan) is based on its multiple elements each of which is functionally distinctive and mutually interdependent.

Effective planning is strategic planning. Strategic planning deals with a new array of factors: the changing external environment, competitive conditions, strengths and weaknesses of the organization, opportunities for growth and sensitivity to the changing environment. In a sense, "strategic planning is a management activity designed to help organizations develop greater quality by capitalizing on the strengths they already have" (Keller 1983, vii). "Strategic planning does not deal with the future decisions, but it deals with the futurity of present decisions" (Lall and Lall 1979, 74). Drucker's (1970) definition of strategic planning asserts that it is a continuous process of making present entrepreneurial (risk-taking) decisions in a systematic way and with a fairly accurate prediction of their futurity. Efforts needed to carry decisions out must be systematic, their results must be measured against the expectations through the process of organized and systematic feedback. Strategic planning is "(1) the analysis phase which includes the assessment of external and internal environments, (2) the mission and goals phase, (3) the objectives and action plans phase, and (4) the resource use, needs analysis, and expenditure strategies phase" (Uhl 1983, 2).

Strategic planning involves participatory and adaptive management. It has two major purposes: to obtain agreement on specific long-range institutional goals and to provide advice to the president or CEO and the college board concerning activities that should be given priority in annual budgets. There are three structural performance phases of strategic planning. Regardless of the variety of planning concepts, and for the purposes of this inquiry, the study will articulate planning in three major ways:

1. emphasis on goal setting, goal evaluation, and goal achievement (this view is policy or decision oriented);
2. emphasis on the effectiveness of planned and implemented objectives (emphasis is on strategic planning); and
3. the role of the feedback mechanisms of planning goals and objectives (emphasis is on the planning model).

For purposes of this review of literature, goals and objectives may be perceived as ends, while budget resource allocation activities are viewed as means for the achievement of goals and objectives. The study views research as a source of valid, accurate, and reliable data needed for appropriate planning technicalities, details, and strengths rather than planning superficialities which may be symbols of mediocrity and weakness. Finally, the feedback mechanism of the planning process maintains the balance between goals and objectives on the one hand, and budget-resource allocation, implementation, and course review and evaluation nexus on the other. All information and activities related to planning can theoretically be put into eight components which characterize the study (Halstead 1974, 17):

1. determining goals
2. identifying problems
3. diagnosing problems
4. establishing premises (assumptions)
5. searching for possible solutions
6. selecting the solution
7. implementing the solution
8. evaluating the results of the solution

Assumptions for Educational Planning

There are eight major assumptions related to planning and higher education management. The assumptions, according to Greneman and Finn (1978) generally focus on the internal and external environments of the college which management needs to articulate in order to identify possibilities and constraints that enable planners and faculty to determine what issues and alternatives should be explored before selecting objectives for implementation. According to Greneman and Finn (1978), the eight major assumptions are:

1. A society's goals, whether economic, cultural, political, social, or technological can be achieved only through the development of human resources. In doing so, the social needs of citizens and individuals will be addressed more effectively
2. The strength of a national program of higher education will depend on the quality of program and services offered by individual institutions. Therefore, the primary purpose of a national system of planning, coordination, and control is to encourage all individual institutions within the system to attain optimum strength
3. The presence of one or more well-performing institution or institutions will not necessarily insure an effective national program of higher education. All institutions in the system must be encouraged to perform better
4. Strength in an institution of higher education is closely associated with autonomy in the making of essential decisions affecting institutional operations. It is difficult to be a strong institution unless the institution is given maximum self-determination in its operations. Self-determination does not,

ipso facto, insure quality; it is only a necessary prerequisite for building quality

5. The coordinating function should be assigned to a single central agency (Accrediting Agency) that does not have responsibility for the operational control of any individual institution. By contrast, the control and management of internal operations of the institution is the prerogative of the chief executive (President)

6. Coordination functions can be carried on with what hopefully will be construed as minimal interference with essential institutional autonomy. Among the necessary functions of coordination are:
    a. Devising plans for the orderly development of higher education in the nation
    b. Collecting and analyzing pertinent data concerning institutional programs, facilities, an finances
    c. Giving advice and/or recommendations concerning the role and functions of institutions in the national system
    d. Reviewing institutional requirements for appropriations and making recommendations to the legislature regarding the financial needs of each institution
    e. Reviewing new programs; degree offerings; and physical facilities to ascertain their consonance with national plans

7. The increasing complexity of society requires human talents of a wide variety and achievement at many levels. The needs of society and the needs of individual self-fulfillment are both well served when a wide diversity of educational opportunities is made available in a manner that encourages their widespread use.

8. In America, students have the freedom and opportunity to attend a higher institution of learning regardless of cost.

In brief, assumptions are a theoretical web which looks like guidelines or idealistic situational principles through which the validity of higher education practices, policies, and parameters are continually refined and replenished. The assumptions also relate to the scope of national and state institutional expectations to individual institutions and their constituents.

Origin and Development of Strategic Planning Theory

The term strategy means "strategos" (Cope 1981, 5) in Greek. Strategos was a military leader or general. The verb stratego means to plan. Originally, planning was a process used by individuals, families, armies, and small groups. As societies evolved in social organization and technological complexity, planning became a science as well as an art of leadership, organizations and management.

Although the intellectual roots of strategic planning are three centuries old, its educational theory and practice are only 40 years old. Intellectually, strategic planning drew the wealth of its ideas from five main sources: geopolitical theory, marketing, field theory, general systems, and contingency and management schools of thought. Each of the schools (sources) has become highly specialized. Five areas of strategic planning identified by Cope (1981) are:

> serving establishing the mission, role, and scope of the institution; analyzing data on the internal operations; analyzing data on the external environment; matching institutional mission and strengths in order to capitalize on opportunities for alternative formulations of policy; and choosing the strategies that are consistent with the institution's values, are economically justifiable, are politically attainable, and are consistent with social needs.

Pearce and Robinson (1982) assert that strategic management connotes a set of decisions and actions which result in the formulation and implementation of strategies designed to achieve the objectives of the organization. As viewed by these two authors, strategic management concerns nine critical areas (4). These are:

1. Determination of the mission of the organization, including broad statements about its purpose, philosophy, and goals.
2. Development of organizational profile which reflects its internal condition and capability.
3. Assessment of the organization's external environment, both in terms of competitive and general contextual factors.
4. Interactive opportunity analysis of possible options uncovered in the matching of the Organization profile with the external environment.
5. Identification of the desired options uncovered when the set of possibilities is considered in light of the organization's mission.
6. Strategic choice of a particular set of long-term objectives and grand strategies needed to achieve the desired options.
7. Development of annual objectives and short-term strategies which are compatible with long-term objectives and grand strategies.
8. Implementation of strategic choice decisions based on budgeted resource allocations and emphasizing the matching of tasks, people, structure, technologies, and reward systems.
9. Review and evaluation of the success of the strategic process to serve as a basis of control and as an input for future decision making.

Sensitivity to dimensions of strategic decisions, issues, and concerns, as the authors argue, require top management decision makers. The responsibilities of the top management decision makers may include setting the mission, establishing objectives, planning strategy, establishing policies, planning the organization structure, providing personnel, establishing procedures, providing facilities, providing capital, setting standards, establishing management programs and operational plans, providing control information, and activating people in the light of the organization's mission.

According to Higgins and Vincze (1986, 4) strategic management is principally concerned with executive actions that involve:

1. The determination of the organization's mission, strategic policies, and strategic objectives
2. The formulation of a master strategy to accomplish those objectives. This strategy is most often based on a grand strategy combining basic action and marketing considerations
3. The formulation of policies to aid in the implementation and control of the master strategy
4. Management through subordinates, the process of implementation, which translates strategic plans into action and results
5. The practices of evaluation and control to determine whether the mission and objectives have been achieved and whether the plans and policies for reaching them are functional (see Figure 2.2).

Recently, Peters and Waterman (1980) wrote *In Search of Excellence*. The document is a study of 17 excellent companies in America integrated into eight by scholarly organizational theorists (March, Mintzberg, Pfeffer, Scott, Salancik, and Weik). The principal conceptual theme for which the authors of the book are united is the organizational culture. They view culture to be consisting of:

Shared values and interpretations of social activities and commonly held definitions of organizational purpose and work orientations, all embraced by the normative perspective taken by members of the organization. ... [W]hen culture is strong and cohesive, it provides a sort of multiplier effect for individual work efforts. Individuals are supported, guided, and given identity by a social web which moves them toward common goals (2).

Peters and Waterman (1980) believe that excellent organizations possess organizational cultures that are filled with value systems—usually around content such as the importance of people, superior quality and service, innovation, informality, and detail. The cluster of values that are the foundation of culture give meaning to the life of the organization. This meaning enables individuals to find purpose in the organization and for their own lives. The role of the administrator of an excellent institution (corporation) is to manage the cultural value system. Typically, the management of

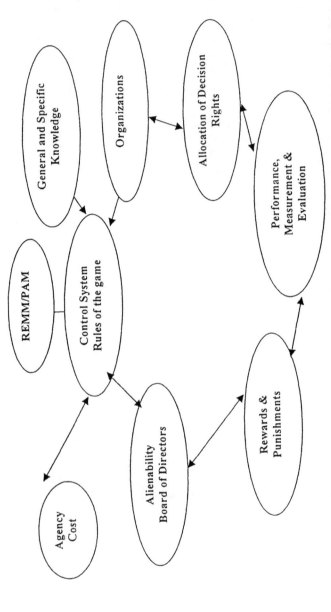

Figure 2.2. The Functional Practices of Evaluation and Control of the Mission

Source: Harris, P.R. and Moran, R.T. 1991. *Managing Cultural Differences.* Houston, TX: Gulf Publishing Company.

culture is implemented through consistent behavioral examples enacted in close proximity to those who perform the essential work of the organization. As culture develops over the years, organizational members come to believe in and act in the light of values that undergird and direct their behavior, and once employees are fully encultured, the need for volumes of specific rules disappears. As a result, members become free to act autonomously, to experiment, innovate, and even fail. Planners who integrate cultural values with management tasks plan strategically.

In relation to schools, Peters and Waterman (1980) consistently view the whole organization to be the unit of culture. Institutional culture can be used as an integrating conceptual framework for increasing the social interaction evidenced in effective schools. The social interaction of effective schooling is more likely to increase the level of cultural change from the base rather than from top-down initiatives.

Although the literature on effective schools does not demonstrate how effective schools and cultures arise, are sustained, and decline, Peters and Waterman (1980) suggest that effective schools (organizations) are those which know the needs of their clientele and devise strategies for addressing them effectively.

In the complex global and high-tech environment, strategic planning involves the ability to manage cultural differences in organizational settings. Harris and Moran (1991) assert that diverse global and regional cultural differences should be managed effectively in order to improve communications with foreign nationals, and work force minority groups. Managing cultural differences effectively will enable business leaders to master business protocol and cross-cultural courtesy for capitalizing on international markets. With the use of wise advice, case study materials, and examples, the authors have demonstrated how to utilize European, Japanese, Middle Eastern, African and Hispanic cultural traits in order to understand, cooperate with, motivate, and lead people in the market place and in other organizational and professional settings. Some of the most important distinctions between Westerners' and Easterners' values include but are not limited to physical appearance, language, religion, family, social attitudes, etc. These influence business practice and relationships. The orient is important for ventures and partnerships.

Jensen (1998) has argued, in *Foundations of Organizational Strategy*, that there are three major components in an organization's (firm's) total strategy. These are its "competitive strategy, its organizational strategy, and its human strategy" (preface). To plan strategically, organizational strategists must understand dualistic and dichotomous relationship between capitalist economic theory of society and the character of human nature both of which become dialectical elements of human competition that generate conflict due to self-interest

Specifically, this strategic and integrated theory of organizations assumes that these organizations are equilibrium systems which are like independent markets. Second, the theory assumes that human beings who have influence in organizations are rational and self-interested. Behavioristically, rationality influences them to be resourceful, evaluative and maximizing in whatever they do. In addition, they integrate the non-rational side of their behavior by trying to avoid pain as they pursue their interests. In a climate of uncertainty and fear, such a dualistic nature of human behavior may cause strategic planners and thinkers to make decisions and take actions that may negatively impact on organizations. In other words, economically, although humans are resourceful, calculating and self-interested maximizers, they are not necessarily interested only in money income or wealth alone. Psychologically, although all people are influenced by income elasticity of demand, the fact that human needs are hierarchical cannot be substituted for higher needs if lower needs have not been met. Third, sociologically, society tends to impose costs on people for violating social norms and conventions. If this influences their behavior due to the benefits they experience, social change is assured. Fourth, politically, if imperfect people (agents) behave altruistically, they care about others and their own personal interests.

Finally, in the realm of strategic planning dialectics, information is not only too costly to produce, but , it is also expensive to transfer between and among agents. In essence, organizations are entities that exist in a system of markets of which "financial, product, labor and materials" (1) are paramount.

> In this diagram (p. 32), you can see the "fundamental conceptual building blocks that form the foundations of organizational strategy. REMM and PAM are the components of the dualistic model of human behavior in which the integrated theory of organizations is based. Because specific knowledge is costly to transfer among agents, facilitating its use in organizations and society means that decision rights must be delegated to the agents who possess the specific knowledge relevant to the decisions. Self-control problems and the conflicts of interest among self-interested individuals then create agency problems when decision rights are delegated to agents with the relevant specific knowledge. Alienable decision rights solve this control problem in capitalist societies, but since alienability of decision rights is not delegated to agents inside organizations, they must create substitute control systems that accomplish the control that alienability provides in the economy as a whole. This substitute control system, the organizational rules of the game, consists of these systems that...allocate decision rights to those agents with the relevant specific knowledge for their exercise ... measure and evaluate the performance of the decision agents, and ... reward and punish agents for their performance (Jensen 1998, 3).

Harris and Moran (1991) have done a comparative study of the cultural differences between East Asian countries and United States of America and that: upon visiting many campuses, educators and planners resolved to write *Academic Strategy: The Management Revolution in American Higher Education* (Keller 1983). The book's motif was to address the causes and effects of the perilous new era of declining enrollments, inflated costs, and shifting academic priorities. In other words, retrenchment. To address retrenchment, he examined the new role of strategic planning and how it is changing the role of professors, trustees, and presidents. Keller (1983, 81) defined planning as:

> a new development of great potential. This type of planning is not the same as the mechanical and deterministic long-range planning that was tried a decade or two ago. Strategic planning deals with a new array of factors: the changing external environment, competitive conditions, the strengths and weaknesses of the organization, and opportunities for growth. Strategic planning is an attempt to give organizations antennae to sense the changing environment. It is a management activity designed to help organizations to develop greater quality by capitalizing on the strengths they already have.

What Keller emphasizes in his strategic conception is not only the prioritization of institutional resources, but the use of participatory management techniques and decentralized decision-making strategies of faculties, academic managers, and trustees. Such an approach is likely to motivate institutions to become innovative, cohesive, productive, and effective.

Strategic Imperatives

William C. Giegold (1978) Professor of Management at Virginia Polytechnic Institute and State University said that three questions may be asked in relation to strategic planning. The questions are:

1. Why are we here?
2. Who are we?
3. Where are we going? (68, 79).
4. Where are we? (Neff, 6-29-87)

Giegold has articulated the above mentioned questions to sensitize the ability of the organization to establish standards for assessing its strengths and weaknesses. Giegold suggests that at any point in time, people, structure, and technology are crucial entities for organizational survival. Analogically, George Keller believes that planning, people, and quality are the crucial organizational imperatives. In terms of contributions, people have skills, attitudes, experience, interpersonal competence, supervisory styles, and other strengths and weaknesses which characterize the human resources of the organization.

The structure in which people function in order to fulfill their organizational roles and obligations is composed of objectives, goals, procedures, policies, and controls which give purpose, direction, interpersonal constraint, and discipline, for the realization of the organizational mission.

Technology consists of the products, processes, facilities, design concepts, patents, and functional know-how which are used by members to carry out the purposes of the organization.

In brief, the three terms (people, structure, and technology) serve as the foundation for identifying strategic activities and serve, in general terms, as a criterion for measuring effectiveness by articulating the needs of the organization's social, economic, political, cultural, and technological environment.

Strategic Versus Tactical Planning

It is useful to show the distinction between strategic and tactical decisions because they differ in ways they are formulated and implemented. To demonstrate the comparative distinction between the two planning theories, George Steiner's and John Miller's (1984, 2-3) dichotomy will be used:

1. *Importance.* Strategic decisions are significantly more important to the organization than tactical decisions. ... Doing the right thing is more important than doing things right.
2. *Level at Which Conducted.* Due to their importance, strategic decisions are made by top-level marketing managers while tactical decisions are made at the level of product and functional managers.
3. *Time Horizons.* Strategies last for long periods of time, while tactics have short durations. Strategic plans might have a ten-year horizon, in contrast to annual marketing plans that delay primarily with tactical issues.
4. *Regularity.* The formulation of strategy is continuous and irregular. The ongoing process of monitoring the environment might trigger an intense strategic planning activity when new opportunities or threats appear. Tactics are determined on a periodic basis with a fixed time schedule, typically designed to correspond to the annual budgeting cycle.
5. *Nature of Problems.* Strategic problems are typically unstructured and unique. Hence, there is great uncertainty and risk associated with the formulation of strategies. Tactical problems, such as setting an advertising level or selecting salespeople, are more structured and repetitive in nature, so the risks associated with tactical decisions are easier to assess. In addition, strategy formulation involves the consideration of a wider range of alternatives than the formulation of tactics.
6. *Information Needed.* Since strategies represent an organization's response to its environment, the formulation of strategies requires large amounts of information external to the organization. Much of the information is related to an assessment of the future and thus is quite subjective. Tactical decisions rely much more on internally generated accounting or market research information.
7. *Detail.* Strategic plans are typically broad statements based on subjective judgements, while tactical plans are quite specific, supported by much more detailed information.

8. *Ease of Evaluation.* Strategic decisions are much more difficult to evaluate than tactical decisions. The results of strategies might become evident only after many years. In addition, it is difficult to disentangle the quality of the decision from changes that might have occurred in the forecasted environment. In contrast, the results of tactical decision are quickly evident and much more easily associated with the decision.

Although it has been possible to thematically differentiate between strategic and tactical planning, there is no generally accepted definition of strategy. Hofer and Schendel (3) define it this way: "An organization's strategy is the fundamental pattern of present and planned resource deployments and environmental interactions that indicate how the organization will achieve its objectives."

This definition creates the awareness that strategic decisions are concerned with resource allocation that is based on an analysis of the interaction between environmental factors and internal organizational capabilities. In this case, strategic decisions determine where an organization places its efforts which identifies markets and submarkets it chooses to participate in, and what products (students in case of school) it attempts to produce for its clientele (markets). These strategic decisions provide direction for the organization's effort, while tactical and operational decisions are needed to implement strategic decisions.

When an organization (institution) experiences growth, it makes decisions incrementally. However, during periods of uncertainty, crisis, and retrenchment, the organization finds difficulty to make immediate and effective adjustments. The difficulty arises because the institution finds itself in a position where there exists debate concerning whether it should fund old programs or it should discontinue them or replace them with new ones; whether the scope of new programs is consistent with institutional expansion or not, and whether it is rationally logical to cut or retire tenured faculty and staff, cut funds, and programs in order to prioritize alternatively and still maintain the mission of the institution. The dynamic, rather than the static, awareness of institutional adaptability is called the "strategic window" (Abell 1984, 395). Abell's decision regarding the strategic window concept can be formulated when the institution analyzes its external environment and relates the condition of that environment to its master goals and objectives—the grand strategy. For the organization to be safe and effective, the strategic window should perpetually remain open, rather than closed. It must help the organization to protect itself against entropy. As it remains open, the strategic window potentially provides an avenue that will propel the institution into the future and "keep the ship of the people afloat."

Writing about Corporate Planners who do things in the opposite way, Professor Hayes (1985, 111) of Management of Technology at the Harvard Business School said the following about strategic management:

With all the time and resources that American Manufacturing Companies spend on Strategic Planning, why has their competitive position been deteriorating? Certainly not because the idea of doing such planning is itself misguided. Nor because the managers involved are not up to the task. Drawing on his long experience with the nuts and bolts of operations deep inside American and foreign companies, the author proposes a different answer. Perhaps the problem lies in how managers typically approach the work of planning: first by selecting objectives or ends, then by defining the strategies or ways of accomplishing them, and lastly by developing the necessary resources or means. A hard look at what the new industrial competition requires might suggest, instead, an approach to planning based on a means-ways-ends sequence. Such a change in strategy makes the organization to compete progressively by experiencing incremental improvements in the firm of "strategic leaps.

The implication of this type of strategic thinking on the provision of higher education can be far reaching. The institution needs to devise strategies for securing resources (funds, personnel, technology, time, and facilities) before it can strategically convert goals, strategies, and programs into ends (objectives) that are realized through research, instruction, and service. Hayes coauthored *Restoring Our Competitive Edge* with Wiley (1984). The book was selected by the Association of American Publishers as the best in business management and economics at that time. What he said has proved to be useful.

Types of Strategic Planning

Ackoff (1970, 6-22) described three organizational postures for strategic planning: satisficing, optimizing, and adaptivizing. By assessing an organization's historic posture toward strategic decision making, planners are better able to understand the opportunities and pitfalls of undertaking strategic planning within the institution. The characteristics of each of Ackoff's postures are discussed below.

1. Satisficing. Ackoff's first philosophy of planning is that of satisficing— attempting to do well enough, but not necessarily as well as possible. Ackoff (1970, 7) noted:

> The satisficer normally sets objectives and goals first. Since he does not seek to set those as "high" as possible, only "high enough," he has to revise them only if they do not turn out to be feasible. Once the objectives and goals are set, he seeks only one feasible and acceptable way of obtaining them; again not necessarily the best possible way.

Satisficers seldom formulate and evaluate sets of potential strategic alternatives since any feasible set will satisfy them. They are more apt to identify past deficiencies produced by current policies than to define future opportunities. Satisficers tend to focus on the financial aspects of their operation, neglecting such elements as manpower planning, physical plant, and services. Financial forecasting and budgeting dominate their planning efforts. Satisficers shy away from organizational changes because of their potential for controversy and conflict. They typically deal with only one forecast of the future as if it were a certainty. This type of planning seldom produces a radical departure from the past, usually leads to the comfortable continuation of current policies, and appeals to organizations more concerned with survival than with development and/or growth. Satisficing seems to be the traditional approach to deduce, however, that this approach is not of much value in a dynamic environment. Change, "in itself," demands that an organization look not to the past but to the future in order to define opportunities and threats and the means to deal with them. Therefore, academic organizations which continue to operate from a satisficing posture will surely find themselves left behind by the rapid changes and economic pressures of today's environment. Preoccupation with budgets, bottom lines, and risk avoidances—all characteristics of the satisficing posture, breeds mediocrity and ultimately organizational decline. Satisficers are conventional rather than strategic planners.

2. Optimizing. An alternative to satisficing planning is optimizing planning. Optimizers make an effort not just to do well, but to do as well as possible. They are constantly searching for a better way, a better product, a better environment. Optimizing is based on the use of mathematical models of the systems being planned for, which attempt to translate organizational goals into quantifiable terms and combine them into a single performance measure.

Optimizers tend to take many elements of the organization and its environment into consideration when developing optimization models and therefore often have a deeper understanding of their organization as a system. However, they assume all parts of the system are programmable, and therefore, fail to control for unanticipated environmental responses. For this reason, optimization is more useful in shorter-range tactical planning than in longer-range strategic planning.

The planning models and systems of optimizers have immense value in providing data for the strategic planning process. However, it must be emphasized that strategic planning is an intellectual exercise, not an exact science. Models provide useful data, but the well informed opinions and even hunches of experienced managers and professionals must be taken into account as well.

Planners who attempt to rely only on the results of quantitative analyses of organizations and environmental scenarios are well advised to note the cautions of Peters and Waterman (1982, 23). They reported that the nation's most successful organizations have a "bias for action." An organization preoccupied by quantitative analysis and data-based decision making stifles the creativity and entrepreneurial spirit described above. In a dynamic and highly competitive environment, higher education institutions cannot afford to be overly rational. Successful organizations realize that environmental opportunities must be created, not simply reacted to. An over-reliance on optimal decision-making techniques and data analysis can paralyze the development of openness and flexibility in an institution. These characteristics are essential to organizational development and prosperity in a dynamic and competitive environment.

   3. Adaptivizing. Ackoff's third planning philosophy, adaptivizing, has three main tenets. The first holds that the principal value of planning is not in the plans produced, but in the process of producing them. This leads to the idea that planning cannot be done to or for an organization, but must be done by the responsible managers. The second tenet holds that the principal objective of planning is the design of an organizational management system which *minimizes* the need for *retrospective* planning—planning directed toward removing deficiencies produced by past decisions. The final tenet holds that our knowledge of the future can be classified into three types: certainty, uncertainty, and ignorance, each requiring a different type of planning.

   For those aspects of the future about which there can be virtual certainty, an organization can develop plans committed to particular actions or strategies with specific policies and procedures. For those aspects of the future for which there is a high degree of uncertainty, contingency plans must be developed. That is, flexibility must be built into organizational policies to allow for response to the opportunities presented when "the future makes up its mind." Finally, for those aspects of the future which cannot be anticipated (for example, technological breakthroughs or radical economic shifts), responsivity, which allows the organization to quickly detect and adapt to environmental deviations, must be built into the organizational planning system.

   Adaptive responses for the two later situations can be of two types: (1) passive adaptation, in which the organizational system changes its behavior so as to perform more efficiently in a changing environment, as has been seen in previous efforts to bring the computer into curricula throughout higher education, and (2) active adaptation, in which the organization changes its environment, perhaps, by addressing new markets or designing new products, so that its own present or future behavior would become more efficient.

   An adaptive organization, therefore, possesses the characteristics of America's best managed organizations (Peters and Waterman 1982, p 13-16): (1) a bias for action, (2) an orientation to the customer, (3) an encouragement of entrepreneurship, (4) a respect for the worker, (5) a value-driven philosophy, (6) a narrow product line, (7) a simple structure and a lean staff, and (8) simultaneous loose-tight properties. The adaptive organization is always looking for opportunities within its defined scope of activities or mission. It encourages product and program experimentation within the bounds of its mission, and allows for occasional failures, for only through such errors can new developments be generated. The focus of the organization is on the customer, not the product. Adaptive organizations realize that no matter how good a product may be, if it's not what the customer wants, it won't be consumed. Quality is the key value of the adaptive organization, and individuals are encouraged and appropriately rewarded to champion new ideas, products, and services that meet the organization's quality standards. Planning is done by the work units, not by the top managers. The adaptive organization recognizes the value of hands-on experience in quality decision making. The structure of the organization reflects a high degree of respect for and confidence in the workers and their ability to contribute to the development of the organization. Finally, commitment is encouraged by a focus on organizational excellence and the creation of a culture that reinforces experimentation, dedication, cooperation, and involvement.

Planning Parameters

The parametric criteria by which the organization's performance is evaluated are its mission, goals, objectives, internal, and external environments and operational and management data bases. An institution's leadership has the power to coordinate the application of planning parameters on the planning environment and creatively to rationalize, not only the relationships among and between the parameters, but also, how the mission which all the parameters embrace, can be achieved.

Mission

The mission of the institution is its identity, or mirror, self-concept, institutional philosophy or public image. Because the mission is the aim, reason, or purpose for the institution's existence and reason for its being, this mission is viewed in terms of what is happening more than in terms of a general statement of intentions or purposes, or goals. In the case of a university, colleges, departments, units, positions (professional ranks), and a variety of funds, facilities, and review and evaluation mechanisms are structurally and purposely designed to enhance the development of that mission.

Martha Hesse (1985), writing about Michigan State University, suggested that the mission of the university is composed of a profile of the university's history and current performances, vision of the leadership, macro-environmental considerations, and distinctive competencies. Fenske, Richardson, and Doucette (1985, 191-192) have conceptually tried to show the hierarchical relationships between missions, goals, and objectives. They say that:

> The common conceptualization of the relationship of institutional missions, goals, and objectives is that of a continuum or hierarchy of decreasing levels of generality beginning with missions and culminating in objectives. Despite this assumed relationship, numerous attempts to aggregate objectives into goals ... they are fundamentally different in nature. Goal statements are abstract, qualitative outcomes that educators hope their efforts will achieve; objectives are concrete, the units of measure used in quantitatively oriented management systems.

Looking at the historical role and place of Oxford University's 800 years of existence, Stewart (1975, 18) says that

Oxford's notion of her purpose has seldom been clear, and often fluctuates. Some see the university chiefly as a research institution, some as a nursery of church and state empire, some as a liberation of the spirit, some as the microcosm of all society, some as a forcing-house for first-class intellects, some as a training ground for economic struggle, some as a channel of accepted wisdom, some as a probe towards new knowledge. ... The progress of this university is no disciplined march of intellectual legionnaires, but more the groping, quarrelsome, skirmishing and sometimes comical advance of a posse of irregulars, blowing trumpets and jostling their way across a soggy sort of battlefield.

As Fenske, Doucette, and Stewart indicates in these two quotations, the institution's role (expected performance or behavior), function, or purpose varies from place to place over time in space. This apparent historical instability of the university's mission does not necessarily mean that the college/university, as it may be perceived by various academic critics and other elitist officials, does not address its mission. What this means is that the servant (institution) of society strives to do things either in the right way or does the right things. Doing things in the right way is to be efficient while doing the right things is to be strategically effective. As Cope (1981) argues, efficiency is a symbol of static, conventional, and mechanistic planning while effectiveness is symbolic of dynamism, change and innovation. While the former is likely to lead to entropy, the latter results in vision, progress, and change. Change brings development while entropy results in eventual decline and death. For all the time the institution is alive, its struggle for existence is based on its attempt to make survival adjustments related to efficiency and effectiveness. When the college or university is neither effective nor efficient, it has no reason for its existence.

Organizational Structure and Design

The structure and design of any organization is determined by economic and ideological forces that are classifiable, or professional and occupational interests or ideological and ethnic values, or resources in terms of physical units and outputs within the whole system. In this light, this chapter deals with theories of organization structure. The chapter overviews traditional theories and presents a detailed review of the more contemporary research and theoretical analysis on organizational design. Of specific interest is the agency's (bureau's) needs for programmatic support, its program technologies and its environment. The purpose of this chapter is to examine both the traditional and contemporary models of organizational structure from the literature on organizational theory. Emphasis is placed on the technical as opposed to the political uses of rationale behind a reorganization of structure. To some extent, the rationale behind a reorganization (structure and design) is political and what scholars have called "rational" (Gortner et al. 1997, 92) organization design. A wealthy variety of research and theory on the advantages of designs that use most technical, programmatic and political objectives is abundantly available.

Organization structures are organized in order to "improve their efficiency by removing duplicative offices and improve the level of coordination" (91). These structures serve more than political ends. Administrators analyze and choose structures on the basis of technical efficiency and other matters. Structures may differ in their "capacity to adequately coordinate task activities, in their degree and form of specialization" (92), and in their capacity to allow agencies "to respond adequately to changing environments and program technologies" (92). Above all, the three major contemporary schools of thought concerning how best to "design innovative and responsive organizational structures" will be highlighted. These schools of thought include the traditional Weberian structuralism, centralization versus decentralization and differentiation versus integration.

Sources of Structure in a Bureau

The formal structure of any organization, e.g., the bureau is the officially prescribed distribution of authority and task responsibility among its offices and officials. The authority of officials to decide, to act, or to delegate responsibility is prescribed in the structure, and there is often some further specification of the conditions or bases for action, command, and intelligence gathering structures which specify how new policies and procedures are to be communicated to the appropriate level for official action. Formal structures prescribe how the bureau's work is to be divided into individual tasks and grouped into departments, offices, and other subdivisions. The relationships between and among all the subdivisions, their unique responsibilities, and their coordination are prescribed in the structure. The prescriptions that define structure are a product of legal, managerial, and professional decisions that evolve with political responsibility.

Internally as well as incrementally, executive and mid level managers develop structures of which rules of procedure for the creation of new projects, routing activity reports, and monitoring compliance are examples. In addition, professional program specialists develop the codes, regulations and procedures for programs that determine specific reporting and generate command structures for program implementation. All written rules are usually inscribed in manuals which form the yardstick for the bureau's operation. Job description, civil service laws of specific jurisdiction, specify the division of task responsibilities. These procedures and rules determine the specific activities of each bureau and how its structure will operate. The next few paragraphs will answer the following questions: (1) What models are used in the creation of these structures? (2) What principles of good and useful structural forms guide the original design and subsequent reorganization of the bureau?

1. Traditional Structural Principles.

Organizational people belief that an ideal structure should conform to the theory of administrative science school. This school of thought believes that a set of universal principles of structure are the key to successful management which is well structured and self-regulating. Max Weber's model has always been used as an analytical tool of bureaucratic management. The main structural elements of the model are hierarchy, delimited authority, formalized rules, and specialization or division of labor (Weber 1947).

Specialization of functions promotes the efficiency of bureau operation. It enables officials to become highly proficient and esoteric. It allows employees to become more productive because complex work is organized into simple and repetitive tasks that increase the speed of production. The ideal type bureaucracy is professionally, technically, and rationally designed. This ideal type bureaucracy is professionally, technically, hierarchically, and rationally designed. This rational order produces stability, consistency, and efficiency. It also enhances predictability. Because of their inherent simplicity, these principles replicated in organizational design. Simon (1965) and Simon and March (1993) have called these principles "vacuous and inconsistent" (Gortner et al. 1997, 93) because they show lack of understanding, intelligence and serious purpose.

2. Centralization and Decentralization.

Centralization and decentralization refer to the degree to which decision-making authority is confined to the top echelon offices and officials of the organization. Centralization is the process of achieving greater control for the purpose of monitoring operations and for clarifying policy making and communication channels. In other words, centralization facilitates control and uniformity in service delivery. Such uses can be critical to the survival and effectiveness of the organization. Organizations decentralize in order to enhance participatory management as articulated in the *National Performance Review* of 1993. Decentralized structures allow greater autonomy in the bureau's divisions and units. More people participate in decision making. Decentralization generated mechanisms for unaccountability and conflict because many decision-makers do not make consistent policies in bureaus. However, it allows managerial flexibility and responsiveness to clientele. Over the years, Alfred Sloan of General Motors has tended to concentrate on using a model called "centralized control of decentralized functions" (97). He used the best of the two "worlds." Based on the observations of contingency research, the effectiveness of any model including centralization versus decentralization depends on the ecological, technical and environmental conditions. In relation to bureaus and other organizations, some of the major "principles of Administrative science" (96) are unity of command, line staff, span of control, and functional and scalar principles.

Principles of Administrative Science

Delegation of Authority- is the transfer of authority and responsibility from a higher to a lower administrative official for purposes of decision-making. Due to accountability constraints, people do not like to delegate authority. They resist by refusing to relinquish power in order to delegate it. Those who delegate do so because they know or, assume that someone will manage the affairs of the organization with a sense of efficiency, accountability and effectiveness.

Unity of Command- Each official is expected to receive commands from and be responsible to only one supervisor in order to avoid confusion, unfair expectations, divided loyalties, and potential for uncoordinated action. Even though the span of control, i.e., the optimal number of subordinates, should be successfully commanded by one supervisor only. In this regard, the American bureaucracy which serves the President and Congress may have difficulty to coordinate its activities due to the fact that its loyalty may be divided between the two masters it serves. This generates conflict, ambiguity and frustration on the part of bureaucrats because they may be confused as to whom they are accountable.

Line Versus Staff- Line services are direct in their contributions to the organization. Staff services are advisory and supportive in nature. Most of the time, contemporary organizations are limited in their ability to distinguished line versus staff issues.

Functional/Scalar Principles (Tall Versus Flat Hierarchies) – This connotes the search for the optimal basis determining the appropriate type and degree of specialization in subordinate officers, and the optimal point at which to add another layer in the hierarchy.

Functional Consolidation – is merging of two or more administrative units that perform similar tasks into a single agency, e.g., fire and defense departments.

3. Differentiation and Integration

Closely related to centralization and decentralization are two basic theoretical concepts of organizational structure that underpin contemporary organization theory and design. The concepts are "differentiation and integration" (Gortner et al. 1997, 97). The two terms express finer or smoother and hierarchical task distinctions. Differentiation is the vertical and horizontal degree of specialization found in organizations. A more differentiated organization has a more complex structure because the volume of work distinguish a variety of clientele groups. The degrees of ways of specialization have policy implications and technical consequences. In other words, all organizations that are socially differentiated, due to technical specialization, are, according to Trist (1963 and 1977), not only sociotechnical systems, but they also are social ecologies.

The greater the level of differentiation, the more formidable the task of integrating or coordinating all these distinct and specialized tasks within and among the subdivisions of the organization. The integration process includes all the mechanisms and procedures by which the differentiated tasks are coordinated and ordered to achieve the organization's purpose. Integration is achieved through the hierarchical chain of command, communication system and also through the processes for task coordination specified in rules, program regulations, plans, and schedules. Staff meetings, program task forces, procedures for circulating memos about policy changes, informal consultations, and even departmental grapevines, all contribute to organizational integration" (Gortner et al. 1997, 97). The greater the level of differentiation, the greater the need for integration and coordination of activities.

When differentiation and integration are balanced, the organization structure can be viewed to be effectively designed. The "greater the level of differentiation, the greater the need for integration" (97). Although organizational members may complain about cuts, programs and procedures, more often than not, what is required is to understand the levels and patterns of differentiation and learn how to make tradeoffs. Alternative structural forms exhibit different solutions to the balancing of differentiation and integration.

4.   Bases of Departmentalization

Division of labor at the individual level results in specialized tasks that must be grouped together to form departments, offices, and other subdivisions. Departmentalization is a basis for grouping tasks and effective utilization and implementation of resources in consonant with specific elements of its jurisdiction. In a traditional sense, bureaus were departmentalized on the basis of policy area or program area, management function, client type, and geography or regional considerations. In the U.S. and in several other countries, departmentalization is based on similarity of program policy (Gortner et al. 1997). Second, in order to make departments or their units more functional, "officials are grouped into offices based on their management specialty" (98). Such specialty may include "program management, policy education, personnel, budgeting or planning" (98). Generally departments, among other things especially the political, technical and professional factors, are largely based on either programs geography or program functions (e.g., personnel) (Filley, House, and Kerr 1976); Management (process), client type (e.g., for corrections – juvenile offenders or criminals); and geography (e.g., soil conservation districts).

Organizational form may include; the "Matrix like NASA" (101). Which has several departments each of which deals with projects handled by organizational teams. Second, TQM which according to Hackman and Wageman (1995) deals with cross- functional problems. The pyramid is the third type of organizational forms that are radically different from the rest.

5. General Concerns of Traditional Approaches

The traditional approach to organizational structure places high value on stability, symmetry, clarity of lines of command, and on fully rationalizing the structure of the bureau. Generally, the universal principle of structure and management sought by the Administrative science still guides many management practices. Its Weberian origins are classic but somehow irrelevant and confusing. As a result, current approaches attempt to flexibly create an organizational form that is responsive to circumstances rather than to find a form that will be universally applicable. Structure can be crafted to accommodate specific environments and work flow reflected in the new trend toward organization design. The new trend will put emphasis on processes of management and production rather than hierarchical structure which disempower, demotivate and alienate employees.

Organization Design: Perspectives on Structure

Organizational design is the complex coordination and integration of organizational structure (Figure 2.3). Theoretically, program goals, processes and procedures rest on the universalistic principles of Administrative Science School. Solutions to problems are handled in strategic and technologically based designs: Administrators, according to Thompson's (1967, 114) view and Gortner et al. (1997), "need a rationale that creates linkages between the environment, technology and structure." Unlike the industrial setting of hierarchy, which is currently under fire for causing a lot of problems, the post industrial organizational forms are increasingly becoming more "Organismic" (Burns and Stalker 1994) and learning "Organizations" (Senge 1990; and Gortner et al. 1997, 115). Complex organizations encourage "interdependency among agencies … and a more stable, effective, interorganization system" (114). The new structures should emphasize "a network rather than a hierarchy of authority and control relations, with open, lateral, and upward communications based on consultation, not just downward commands … tasks and workflow are flexible and subject to continual redefinition on the basis of new information" (Perrow 1960, 33-34).

In the new economy (high tech) self-correcting organizations (Landau 1973), organizational learning through single-loop, double-loop (conflict stage) and deutero learning stages, (Argyris and Schon 1978) and self-designing organizations (Hedberg, Nystrong, and Starbuck 1976) must have "a different culture than the traditional, hierarchical, authoritarian ones of the past" (Gortner et al. 1997, 118). These approaches include the traditional and the universalistic prescriptions of the administrative science school and antidesign theories that are increasingly becoming irrelevant. Structures can be designed with the use of technology and application of interdependency models. Given this reality, it is

Figure 2.3. The Structure of Organizations

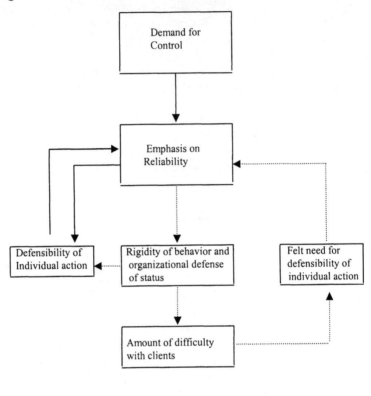

_____ Intended results

- - - - - - - - - - - - Unintended results

Source: Pugh, D.S. 1984. *Organization Theory: Selected Readings.* London: Penguin Books, p. 32.

important to know that structure can support or impede the efficient coordination of work process although the former does not define the process. Careful planning should match structures to technology, environments, and program design and development. In such structure, there is need to reinforce rather than hinder program administration, implementation and evaluation.

All organizations create mechanisms for carrying on activities that are instrumental to their goal achievement. The regularity of the activities are entered around the processes of allocation, coordination and supervision of the organization's structure. Organizational structure may be viewed as a form of bureaucratic technical efficiency (Weber 1947) or bureaucratic dysfunctionalism (March and Simon 1958). March and Simon have tried to assertively show that imperfections of the bureaucracy could be, paradoxically and ironically speaking, "just as great a cause for its perpetuation as its efficiencies" (Pugh 1987, 13). In his studies of firms in stable and adaptive environments, Burns (1963) comparatively contrasted bureaucratic with organismic structures. Bureaucratic structures are mechanistic in orientation. For instance, in relation to organismic authority, task allocation and communication are very adjustable while the bureaucracy's rules and procedures are extremely rigid – due to their constitutional and political mandates. Woodward (1958) strongly suggests that the structure of the manufacturing arena is strongly related to the technology of production. This proposition provokes debate concerning whether all organizations are similar in their possession of the basic principles of structure. Pugh (1987) has described the research he carried out with his colleagues by measuring "the range of degrees of specialization, standardization and centralization of authority structures" (13-14). They also investigated the "effects of contextual factors such as size, technology, ownership, interdependence, etc., on the characteristic differences found" (14). Lawrence and Lorsch (1967) analyzed the degree of structural differentiation that is necessary for "a firm to function in a particular environment and the corresponding integration mechanisms required for it to be a high performer" (Pugh 1987, 14). Crozier (1976) used organizational structure to analyze "recurring strategic and tactical games played by individuals or groups in organizations" as they use power for bargaining purposes. Finally, in relation to the structure of organizations, Jaques (1976), in his *A General Theory of Bureaucracy* shows that the basic depth-structure of an organization is established by and based on "the manager-subordinate relationships which have different time-spans of work discretion" (Pugh 1987, 14). All these scholars have shown that structure has nothing to do with processes, but something(s) to do with hierarchy.

Hage and Aiken (1970) conducted case study research on organizational change and dynamics. Having studied a variety of firms, these authors identified seven points for strategic organizational climates. The Hage and Aiken's seven structural characteristics of adaptive or dynamic organization include:

1. Organizational complexity, defined as the number and professionalism of occupational specialties in the organization, is positively associated with the ability of the organization to respond to external change, because professionals are often extremely oriented to the developments in their fields and bring them to the agency.

2. Centralization of authority in the upper echelons of the bureau slows the rate of change because decision criteria are static and lower ranking personnel, who often see the need for change, are most directly excluded from decisions.

3. Formalization, the degree to which tasks are highly codied into rules and standard operating procedures, slows the rate of program change. When large portions of program and management activities are rule governed, change is delayed and perceptions of the possibility of substantial change are limited. Extreme formalization also slows the process of implementing change, as a whole set of rules must be developed and coordinated with existing ones.

4. Stratification, the differentiated distribution of rewards among employees to emphasize rank, decreases the rate of change. Stratification creates insecurities and fears of loss of status. It also discourages negative reports on organizational performance and open discussion of problems with superiors.

5. Emphasis on a high volume of production lowers the rate of change since change, almost of necessity, disrupts production.

6. Greater emphasis on efficiency delays change because new program ideas are usually oriented first to improvements in quality, not efficiency. Thus, program changes will only be adopted when they have developed to the point of high operating efficiency.

7. Higher levels of job satisfaction are also associated with greater rates of change since satisfaction increases commitment to organizational success and enables the organization to overcome the strains involved in change (Gortner et al. 1997, 113).

Self-Designing Bureaus and Organizations

Complex public and private organizations (firms) could be part and parcel of the boundary – spawning cooperative, coordinating or competitive institution for resources and program jurisdictions. Informed organizational administrators would tend to create a climate of, or a climate for stable and effective interdependency of organizational systems (Litwak and Hylton 1962; Benson 1975; and Lindblom 1965). Thompson (1967), who argued that organizations are professionally and technologically managed in order to accomplish certain organizational and structural processes of the environment, tend to "boundary-span" between the bureau and the environment. The boundary spanners are roles that are played by certain individuals for the purpose of "buffering" the core technology from external interference. In relation to external interference and possible disruption of organizational operations, "under norms of rationality, organizations facing heterogeneous task environments seek to identify homogeneous segments and establish structural units to deal with each" (Thompson 1976, 70).

Korten's (1980) organizational model of self-designed structures that "learn" (Gortner et al. 1997, 116) advocates "emerging knowledge of program development needs rather than ... to traditions or excessive needs for internal security and control" (116) of structures and technologies. These structures need to be tailored to meet program needs.

Korten studied effective Third World programs in terms of their diversity of goals, sponsorship, size and funding sources. He argued that with the exception of those which did not succeed, the successful programs that were developed depended "on the learning capacity of the implementing organization" (116). Korten (1980, 498) discovered that "The learning organization embraces error." This organization does not deny if the program identifies problems, corrects them, and uses available means, regardless of source, to solve the problems. Second, the learning organization capitalizes on existing local knowledge, expertise and technology in order to remedy the program problems. The program targets and means for reaching them enable program developers to be informed about the priorities and hardships of the target group. Third, for learning organizations, linkage of knowledge to action enables the organization's implementation leaders and users to socialize with "the teams that created the original program" Korten 1980, 429). In other words, this approach tends to ensure that the dedication and enthusiasm of the project initiators (champions) is not lost but is "used and rewarded" (Peters and Waterman, 1982). Also, policymaking teams should never be separated from the implementation ones because these "clients, researchers and administrators" (Gortner et al. 1997, 116) form the necessary reservoir for viable and creative adaptation of the program. In the Third World, program planning, development, implementation and evaluation can be a participatory endeavor. In the U.S., program development clients lack a set of unified demands. As a result, several problems related to program procedures, staffing, and funding may create constraints in the process of program development and implementation. Some of these programs are associated with American judicial, legislative, executive and bureaucratic mandates that take a long time to satisfy ambitious, parochial and diverse political constituencies.

Hedberg, Nystrom, and Starbuck (1976) just as Landau (1973) have shown that self-designing bureaus and organizations use program development processes which put pressure on them to enhance flexibility and create mechanisms for sensitizing opportunity and knowledge that are necessary for organizational self-redesignig. In some ways "Perrow's nonroutine structure is comparable to Burns' and Stalker's 'organismic' system (Gortner et al. 1997, 117). The former four scholars are less interested in structural forms that portray decision-making channels which will unrigidify organizations by forcing them to reappraise themselves continuously. The "minimalist" processes that prevent complacency and promote the continuous drive for organizational self-design or "self-renewal" include but are not limited to:

1. Acting on minimal consensus rather than waiting for unanimity.
2. Striving for only minimal contentment among personnel, which sharpens their desire for change and their search for alternatives.
3. Working toward only minimal affluence since even though a 'small buffer of flexible resources is an asset ... too much affluence breeds complacency and contempt for new opportunities.
4. Placing only minimal faith in plans or goals. Even though they are needed to direct immediate action, they should be discarded easily.
5. Attempting to be only minimally consistent since total consistency impeded the pluralistic bargaining process that produces incremental changes, thereby forcing a delayed and destructive revolution to achieve any change.
6. Aiming only for minimal rationality in procedures. Even though basic managerial processes must be established, highly coherent and fully rationalized structures convey a false sense of control and prematurely define new problems and opportunities rather than encouraging their exploration. Some structural and procedural ambiguities will keep the organization in a state of readiness for change (Gortner et al. 1997, 118).

Having studied learning organizations, Senge (1990) argued that they "must have a different culture than the traditional, hierarchical and authoritarian one of the past." His concept of culture means "the perspectives, values, beliefs, myths, behavior patterns, and so on commonly held within an organization" (Gortner et al. 1997, 18). Senge (1990) asserts that learning organizations have five technologies that are critical to organizational success. They consist of:

1. **Systems thinking.** The ability to contemplate the whole of a phenomenon instead of any individual part of the pattern.
2. **Personal mastery.** The discipline of continually clarifying and deepening one's personal vision, of focusing one's energies, of developing patience, and seeing reality objectively.
3. **Mental models.** The process by which individuals learn how to surface and challenge the other individuals' mental models (deeply ingrained assumptions, generalizations, pictures or images) that influence how one understands the work and, therefore, takes action.
4. **Building shared vision.** The skill of unearthing a shared 'picture of the future' that binds people together around a common identity and sense of destiny, therefore fostering genuine commitment and enrollment rather than compliance.
5. **Team learning.** The skill of sharing 'dialogue,' the capacity of members of a team to suspend assumptions and enter into a genuine 'thinking together,' and learning how to recognize the patterns of interaction in teams that undermine learning (Senge 1990, 6-10; and Gortner et al. 1997, 18-19).

The underpinning concept behind the self-designing organization is for it to remain with tension and radical dynamism like the organismic model. However, the self-designing organization is different from the organismic one because the former uses different strategies for the creation and maintenance of its dynamism. Such dynamism has power that makes the status quo difficult through rule setting that makes change easier and achievable. Such kind of dynamism is inherent in TQM processes whose synergistic vision is shared with self-designing organizations.

Organismic and Mechanistic Systems

To effectively define the organismic system requires the need for its comparison with the mechanistic systems. First, organismic organizational system is characterized by:

1. The contributive nature of special knowledge and experience to the common task of the concern.
2. The realistic nature of the individual task, which is seen as set by the total situation of the concern.
3. The adjustment and continual redefinition of individual tasks through interaction with others.
4. The shedding of responsibility as a limited field of rights, obligation and methods. (Problems may not be posted upwards, downwards or sideways.)
5. The spread of commitment to the concern beyond any technical definition.
6. A network structure of control, authority, and communication.
7. Omniscience no longer imputed to the head of the concern; knowledge may be located anywhere in the network; this location becoming the center of authority.
8. A lateral rather than a vertical direction of communication through the organization.
9. A content of communication which consists of information and advice rather than instructions and decisions.
10. Commitment to the concern's tasks and to the "technical ethos" of material progress and expansion is more highly valued than loyalty.
11. Importance and prestige attached to affiliations and expertise valid in the industrial, technical and commercial millieu external to the firm (Burns 1963; and Pugh 1984, 46-47).

Organismic organizational systems are suitably adapted to unstable organizational climates which are prone to a variety of prevailing problems. Specialist roles that exist in hierarchically mechanistic settings are unheard of in organismic organizational environments. Responsibilities, functions, methods, and powers of organizational participants require continuous definition and redefinition. The definition and redefinition of these tasks is a group or collective rather than an individual exercise. Collective or group activity enables the organization to learn, share responsibility and tasks and try to solve common problems. Individuals work for a specific and overall purpose of the organization. "Interaction runs laterally as much as vertically, and communication between people of different ranks tends to resemble lateral consultation rather than vertical command. Omniscience can no longer be imputed to the boss at the top" (Pugh 1984, 45). Unlike the individual in mechanistic systems, the person in the organismic organizational realm is committed to the organization. The mechanistic system tells the individual what to do, how to do it, what does not concern him/her, what is not expected of him/her, and what others are responsible for. Contrary to the mechanistic system, the organismic organization allows the individual to be "independent," exploratory, boundaryless, responsible, competent and curiously innovative and productive. In other words, organismic systems create a climate for open and free exchange of information flow that can be used for dynamic change.

Second, mechanistic Taylorism is adapted to stable organizational environments. In mechanistic systems, specialists handle problems, tasks and concerns. Each specialist "does his or her own thing" regardless of the overall purpose or mission of the organization. Only the top person approves or appraises the job and work of the individual by seeing its relevance to the whole organization. "The technical methods, duties and powers attached to each post are precisely defined and a high value is placed on precision and demarcation" (44).

Vocational and professional interaction in the organization is vertical (superior-subordinate) rather than horizontal and collegial. An individual operates in the context of the dictates and prescriptions that govern the role he/she plays in the organization. Such a hierarchy of values portrays the top person to be omniscient. This charted and complex hierarchical management system works like a control system that allows decisions and instructions to "filter" as they descend "through a succession of amplifiers" (44). In other words, mechanistic systems are rationally bureaucratic and characterized by:

1. The specialized differentiation of functional tasks into which the problems and tasks facing the concern as a whole are broken down.
2. The abstract nature of each individual task, which is pursued with techniques and purposes more or less distinct from those of the concern as a whole.
3. The reconciliation, for each level in the hierarchy, of these distinct performances by the immediate superiors.
4. The precise definition of rights and obligations and technical methods attached to each functional role.
5. The translation of rights and obligations and methods into the responsibilities of a functional position.

6. Hierarchic structure of control, authority and communication.
7. A reinforcement of the hierarchic structure by the location of knowledge of actualities exclusively at the top of the hierarchy.
8. A tendency for vertical interaction between members of the concern, i.e., between superior and subordinate.
9. A tendency for operations and working behavior to be governed by superiors.
10. Insistence on loyalty to the concern and obedience to superiors as a condition of membership.
11. A greater importance and prestige attaching to internal (local) than to general (cosmopolitan) knowledge, experience and skill (46).

As a rational and mechanistic "jungle," to be effective in communications, and in spite of its insistence on using mechanistic principles, the ideology of bureaucratic formality which is also the ideology of industrial management-the bureaucracy, tends to employ liaison specialists in order to penetrate bureaucratic tough and enhance effective communications. Sometimes special committees are selected to expedite the communications structural operations without which the system may develop pathologies that may "strangle" the organization. In general, "out of date mechanistic organizations are perpetuated and pathological systems develop, usually because of one or the other of two things: internal politics and career structure" (50).

There are three theories which rationalize organizational structure. First, the classical Weberian theory of scientific management views the organization to be a hierarchy (formal organization) in which labor is not only motivated by material rewards, but it is also highly specialized for efficient production. This theory which contains both the motivation organization theories in one, receive unity of control through a centrally placed bureaucratic or charismatic system of authority which uses mechanistic techniques to account for the efficiency of taskful purposes, processes, and satisfaction of clientele needs (Etzioni 1964).

Secondly, the development of the Human Relations Theory (school) in America took into notice that material rewards which motivate a person to physically become an appendage of the machine did not motivate workers well enough. As a result, the human relations school (informal organization) advocated that workers have noneconomic, social, psychological, emotional and cultural needs which organizations should nurture and communicate if they expect workers to be satisfied and productive. The proponents of this school are Mayo and Lewin who placed emphasis in participatory management in decision making. Since the critics of this school believe that the human relations school deals with the management of workers' emotions, workers are manipulated to serve the needs of top management rather than their own needs (Etzioni 1964).

Finally, the third school is the structuralist approach which is a synthesis of the formal and informal organizations. While the human relations school recognizes organizational harmony, the structuralists recognize that organizations are in a dilemma: There are inevitable strains which can be reduced but not eliminated—between organizational needs and personal needs; between rationality and nonrationality; between formal and informal relations; between management and workers; and ... between ranks and divisions (Etzioni, 38).

In this arena, the roles of management and workers come into conflict as each group tries to fulfill their own rights and obligations, respectively. Although the conflicting obligations alienate the workers, the conflicts can be managed and minimized but not eliminated. These conflicts generate the impetus for creativity, organizational health, and effectiveness. By itself, this organizational arena provides a conducive climate for planning strategically. When organizational leaders view the structure of their organization in light of the three schools of thought, they can be able to make better strategic decisions which can perpetuate the dynamism of their organizations.

Perceptions of Strategic Decision Making

A dynamic organization has a motivating organizational climate in which planning participants play diverse roles in strategic decision-making processes. The six main models (styles) of strategic decision making are anarchy (accident), compromise-consensus (collegial or team approach or groupthink), mechanistic (bureaucratic or Machiavellian), conflict-resolution (debate), and rational. These decision-making models are also leadership styles. Although each style has advantages and disadvantages, the rational model, regardless of its uncomprehensiveness in goal and objective setting, and in spite of its narrow participatory base, is not only the ideal (Chaffee 1983), but also the most common management style in organizational settings. However, in the above mentioned criticism of the rational model, "What is desired is not homogeneity of response, but diversity in participation." Rationality is a style of formalized planning embedded in the nature and theory of strategic decisions (Chaffee 1983).

1. The Essence and Theory of Strategic Decisions

Strategic decision making is synonymous with "strategic choice, strategic planning, or simply strategy" (Pennings 1985, 1). Though "strategy" has its origin in the military sciences, it has acquired organizational, semantical, directional, heuristic, cultural, and eclectic dimensions.

Military strategy is not only the art of war, but it is the science of "moving and disposing troops so as to impose upon the enemy, the place and time and conditions for the fighting preferred by oneself" (2). This military analogy is limited, however, because unlike the mobility and flexibility of armies, organizations are comparatively sluggish, inert, clumsy, and fixed in place and time. In the light of its military linguistic roots, strategy is long-term and comprehensive while tactics are short-term. Hence, strategic and tactical planning become logical derivatives. Organizationally, strategy means:

1. A statement of intent that constrains or directs subsequent activities (explicit strategy);
2. An action of major impact that constrains or directs subsequent activities (implicit strategy); and
3. A "rationalization" or social construction that gives meaning to prior activities (rationalized strategy).

On the other hand, cognitive representations of the phenomenological or interpretive "schools of thought" hold the assumption that organizations, consist of people whose collective experience leads to convictions that represent the image of their organization and its strategy. Strategy, in this case, is viewed as an external posture of the organization's identity or mission. This external organizational reality or mission is the organization's socially constructed reality.

Strategic decisions may be formulated, implemented, and evaluated in a directional dimension within the organization (vertically integrated, horizontally diversified, and perhaps "concentrically coordinated").

Empirical findings from private and public institutions and management consulting which are involved in the praxis of strategic decision making provide heuristic reflections on the theory of strategic decision making. Five heuristic observations on the theory are evident.

First, Chandler (1962), a business historian who was associated with strategic and paradigmatic organizational structures examined the evolution of large corporations and the connection between them and the environment, strategy, and organization structure. His analytical findings "suggested that strategic diversity from one product to a multiproduct focus was more effectively dealt with through divisional organization designs" (15). The introduction of designs was often impeded by organizational inertia and commitments to the status quo.

Second, Nelson and Winter (1982), writing on institutional economics (resource-dependence research in organization theory), concluded that organizations are "viewed as establishing favorable exchange relationships with interdependent actors in their external environment" (15).

Third, in industry where oligopolies exist, labor is highly specialized, and competition is predictable, the situation is viewed as a community or "niche" which is able to secure necessary external control. If the environment is volatile and highly diffuse, it will have a narrow niche width which is not very attractive. In this case, an environment which is highly competitive, has a broad niche width, and is not volatile, will be attractive to strategic decision making. In other words, the nature of environmental posture or environmental focus, or design, will influence organizational strategy.

Fourth, March and Simon (1958) have developed the bounded-rationality paradigm through which they perceive strategic decision making as a process rather than an outcome. They see outcomes as secondary, treated as "a cognitive construction for retroactive sense making" (Pennings 1985, 16). Bounded-rationality paradigm perceives organizations to be composed of subgroups which are, from a structuralist perspective, characterized by goodness and bad-ness, unity and diversity, loyalty and disloyalty, etc. In their subgroup dichot-omy, organizations vie for power though their interests are parochial and incon-gruent. In this scenario, dominant organizational coalitions try to minimize the undesirable consequences of bounded rationality and power differentials. By so doing, dominant coalitions behave strategically because rational actors (partici-pants) in the coalition help to create unison. In addition, organizations adopt a course of action that is the result of a negotiation among internal and external interest groups. Empirical literature on public policy, especially the works of Allison (1941), has demonstrated that bounded rationality, political, and rational strategic decision-making models were used during the 1961 Cuban Missile Crisis.

Fifth, Pennings says that Wildavsky (1979) and his students reviewed the value of zero-based budgeting and criticized organizations for inertia. They said that:

> the inability of decision makers to dissociate themselves from their roles and to be-come proactive rather than reactive, and the difficulty in dovetailing the plans with their execution. The institutionalization and routinization of formal planning sys-tems might lead to the crystallization of action generators that lead their own life, uncoupled from relevant strategic events (for example, Starbuck 1983).

Actions are triggered not because the planning activities required scanning the internal and external environment for information that induces such actions, but by the routinized planning cycles and their rigid deadlines. The planning systems are imposed upon the organization—for example, by legislative wave or by executive order—and, although the organizations at various levels are required to synchronize their planning activities, these activities become increas-ingly vitalized and devoid of strategic significance (20-21).

Nonparticipatory practices in rational decision-making produce organiza-tional inertia.

Culturally, strategic decision-making theory may be viewed from the prac-tical viewpoint in such a way that organizations are "systems of symbols, val-ues, and myths that can be examined on their deeper logical structure (Pennings 1983, 2). The methodology for conceptualizing and analyzing such systems is anthropological structuralism. Structuralists analyze and expose a system's cul-ture to its base configurations of polar opposites. The knowledge of the prevail-ing opposites helps to explain how people interpret their reality and how their culture shapes their behavior. Strategic planners, likewise, analyze the culture of their organizations and explicate their rudimentary configurations. Strategic changes follow the modifications of the configurations of organizational values and symbols. Such organizational modifications help people to acquire "new cognitive schemata … or 'mantra'—a form of mythical thinking" (25).

Finally, strategic decision-making theory is a product of strategic interdependence "mutual or expected rationality" (29) of a variety of disciplines. The interdisciplinarity of strategic decision-making makes the theory quite illusive. The illusiveness of strategic decision making is, therefore, a critical and crucial issue in strategic theory and practice.

C. Decision Making Models

Introduction

The purpose of this section is to offer a comparative, descriptive, ad prescriptive variety of the paramount decision making (policymaking) theories in bureaus and other organizations. The comparison contrasts these theories (methods) in terms of search, analysis and choice perspectives. Regardless of the weaknesses, strengths, and criticisms of each technique and its underpinning assumptions, the prospects for contingency theory or synergistic evolution are examined in the implicit light of control and communication of the decisions made.

Decision Making

Decision making is one of the most complex and overtly political activities in organizations. Though most basic policy decisions are formally made by elected officials and courts, administrative decisions about program implementation, staffing, and budget have significant and lasting effects on public policy. The methods, or procedures, or theories or techniques that bureaus employ for decision making also have important political consequences. The decision method affects who participates, how agenda are established, which alternatives are considered, how they are compared and analyzed, and which values will dominate in the final selection. The selected procedures for administrative decision making affect the substance of choice. Whatever method is used depends on the problems it tends to solve and the purpose of the program articulated.

The bureaus, in order to be innovative, tend to rely on standard operating procedures, scenarios that March and Simon (1993) call *performance programs*. Performance programs are the ways in which officials come up with alternatives that are specified or programmed in advance. Programmed decisions are fully codified with respect to both the identification of options or preferences and the method and criterion for choice. The "high degree of programming does not only serve to make the bureau stable, consistent, and predictable, as required of an agent of law, but, it also makes the bureau rigid and reduces the possibility for innovation."

The Methods

Table 2.2 is an illustration of the paramount elements of decision making in public agencies. The differences which result in the success or failure of each of these methods could be understood in the light of the culture of "participation, accountability, and organizational setting" (364).

The Rational Model for Policy Analysis – Theory

The rational method of decision making is used in the public and private sectors. It is mainly used for analyzing efficiency and return on investment; in this respect the rational approach is the ideal model for decision making. The emphasis is on efficiency, which makes it possible for policy—goals set by policymakers to be viewed in relation to the role of the bureaucracy. Research on administrative behavior has been used to criticize rationality for its unrealistic and idealized assumptions. Continually, it is challenged for objectivity, suitability, and description. The model has been modified for use in the context of policy analysis and systems analysis. These approaches are costly and elaborate.

Rational choice is rational because it tries to select the most efficient means or instrument to realize a given purpose or goal. The model is also called "instrumental rationality when it is used for identifying the alternative that produces the most of the desired effect or greatest level of return" (226). It promotes the value of efficiency. In contrast to instrumental rationality, substantive rationality is concerned with the values of 'goodness' (226) of the goal or purpose itself. What is substantively rational is the subject of political philosophy and legislative, judicial and administrative rationality and deals more with "means rather than ends" (226).

The four stages of instrumental rationality are as follows:

1. The goal (end) of the policy is considered a given for the situation under consideration. The assumption is that external policymakers set goals. Also feasible alternatives which are means for accomplishing goals are given. In principle, search, which is not the process for determining several preference-based alternatives is not controlled by administrators, who determine alternatives, but is controlled, through selection, by political and technical experts.

2. Second, alternative programs or procedures are "subjected to a thorough analysis to identify all the consequences, desirable and undesirable, intended and unintended, that are associated with each alternative" (226). The

Figure 2.2. The Functional Practices of Evaluation and Control of the Mission

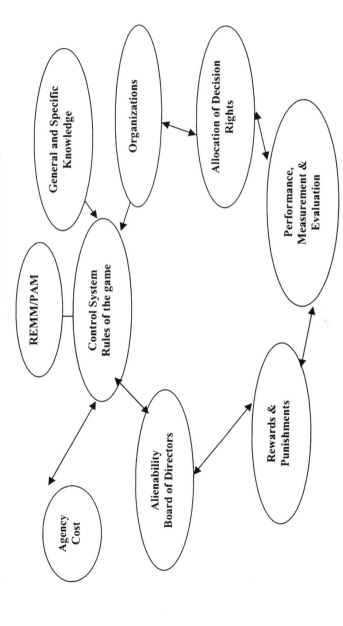

Source: Harris, P.R. and Moran, R.T. 1991. *Managing Cultural Differences.* Houston, TX: Gulf Publishing Company.

consequences may be uncertain and risky. The analysis of alternatives is experimentally and scientifically forecasted.

3. Third, the alternatives are ranked in accordance with consistent and consecutive preferences and their respective consequences. Each alternative has different consequences which are ranked to correspond with the right alternatives.

4. Finally, the choice criterion is to optimize rather than maximize benefits or to select the alternative with the highest value. In essence, the rational decision method is used as an advisory tool by policymakers when goals and policies are at stake. It is administratively, directly, and immediately used in order to identify efficient programs and operating procedures.

March and Simon (1993) have criticized the rational method of policy analysis. They argue that three unrealistic assumptions characterize the model. First, "it is not clear how or by whom the alternatives" (Gortner et al. 1997, 227) that are to be analyzed and ranked are identified. Not all possible alternatives are examined. Imagination is limited, and selective perception is common. What sample of options is identified and studied? On what basis are the options selected? The model does not specify this; it assumes that the alternatives are selected by policymakers. The "objectivity of the search process and its fidelity to the principle of efficiency are called into question if political considerations determine which possible programs will be analyzed" (227).

The second criticism, according to March and Simon is the false assumption based on the belief that "risk and uncertainty" (227) will be known. In other words, consequences are either over or under estimated. On the other hand, whole categories of consequences known as 'unanticipated consequences' (227) are missed.

Finally, March and Simon have criticized the classical rational method for its assumption, that the decision maker, you and me or individual or group "has a consistent preference ordering for the consequences of the alternative" (228). Generally, "many consequences, desirable or undesirable, a company a program" (228). To ensure the effectiveness of the rational method, comparisons among a set of alternatives and their consequences and vice versa, must be made.

The problem of finding a consistent preference ordering for the various consequences of different alternatives is an important theoretical stumbling block for policy analysis. Even though, "analysts transform all types of consequences into one, money" (228). Cost-benefit analysis is a key form of policy analysis. This technique is based on "comparing the monetary value to society of all costs and all benefits of each alternative" (228). The only one kind of consequence is monetary and the optimal solution alternative that maximizes net benefit to society is the 'best' one that can be selected.

According to Pareto (Italian economist and sociologist), "change should be made if at least one person benefits by it and none are worse off" (288). This is kind of utopian. However, the Kaldor-Hicks (British economists) criterion which is applied very often states "that if a policy change makes the 'gainers' so much better off than they can compensate for the 'losers' and still come out ahead, the policy should be undertaken" (288). In actual practice, this criterion suggests that "we maximize net benefits, that is benefits minus costs" (288). This though is undemocratic since it does not deal with equity issues. As a rational policy analysis method, the drawbacks of this method raises issues as to whether its "intangible benefits and costs can be assigned monetary worth" (288). As a result, the "debate raises questions about race, gender and other 'human' political issues about which there is intense disagreement" (228-229). Even when estimates are done or designed with statistical accuracy and plausibility, evidence indicates that the beneficiaries of the system are not minorities and women; but rather, white males.

Another drawback of cost-benefit analysis as the cornerstone of a decision-making method is that it substitutes judgement based on economic factors or technical efficiency for professional judgement (Cohen 1980). Such a decision might undermine the psychological and political (strategic) importance of such a decision in the case of military related decisions that concern whether a ship is more effective even when it is more costly than a cheaper one which can do the same functions but less effectively because of its strategic vulnerability.

Finally, in spite its politically inclined cost-benefit method, those who use rationality argue that it is an "objective and apolitical in a partisan sense" (230). However, as a policy making tool, "its role is advisory rather than determinative" (230). This shows not only who makes decisions and how the decisions are made, but it also shows that changes in the political system are inevitable. For instance, such changes may be associated with Democrats who tend to "favor low discount rates" (230) while Republications tend to favor higher discount rates" (230). Democrats argue that lower discount rates are components of cost-benefit analysis which allows projects to be efficiently funded when viewed by budgetary agencies and taxpayers.

The Rational Model

Essentially, the rational way of making decisions is based on individual reason. Individuals or groups of individuals may set goals and objectives for their organization. They can generate and examine all alternatives for achieving organizational goals. They can be able to predict the consequent consequences of each adopted alternative. They can compare the consequences in relation to the agreed goals and objectives. It is true that because of individual values which people choose for themselves, and devise a machinery for implementing and evaluating programs which promote the values, goals are "fluid and conflicting"

(Van Vught 1985, 596). They are fluid and conflicting because, as McNeil (1973) says, the rational model through which the values are articulated, lacks comprehensiveness of intellectual diversity. However, since an eclectic rationalist perspective of the rational model possesses collective views from other models, it can be used to criticize values in the process of decision-making; collective and rationally organized participatory discussions enable values to be collectively formulated, integrated, and shared by the group or by organizational members. In the light of the collective rationalist view, values can be criticized, liberalized, "deauthoritarianized," and democratized. The liberalization, deauthoritarianization, and democratization of the rational model is a logical imperative, especially in higher education and other organizations and corporations.

Lawrence, Pennings (1985, 375) argues that the rational planning approach rigidifies behavior because the future is unpredictable. This phenomenon of an unpredictability pushes behavior from its goals. As a result, organizational people spend much more time in executive behavior programs than they do in strategic planning. In this case, people's use of time to program behavior blocks rationality, hence its rigidity.

These strategies, according to Pennings, may be used to reduce the rigid aspects of rational planning. First, organizational behavior can be programmed to contain healthy rationality. Policy decisions can be made retrospectively to guide future behavior. Second, institutional planners should employ participatory decision-making strategies. The collegial decision-making strategies, such as the collegial and informed consensus rather than the authoritarian-control and logic-driven models of judgmental and analytical reasoning processes should be used. Third, time strategic interdependence or eclectic rationality should be applied. Eclectic rationality is balanced and flexible management. Unlike the rational model and MBO, "eclectic rationality" will not stifle creativity.

Grandy and Warner (1986), writing on *Philosophical Grounds for Rationality*, indicated that rationality, notwithstanding its narrow and stifling intellectual base, could be understood better by examining its meaning, reasoning style, psychological explanation, and ethical reality. Rationality is communication which is "reason-governed activity" (Grandy and Warner 1986, 1). It is also "a purposive reason-governed endeavor" (1). As Grandy and Warner point out, Kant and Locke assert that rational reasoning consists of the entertainment and acceptance in thought and speech of a set of sequential ideas each of "which is derivable by an acceptance principle of inference from its predecessors in the set" (9).

Rational reasoning has a narrow intellectual base which stifles creativity because many people who plan rationally, or for whom rational planning is done, are qualitatively selected. They are selected because of inherent conventional, situational or natural limitations of rationality which is ability to argue argumentatively. Arguing is a skill, more than the ability to see logical connections. A planner's ability to make argumentative utterances will be effective when the meaning of the words and intentions are known. The meaning is systematized and systemized if it is shared rationally and conventionally. Systematic and conventional rationality is elocutionary, persuasive, and effective communication (Grandy and Warner 1986, 598).

One way in which rational planning is used is in the policy area of institutional management. In respect to policy-oriented issues, Van Vught (1985) suggests that actors who participate in the formulation, analysis, and integration of values can agree on the policies they make because they "purge the private, selfish, or idiosyncratic preferences in open and public debate" (598).

Organizational theory has three main dimensions which characterize policy-networks within the rationalist tradition (perspective). These dimensions include: (1) centrality – the number and the length of linkages between one organization and all other related organizations; (2) complexity – the extent of functional dissimilarity (differentiation) of goals, services, products, or target populations among related organizations; and (3) density – the extent to which members of a population or network are directly related (connected) cohesively. Rationality, a "policy-network can be seen as an operational elaboration and an institutional approximation of the rationalist idea of collective decision-making and policy development by means of the 'community of discourse'" (602).

Ellen Chaffee authored *Rational Decision Making in Higher Education* in 1983. Summarizing the essential features of the rational decision, Chaffee concluded that there should be:

1. A clear set of specific values or objectives which serve as criteria for particular decisions;
2. An organizational atmosphere of stability, confidence, and predictability;
3. Consistency, on the part of the decision-maker, with prior practice and with understood principles of decision making within the institution;
4. Provision for analyzing a particular situation as strategic, tactical, or operational and for determining whether the classification is permanent or temporary;
5. Provision for determining who should make the decision, who will be affected by it, and to what degree each party should participate in the decision-making process;
6. A mechanism for generating as many alternative solutions to the problem and for presenting those alternatives for simultaneous considerations;
7. A means of assessing the likelihood that a particular alternative will produce results that correspond with the value structure;
8. A process for evaluating the degree to which such correspondence has been achieved and for feeding the evaluation back into the decision process (60-61).

It is evidently clear that among other things, the rational model of planning is associated with institutional or societal goals. The goals rationally evolve from institutional operations and needs. Experienced goal framers formulate goals in a social climate conducive to goal articulation, clarification, implementation, and evaluation. The purpose, intent, and implication of goals (ends) are focused on the needs and means of the organization which uses the goals. When these goals are constructed in a psychologically and socio-politically stable climate, they can hardly get into conflict with declared institutional and cultural values. The tendency to eliminate conflict between and among goals and values enables management, irrespective of the rigidity and creativity-stifling characteristics of (rationality), to reduce or minimize its negative attributes (Chaffee 1983).

The rational model, according to Havelock (1973), emphasizes a problem-solving process which has six stages: 'building relationships; diagnosing the problem; acquiring resources; choosing the solution; gaining acceptance; stabilizing the innovation." By comparison, Halstead (1974) argues that the rational strategy has six components, namely "determining goals, identifying problems, diagnosing problems, establishing premises, searching for possible solutions, selecting the solution" (17). Kitchen, whom Halstead has cited, indicates that an alternative strategy of rational planning involves six of the following: "Sequential steps: (1) identification of problems; (2) diagnosis of the problem situation, (3) clarification of the diagnostic findings; (4) search for solutions, (5) mobilizing for change, and (6) making the actual change decisions" (17).

March (1994) is a renowned professor at Stanford and an authority in decision-making. He asserts that decision-making is fundamentally central to individual, group, organizational and scientific life and enterprise. Drawing from a broad interdisciplinary perspective of the social and behavioral sciences, March tries to vividly and paradoxically show how decisions are made as opposed to how they ought to be made. In this endeavor, he addresses four controversial and paramount issues that persistently affect the province of organizational decision-making.

First, decision-making is based on alternative assumptions and actions whose expected consequences…are not known with certainty (March 1994, 5). Rational choice decision-making processes are preference-based because the consequences are examined or evaluated relative to personal preferences. "Alternatives are compared in terms of the extent to which their expected consequences are thought to serve the preferences of the decision maker" (2). Such rational choice processes are humanistically and theoretically rooted in "microeconomic models of resource allocation, political theories of coalition formation, statistical decision theories" and strategic, situational, demographic, and global survival theories (3). For instance:

Decision makers do not consider all consequences of their alternatives. They focus on some and ignore others. Relevant information about consequences is not sought, and available information is often not used. Instead of having a complete, consistent set of preferences, decision makers seem to have incomplete and inconsistent goals, not all of which are considered at the same time. The decision rules used by real decision makers seem to differ from the ones imagined by decision theory. Instead of considering 'expected values' or 'risk' as those terms are used in decision theory, they invent other criteria. Instead of calculating the 'best possible' action, they search for an action that is good enough' (9).

Human inability to know about the possible consequences, to use incomplete and inconsistent goals, and to use a different set of rules for decision-making rather than decision theory shows that rationality is limited (bounded) at the individual, organizational, societal and scientific levels. Rationality is bounded (limited) because of "attention, memory, comprehension and communication" (9) problems. As a result, decision makers tend to satisfice or use problem-solving heuristics rather than maximize or optimize (Sagini 1987). This may result in slack or uninnovative organizational experiences.

Second, the bounded element of rationality tends to make the decision-making process to be characterized by inconsistency and ambiguity rather than clarity and consistency. Decision makers take risks inadvertently in order to avoid them. They make errors by estimating potential risks. Whether they are successful or less so, knowledgeable or ignorant, they have to make decisions in a competitive, global and sometimes turbulent environment. They do so in order to demonstrate that they are rational (intelligent, calculating, successful, spiritually and coldly materialistic or sane) in a procedural or substantive sense. Logically, the consequences are defined by alternatives, expectations, preferences and decision rules.

Third, though decision-making is thought to be an important and paramount organizational activity, leaders create climates for certain decisions to be implemented and for others, especially those which do not promote their interests, not to be implemented. The climate is political and conflictual. Trust and distrust are elements of "decision struggle."

Since inconsistencies lead to complications, decision makers need to "convert inconsistent partnerships into teams by aligning preferences and identities" (139). This strategy may lead to concerns about "contracts, incentives, selection, socialization and attention" (139) that tend to reduce or eliminate inconsistencies.

Ultimately, the significance of certain operational, tactical or strategic decisions is not necessarily based on the outcomes alone, but, it also is based on the individual, organizational or social meanings these decisions create and sustain. Metaphorically, decision-making, as Harold Lasswell has stated, is a power struggle concerning "who gets what, when, and how" or coalition building or partnership making that is essential for group, team or organizational agreements.

Finally, the outcomes of decision processes may not be solely attributed to the actions of individuals alone. They are attributable to the iterative, synergistic, and interactive influences of a variety of factors, forces, and climates that are reflective of individual, organizational, societal, environmental or global conditions.

In other words, while decisions happen based on the logics of consequence and appropriateness, the same decisions are bedeviled with the calculus of interpersonal and intrapersonal ambiguity in the realm of preferences, identities, experiences and meaning. Using intelligence to articulate "anticipatory rationality and history-based rule following is a wise way of engineering decision making. To be effectively engineered, decision engineering is characterized by improved 'adaptiveness, the use of knowledge and the creation of meaning'" (222).

The decision to launch the Challenger was an example of irrationality and irresponsibility. The blame of irresponsibility and irrationality has been critically examined by Vaughan (1996). If the political, bureaucratic and corporate elite had made launching decisions rationally rather than secretly, the catastrophe would have been averted. Making such a risky decision to launch when they knew that the O-rings were faulty is a clear demonstration of how the culture of deviance dominates organizational settings.

The Challenger tragedy represents an important case for understanding the social basis of technical failure under cold-weather conditions of a pair of O-rings used as seals in the solid rocket booster (SRB). The tragedy had a sociological as well as a technical cause. However, NASA and the SRB contractor, Morton Thiokol, had advance warning of the possibility of O-ring malfunction in cold weather. Yet, the decision was made to launch; understanding the tragedy thus requires understanding this decision. Diane Vaughan (1996) has written an exhaustive, theoretically sophisticated, and most persuasive account of the Challenger launch, which questions the conclusion reached by earlier investigators. The view that the tragedy reflected "amoral calculation" by mid-level managers who suppressed safety concerns makes little sense, she argues, in view of NASA's normal concern for safety and the disastrous consequences of ignoring risk. Understanding individual actors to explore the organizational and environmental context in which it happened makes sense. Invoking anthropological ideas about "thick description," she plunges the reader into the culture of NASA and engineering and the history of the ill-fated-O-rings. According to Vaughan, the Challenger launch decision was made by moral individuals who responded to production pressures but consistently abided by the set of rules governing the definition of safety and risk. Engineers and managers were aware of problems with the O-ring damage using consensual procedures consistent with engineering and industry principles. Incrementally, they came to the conclusion that the O-rings were "safe" because they were redundant (a second O-ring would back up the first). The work groups belief in the acceptability of this risk was supported by larger organizational and environmental contingencies. Engineering culture accommodated technical compromise, and the original "technical" culture of NASA had been modified to include bureaucratic and political concerns, requiring the balancing of all three. Vaughan also shows how "structural secrecy" made it difficult for NASA administrators to "know" that there was a safety problem. Organizational inertia made it difficult to overturn previous conclusions about safety; specialization limited understanding, as did technical jargon and the over-abundance of information; regulatory mechanisms were ineffective. On the eve of the launch, decision makers at NASA were concerned enough about the effects of cold temperature to ask a teleconference with Thiokol. Thiokol engineers recommended against the launch, arguing that risk increased unacceptably in cold temperatures. However, they did not have unambiguous hard data with which they were to back up their recommendations. This prevented an effective formal challenge to the brief in the O-rings safety. Various obstacles to communication limited the effectiveness of the warnings the engineers were able to send out. On the other hand, Vaughan mounts an effective critique of the amoral calculation hypotheses, she provides abundant evidence indicating that procedures were followed and that there was a pervasive belief in the safety of the O-rings; similarly, she shows that the view that rules were violated is based on an understanding of NASA's procedures. Nevertheless, Vaughan may read more into this than is warranted. She admitted in her conclusion that the normalization of deviance may, in other contexts, facilitate misconduct, so why not in the Challenger case? There is no clear evidence that individuals used the rules to cover up their conscious transgressions. But Vaughan's argument that there was no malfeasance too often boils to a simple insistence that actors followed the rules of decision-making which tend to assume what needs to be proven.

This is particularly important as Vaughan appears to have relatively limited access to events at Morton Thiokol. Since engineers there eventually cautioned against cold-weather launch, and since Thiokol managers excluded the engineers from the launch decision, it is conceivable that concern about the O-rings prior to the Challenger incident was greater than it appeared. Circumstantial evidence to this effect exists, since when NASA asked for a teleconference on the question, the Thiokol engineers responded with an extremely unusual no-launch recommendation, even in the absence of "hard" evidence. If nothing else, Vaughan's account does not allow us to dismiss completely this alternative hypothesis. These conclusions Vaughan draws from her analysis are also persuasive and reasonable, but could be expanded. She makes a strong case that the focus on the middle management malfeasance distracts from the real responsibility of organizational and political elite's (Reagan's) in shaping the decision-making environment. It also makes technical decisions seem deceptively routine. Most importantly, it draws attention away from the ways in which routine organizational practices can "normalize" deviance.

Vaughan could add that Thiokol's apparent willingness to express its concerns about the O-rings only after NASA asked and NASA's aggressive reaction to the unusual suggestion by a contractor that launch be delayed may suggest that interorganizational hierarchy played a role in structuring this (and perhaps other) technical decisions. Finally, her analysis reveals the limits of engineering culture. Engineer's willingness to balance technical, economic, political, and bureaucratic pressures reduces the chances that concerns about O-rings safety would be voiced in unambiguous ways. And engineering "craft," as Vaughan calls it, which construct lasting conclusions on the basis of necessarily imperfect knowledge and best estimates, may encourage certain matters which should be routinely questioned. In the realm of rationality, the decision to launch the Challenger was a political rather than a technical one. The business and political elite's interests rather than the interests of organizational managers and scientists dominated the launch decision-making machinery. The judgment of experts, the evaluation of consequences of a faulty decision were ignored. The decision was carried on hastily and secretly rather than professionally, and responsibly. These secretly and politically based influences which dominated technical and professional judgement of scientific experts were followed by ineffective, disastrous and irresponsible consequences whose responsibility was erroneously blamed on the technical experts as the real culprits had hidden behind the former's aprons.

Types of Strategically Designed and Rational Decision-Making Models

The Incremental Model

During the 1950s, behaviorism evolved as a study (theory) of decision-making with a concern for descriptive accuracy "not met by the prescriptively oriented rational model in its original form" (231). At the same time, decision theorists advanced other empirically accurate and classic models such as incrementalism and satisficing.

The incremental model is used to make decisions through the bargaining process. Participants use it to allocate resources in terms of "budgets, personnel, program authority or autonomy" (231). Participants agree on one alternative because it is selected as the best one. Benefits of each alternative are incremental but small and status quo oriented (Lindblom 1959). Such incremental decisions are reached through compromise. The decisions change programs and policies in small and sequential steps or stages in order to maintain the status quo. The bargaining participants employ "persuasion, debate, and negotiation" rather than rationality (Gortner et al. 1997, 231). Proposals, counterproposals, and negotiation may generate minimum conflict before new ideals are made.

Incremental solutions focus on "tangible programs and projects rather than on more abstract goals and policy statements" (231). It is easier to "bargain over resources than over ideology, principles and goals" (231). Consequently, decisions made through incremental approach "tend to be crisis oriented, internally fragmented, ... contradictory, and are characterized as a series of changes in program activities rather than a specific statement of policy or organizational outcome" (231).

Though the incremental method is well suited to describing the activities of political decision-making groups such as legislatures, it also allows for a good description of budget and policy decision-making in bureaus, where multiple levels and divisions are involved in program development. In terms of administrative decision-making, persuasion and bargaining are part of the official linkages to professional, organizational, and constituency interest.

According to Lindblom (1959), the incremental model can be summarized as follows: First, "clear value preferences are rare despite what the rationalist model claims" (Gortner 1997, 231). In general, decision makers can attach preferences only to specific proposals that may reflect abstract goals and values only indirectly. This is why incremental decision makers bargain over programs. Second, policies and programs are not distinguishable from ends (goals and values). Third, the test of 'good policy' is that the actors agree on it even though they may not be able to agree on its underlying values. Fourth, the analysis of alternatives is limited both in number and depth by considering only a few alternatives which are normally considered. Although the incremental model looks to be a fragmented process, in reality, it symbolizes a "decentralized pluralistic system that automatically coordinates itself as actors compete for support" (Gortner et al. 1998, 232). The pluralistic assumptions of the incremental model justify the essence of its existence. It reflects the working of the political system. Decisions portray a series of successive approximations to multiple desired ends or values. In brief, its multiple goals serve a pluralistic society better.

Innovation and Incrementalism

Lindblom (1959) shows that the method's bargaining process articulates limited change. Other theorists see the bureaucratic organization to be responsible for limited search that favors options close to the status quo. Incremental changes are easier to correct if found to be wrong. The tendency of administrators to spend time on immediately pressing projects and to react to crisis rather than to plan is observable. Competition between the old and the new elite who use the model, is common in bureaus (Downs 1967). The bureaus use rules that are imposed on them by external actors – legislatures. The rules, which claim to be "fair" rather than "effective", are not bureaucratic but political in character (Wilson 1989). Wilson argues that the bureau or agency, in addition to its major goals, must serve a large number of contextual goals – that is descriptions of desired states of affairs other than the one the agency was bought into being to create. For example, a policy department not only must try to prevent crime and catch criminals, it must protect the rights of the accused, safeguard the confidentiality of its records, and provide necessary health services to arrestees. These other goals define the context within which the primary goals can be sought.

Satisficing-Incrementalism

Satisficing resembles the incremental method. The method is used for organizational decision-making offered by March and Simon (1993). It is simpler than rationality though it is closer to rationality than to incrementalism. Satisficing "takes the perspective of a single decision maker or a unified group and attempts to optimize, rather than maximize the returns or results from the choice among sequentially possible alternatives. Search is also sequential and is status quo oriented. Simon and March compare it with the rationalist model by saying that "the difference between searching a haystack to find the sharpest needle in it and searching a haystack to find a needle sharp enough to sew with" (162). Satisficing tends to describe how individual decision makers act. The incremental model is a group and an interactive decision-making model as comparable to larger groups particularly the political environments.

Mixed Scanning

Mixed scanning is a variant of the incremental model. It tries to rectify the limitations of the model. According to Etzioni (1967), mixed scanning is dualistic because it is a method of search and decision-making "which does not fully accept either the rationalist model, which is expensive and slow, or the incrementalist model, which is biased toward status quo groups and issues" (Gortner et al. 1977, 235). Mixed scanning is both fundamentally descriptive and prescriptive because it criticizes incrementalism at the "Value-ordering level of decision making."

Aggregate Methods of Decision-Making

Aggregate methods is a third strategy for decision-making in public and private settings. These approaches are descriptive and problem solving oriented. Examples include the use of consultants, e.g., the Delphi technique and the normal group technique (NTG). Generally, these techniques are coached on how to generate a wide range of alternatives (236). One alternative is finally selected through some voting or consensus process. The final choice is said to be an accurate aggregation of individual preferences rather than a negotiated synthesis of preferences characteristic of incrementalism. These aggregate methods allow groups to: (1) generate a broader, more diverse, and more innovative set of alternatives than either the rationalist or incrementalist methods; (2) to avoid the stifling influence of status and claim of expertise by some participants; and (3) to avoid the constraints of *overoutinized* standards operating procedures (237).

Brainstorming is encouraged, and premature criticism of new ideas is avoided. The "hallmark of these techniques is that they attempt to maintain a healthy, well balanced level of group interaction without impressing excessive conformity or allowing excessive conflict" (237). The groups which use the techniques in question are "agency staff, external expert advisory councils, and elected boards and councils" (237). These techniques are frequently used for "planning, for identifying and setting priorities among resources, and for goal setting" (237). For details, see pages 237-239.

The Garbage Can or Nondecision-Making Model: (Organizational Culture)

Garbage can decision theory tries to accurately describe decision-making in organizations. Doing that goes beyond the incremental model in identifying the limits of rationality. March and Olsen (1979a) have argued that "incremental and satisficing models posit a level of clarity of intentions, understanding of problems and predictability in the relationship between individual and organizational actions that is unrealistic for most organizations" (Gortner et al. 1997, 239). These scholars argue that decision-making is a rather unreliable and ambiguous process for selecting courses of action. In reality, it serves as a "forum for individual and group expression of conflict, values, myths, friendships and power" (239). Hence, organizational decision-making is "more expressive of social and personal needs than it is strictly instrumental" (239).

The garbage can model views rationality as a single-goal oriented model of decision-making. As such, the garbage can model views "A choice opportunity as a garbage can into which various problems and solutions are dumped ... by participants. The mix of garbage in a single can depends partly on the label attached to the alternative cans; but it also depends on what garbage is being produced at the moment, on the mix of cans available, and on the speed with which garbage is collected and removed from the scene" (Cohen, March, and Olsen 1979, 26).

Nonmetaphorically, decision-making is an expressive human activity whose opportunity helps to fulfill roles and planned commitments. This activity defines "virtue and truth by interpreting events and goals, distributing glory and blame, reaffirming or rejecting friendships and status relations, expressing or discovering self-interest or group interest, socializing new members, and enjoying the pleasures of a group choice" (March and Olsen 1979b, 11-12).

Based on the garbage can perspective, the rational and incremental models err in assuming too much certainty and knowledge in decision-making. Realistically speaking, "most decision-making situations are plagued with ambiguities of many sorts: objectives are ambiguous; there is no clear set of preferences that present the organization's intentions; causality is obscure; technology is difficult to define, past events are not easily understood; past events are interpreted differently by participants; and attention and participation of key actors is uncertain since other activities and other decisions compete for their time" (March and Olsen 1979b, 12). When using this model, "decisions reflect shifts in the goals, beliefs, and attention of participants. Goals are defined—to the extent that they are very clearly specified – only in the process of considering particular proposals and debating whether to accept or reject them" (240).

Anderson (1983) asserts that decisions are made through a series of binary (Yes-No) choices of specific plans. Both Anderson and March and Simon (1993) indicate that the decision makers did not necessarily select choices they thought would solve the problems. Instead, they thought they would solve the problems. They predictably reasoned the consequences that are not expected to have either very dangerous or very successful results "a bland alternative" (240).

Interpretively, and as Olsen (1979) has also observed, the garbage can model is an artifactual or non-decision model which focuses on the unconscious and unintentional aspects of decision-making. Phenomenologically, decisions are socially acceptable reconstructions of past reality that has occurred. It may be a fictitious way of reconstructing of social reality.

Contingency Theory

When each of these methods (rational, incremental, aggregate, and garbage can) is synergistically or syncretically used to make organizational decisions, they become contingent or an assemblage or theory. Theoretically and empirically, this is possible; however, the reality of it "involves political choices about who will control what kinds of decisions" (Gortner et al. 1997, 247). The more scientific name for garbage can is organizational culture.

Decision-Making: The Role of Management

Every organization needs to be managed in order to effectively coordinate and control its tasks, processes and operations. Of the most classical and contemporary theoretical and management gurus who have controversially discussed the principles of management and yet, have remained current in their influence include but are not limited to Fayol (1949), Taylor (1947), Sloan (1964), Vickers (1961), Simon (1960), March (1976), Lindblom (1959), and Vroom (1974).

First, Fayol (1949) argues that there are 14 principles of management which influence managers to make decisions. These principles are "divisions of work, authority, discipline, unity of command, unity of direction, subordination of individuals to the general interest, remuneration, centralization, scalar chain

(chain of command), order, equity, stability of tenure of personnel, initiative and espirit de corps," i.e., unity of command because unity is strength. According to Fayol, the principle of authority, responsibility, unity of command, good order, espirit de corps, are paramount in management parlance. As elements of law, rules, procedures and regulations, these principles are proverbs of administration. If these proverbs are abused, misused or misapplied, they are sanctioned or sanctionable with "remonstrances, warnings, fines, suspensions, demotion or dismissal" (139).

Second, Frederick Taylor asserts that when principles of scientific management are effectively applied, or when time is well managed in relation to their application, productivity is larger and better for both the employers and employees alike. The same productivity gets magnified when management provides a suitable climate that is conducive to "initiative and incentive" (Pugh 1984, 157). Such incentive driven initiative becomes progressively instrumental to the implementation of four principles of scientific management. These principles include:

1. Immense and systemized knowledge based on realistic experience.
2. Labor must be selectively and progressively recruited, developed, trained and taught in order to retain those who are excellent in terms of natural ability, skills and accomplishments.
3. Principles of scientific management are rooted in an integrated theoretical and practical science.
4. Finally, scientific management is characterized by division of labor whose power and authority rests with its specialization and social differentiation.

Third, according to Sloan (1964), the management of General Motors, the largest American corporation in the world, was largely characterized by "decentralization with coordinated control" (Pugh 1984, 177). Motivation and opportunity were critical to the success of the corporation. The former was provided by incentive compensation, the latter by decentralization. However, based on the success of recent Japanese management practice, decentralized centralization seems to hold much more water than coordinated decentralization of Sloan. Through decentralization, the organization prospered in terms of "initiative, responsibility, development of personnel, decisions close to the facts, flexibility—in short all the qualities necessary for an organization to adapt to new conditions" (177). Coordinationwise, General Motors experienced magnificent efficiencies and economies of scale.

The concept of decentralized coordination portrayed a strong relationship, in terms of decision-making, between the central administration on the one hand and the "autonomously" coordinated divisions and highly specialized staff. Major policy committees consisted of specialists from the central administration, coordinated separate divisions and the specialized line staff. Divisional goals were structured as miniature reflections of the strategic and centrally managed organizational policy whose operational objectives were implemented by the line staff. The staff's contributions touched the field of "styling, finance, technical research, advanced engineering, personnel and labor relations, legal affairs, manufacturing and distribution" (179). In a sense, decentralized coordination of the organizational structure was the "linking pin" and engine of productivity and adaptability. In recent memory, the pin and engine of productivity has undermined its adaptability due to the fact that it concentrates on traditional hierarchical structures rather than labor and the processes of productivity. In other words, the organization tends to use bad judgment (Vickers 1961), and antiquated organizational designs (Simon 1960) and rationally selected alternatives of choice whose reasoning and intellectual formulations may be based on ideological, cultural, traditional, economic, social and demographic biases rather than on scientific objectivity (March 1976). Biased decisions are a product of "technology of foolishness" (Pugh 1984, 224) rather than one of scientific rationality. In other words, made decisions, regardless of their inherent objectivity or subjectivity, may be a product of the science of "muddling through" (Lindblom 1959, and Pugh 1984, 238). One of the best decision-making models that will enhance managerial productivity is the normative model (Vroom 1974). Its predictive utility rests on the deep and integrative foundation that is rooted in conceptual, empirical, and rational description and analysis. For instance, Vroom's decision tree tends to be so normatively dynamic that its influence remains to be continually solvent.

Scientific Visualization of Organizations

For centuries, and even for several millennia, organizations have been traditionally perceived as normative and hierarchical structures whose processes intrinsically and stably maintain and perpetuate the status quo. A generation ago, recent scientific developments and inventions in the information sciences have immensely contributed to the perceptual logic and modeling of organizations. In the 21st century scientific visualization of organizations will dominate the field of organizational forms by superseding "antiquated" and dysfunctional bureaucracies (Benveniste 1994; Bergquist 1993; and Pinchot and Pinchot 1993). In other words:

> The ability to simultaneously visualize both key variables of interest and relevant organizational entities should allow for easier and more widespread analysis and diagnosis of organizational issues. ... Many areas of science and technology, ability to mathematically visualize obscure or shrouded processes, which is the essence of scientific visualization, has led to innovations and insights (Marknam 1998, 1).

The development of graphical data which is amenable to simultaneous display of complex organizational structures as opposed to the traditional and simple hierarchical organizational charts is a major scientific and technological accomplishment (Keidel 1995). These scientific innovations have enabled organizations to be analyzed through the use of multilevel procedures, develop their graphical display nomenclature, and to reconstruct a scientifically embedded explanatory philosophy for organizational modeling which is vital for research and practice. Human ability to scientifically visualize natural phenomena has dramatically increased with all types of research agenda. Some of the visualized organizational designs, processes, and forms may be biomolecular, spherical, microscopic (biomolecular modeling) or macroscopic (interstellar cartography) in their physicality. Such structural designs may influence their behavior. Further research on entities in terms of individuals, dyads, groups and departments requires interdisciplinary analysis.

In the medical field, the use of computer visualization has been dependent on "computer imaging in conjunction with new scanning technologies and ... the requisite software for visualizing intelligent volumes" (Hhone, Pommert, Reimer, Schiemann, Schubert, and Tiede 1994). Moving beyond simple x-ray procedures, computerized tomography, through the application of Fourier analysis, help visualize the density of the 3-D layers of a human body by 'stacking' the 2-D x-ray slices. The same principals of computing tomography, when applied to position emission tomography (PET) can visualize metabolic activity (Friedhoff and Benson 1989).

Theoretically, visualization information processing can be visually and psychologically be displayed to (1) increase information density of the display, (2) reduce elapsed study time of information, and (3) improve the corresponding level of understanding regardless of a person's inborn visualization ability (Markham 1998).

In brief, in the next millennium, the traditional way of perceiving organizations in terms of the hierarchical chart may be challenged by new ways of viewing them. This single-level analysis approach (individual employees, supervisor work teams, project teams, profit centers, divisions, corporations, etc.) will be places with platonic geometric solids i.e., (individuals are represented by a circle, dyads, work groups or teams = polygon, departments = rectangle, the organization = triangle etc.). Their morphology, organizational cartography and virtuality may become new elements of their "transorganizationalism".

The PC as a Decision Making Tool

Computers are intelligent systems which help modern organizations to make complex decisions. These systems which are capable of organizing, processing and modeling difficult decisions, The role of PCs in the organization is that of decision-support and computation. This role is called decision support system (DSS) (Gortner et al. 1997) and has been in use since the 1960s. With the initiation of VisiCalc, managers were encouraged to use the spreadsheet

such as Microsoft Excel, Novell Quattro Pro and Lotus 1-2-3, all of which are programs that use high quality graphics to organize and impressively manipulate build in functions that are complex "statistical, mathematical and financial operations" (403). These sophisticated operations of the DSS are expert systems regulated by programmed and "sophisticated logic, decision rules, and 'interference engines'" (403). New managers need to be fully equipped with skills for operating these systems. They must be familiarized with "processing tasks that crosscut traditional job categories" (403). Public employees must be well trained to assume roles formerly played by statistical analysts and accountants. Such training will enable the manager to detect abuse and be able to bring it under control.

The DSS are based on the use of artificial intelligence and decisions made are rooted in the rational model. Both DSS and expert systems are used incorporate offices and public agencies. In the public arena, the programs are built to deal with "hazardous materials management, land-use planning, and contracts negotiation" (404). As a decision making tool, the PC Tayloristically enhances managerial and professional efficiency and effectiveness.

Decision Making

Decision making is now recognized as a core activity of public administration. The traditional managerial approach to public administration favors comprehensive and institutional management and rational decision making aimed at maximizing efficiency, economy, accountability, and effectiveness. Specialization, premise controls, hierarchy, formalization, and regulations are means of limiting alternatives in order to promote effective decision making. The rational comprehensive model emphasizes clear objectives, comprehensive consideration of means, a choice of means that are informed by explicit values, and operational criteria. The rational comprehensive model is difficult to apply generally in public administration in the U.S. because (1) policy objectives are often ambiguous, (2) it requires proactive administration whereas in practice public administrators tend to be reactive, and (3) agency missions overlap in such a way that it is difficult to deal with problems comprehensively. The new Al Gore initiated public management NPM favors decentralized decision making based on market criteria. It also favors a great deal of employee discretion. The effect of this approach, according to the NAP theory that organizational decision making will be more concerned with customer satisfaction and technical efficiency. The success of the NPM approach will ultimately depend on recruitment and socialization that ensures that decision making is technically, politically, and legally correct.

The political approach to public administration favors incremental decision-making. Here it is accepted that policy objectives may be purposely kept vague in order to build political consensus and support. Means and ends are not treated as distinct. The question in making a decision is more "what steps can be taken in the general direction desired" rather than " what are the best means to a specific objective." The test of a good decision is the extent of political support or consensus that it enjoys. The consideration of possible or potential alternatives is limited.

The incremental model has several limitations: (1) it can lead to hyperpluralism or gridlock as coordination becomes more difficult, (2) small incremental steps in decision making may lead to undesirable or unforeseen consequences, (3) it can produce circularity in policy making, and (4) it is not compatible with large-scale policy shifts. The debate over rational comprehensive decision making versus incremental decision making is partly a debate over alternative political systems and values. Rational comprehensiveness has a centralizing bias, whereas incrementalism favors representative, pluralistic decision making. The rational comprehensive approach also favors limited public participation, while the incremental model favors widespread popular participation. Despite their differences, either approach can work well or fail, depending on the circumstances in which it is used.

The legal approach to decision making emphasizes adjudicatory procedure, which is a special form of incrementalism. It is a form that is bounded by formal rules. Adjudication can be prospective as when a public utility commission considers a rate hike for a company under its jurisdiction. It can also be retrospective, as when it concerns the legality of past behavior. Adjudication is especially valuable when decisions turn on matters of individual intent or unique events. It is also useful when a number of subjective criteria must be weighed. However, in spite of its merits, adjudication also has drawbacks: (1) it is time consuming, (2) it places individuals or the parties to a case in an adversarial, rather than cooperative relationship, (3) it can lead to circularity in policy making, and (4) the rules or laws resulting form adjudicatory decisions may be obscure. These decision-making approaches can be synthesized somewhat through an approach called "mixed scanning." This approach tries to take a rational-comprehensive overview of public policy, while at the same time allowing many policy decisions to be made in an incremental fashion. Mixed scanning can help to avoid inappropriate centralization of decision making and also the policy "draft: that is sometimes associated with the incremental approach. The benefits of mixed scanning can be achieved through strategic planning which requires the assessment of the impact of foreseeable environmental shifts.

Whatever approaches are taken, some pitfalls can be avoided. Among these are (1) misplaced priorities due to unclear goals; (2) confusion of the public interest with that of a clientele group or a constituency; (3) overly rigid adherence to rules; (4) oversimplifications of reality; (5) overquantification at the expense of qualitative factors; and (6) reluctance to engage in policy and program evaluation to obtain feedback. A major question for the future is what role new information technologies will play in administrative decision making.

2. Decision-Making Models – Leadership Styles

The six major decision-making models (leadership styles) that were empirically investigated by the study can be used to make strategic decisions. The process through which strategic decisions can be and are made by using these models and are not only methodologically theoretical, but also theorizable. The models, as mentioned earlier (Sagini 1991), include:

1. Rational: directed by values based on supported data
2. Collegial: directed by consensus
3. Political: directed by conflicting self-interests and power
4. Bureaucratic: directed by traditional administrative pattern
5. Anarchical: directed by accidents of timing and interest (Chaffee 1983, 3)
6. Compromise (Paolillo and Jackson 1986, 3.88)

Essentially, none of these six models is practically ideal. Each has weaknesses and strengths. Some are more popular than others. However, regardless of their utilitarian complexities, the main advantage of using models to analyze events is that models create a distance between decision makers and decisions. Such a distance helps administrators from being directly associated with each decision that has been or will be made. In some cases, they can distance themselves from unpopular and illegal decisions. By so doing, they serve to make corrections that enhance organizational stability and progress. Writing of the essence of strategic decision-making models in courts, Pennings, whom this research cited earlier, said that:

> The use of the multiple models might have important heuristic and diagnostic values, because they provide alternative postulates about the content or process of strategic decision making. By explicitly stating these postulates, one might become sensitive to the capabilities that surface from contrasting different models. Indeed, they resemble aspects of strategic phenomena (19).

Pennings' position implies that when more models are used for making decisions, decision makers receive comprehensively constructed strategic decisions whose usefulness is likely to be more effective than decisions made through single models. This comprehensive approach to decision making is a form of holistic or eclectic strategic management.

Writing on three political models (bureaucratic-structural, social-consensus, and personal-rational), Rutherford and Flemming (1985, 433) stated that, "three models which gave insight into the factors that promote or inhibit change in institutions of higher education ... Although each offers a distinctive, perspective, a number of recurrent themes are identified where the models support and complement one another."

The usefulness of the three or more models can be great for innovative purposes in organizational settings. In relation to college and universities which are organized anarchies because they exhibit, "Problematic goals (i.e., inconsistent and ill-defined preference that are constantly changing); unclear technology (i.e., unsystematic and ill-understood problem-solving procedures); and fluid participation (i.e., variability in the amount of time and effort that members devote to the organization)" (434)

The usage of a variety of models can be complementary in helping senior academics and administrators to face the challenges of the future with greater insight and confidence. In addition, an organization like a college or university, is a system largely based on subject departments rather than on a central administration; a value system which stresses the autonomy of both the individual academic and departments; a decision-making system which relies on a complex committee structure to encourage debate and dissent but one in which the actual decision-making process may be obscure; and perhaps, a covert power system which is mainly controlled by departmental heads. Such a complex organization needs to use an eclectic decision-making strategy which enables it to solve its more urgent, diverse, and pressing problems (Rutherford and Fleming 1985).

The effectiveness and success of the model or models depends on the character of managers who use them. The managers must act as leaders who have ability to guide, motivate, and integrate the efforts of others. In this case, the planner's job is to, "Perfect a team culture that (1) promotes and sustains efficient performance of the highest quality, (2) fosters and utilizes creativity, (3) stimulates enthusiasm for effort experimentation, innovation, and change, (4) takes learning advantage from problem-solving situations, and (5) looks for and finds new challenges" (Blake and Mouton 1964, ix).

What Blake and Mouton indicate is that strategic decision-making models, per se, have no significance and relevance in management unless planners who are skilled in their effective utilization are willing to use the models for efficiency, innovation, and change. The planners, as Bittel (1972, 2, iv) says, must know about nine "Master Keys" of solving problems, focusing on performance criteria, acting from a plan, managing by exception, developing confidence in others, employing the power of training, and knowing one's true self.

It is apparently clear that recent management circles prefer an eclectic or holistic approach to decision making, rather than a nonholistic one. This holistic view seems to be strong because of the complementary and interdisciplinarian character of comprehensive strategic decision making. The comprehensiveness of strategy is a form of strategic interdependence. Strategic interdependence can be rationalized in the context of the rational model. In other words, the rational model can be manipulated to help decision makers make their decisions by using the political, bureaucratic, collegial compromise, and of necessity, anarchical approaches (Pennings 1985, 19), and Rutherford and Fleming 1985, 433-334).

D. The Rational Model and Structure – Leadership Styles

Webster's model is used to describe organizations which establish structure that enable them to achieve their aims. These aims are carried forward through the regularization of allocation, coordination, and supervision of activities. The modern structured society is governed by bureaucratic authority whose specialization is based on immense technical efficiency. Bureaucratic authority is a legal administrative staff (Weber 1947). Their effectiveness depends on their mutual interdependence in terms of:

1. Rational norms and values that demand expediency and obedience,
2. Abstract principles that are rationally and legally used as rules for the pursuit of the corporate group interest,
3. People with authority who have offices, power, and status that give them legitimacy to issue commands to their subordinates who are also, just like their superiors, governed by the impersonal rules of bureaucracy,
4. Bureaucrats or members obey authority because they belong to a corporate group that obeys the laws of the association, organization, commune, church, or state, and
5. In respect to number three above, members obey the delimited impersonal rational order or authority rather than individuals or organizations per se.

The rational legal authority in which the bureaucratic order is an example is a system of values whose official duties are grounded on laws. The bureaucrats have competence, which enables them to exercise expert authority in specialization or division of labor. Because the competent bureaucrats are specialized, they have power and authority to make decisions, enforce laws, and supervise organizational functions. The supervision of organizational functions is an administrative, coordinating, and allocative responsibility which private and public organizations deal with and promote. Bureaucratic organizational offices are patterned on the principle of hierarchy. This means that subordinate offices are controlled and supervised by superior offices. In other words, the authority of offices and officials is rank ordered on the basis of a descending scale of subordinate relationships. The conduct of each office is regulated by a plethora of technical rules or norms. In Weberian view, rules that are technical are used to "prescribe a course of action which is dedicated primarily on grounds touching efficiency of the performance of the immediate functions" (18). Also, by "norms he probably means rules which limit conduct on grounds other than those of efficiency" (18). The office holders have fixed salaries, they are pensionable and can be demoted, dismissed or resign if they do wrong. Their superiors promote them on the basis of seniority and achievement. In essence, rules and norms are prescriptively used for maintaining conduct and conformity in problematic or-ganizational settings.

The bureaucratic organization is a rational and formal organization whose disciplined officials, employees, and workers do not own and are not expected to own the organization's "non-human means of production and administration" (18). They are provided properly in the offices or premised but are not allowed to live there. Their fulfillment of these expectations will protect them from con-flict of interest in order to enhance efficiency and accountability. Given this reality, the incumbent (judge or official) cannot appropriate his/her official posi-tion. Definitively, he/she cannot make a public office or use it for personal gain. Office in this context is the institutionally defined status of person or work premises that is called bureau.

Given the demands for accountability, which is a legal supervisory re-quirement, "administrative acts, decisions, and rules are formulated and re-corded in writing" (19). Mandatory oral discussions rules, proposals, decisions and orders need to be recorded in writing.

Rational Types of Legitimate Authority

Rationally, there are three types of legitimate authority that is bureaucratiz-able. First, the legal-rational type is the basis for bureaucracy particularly com-mon in Western society. This typical Western bureaucratic system is character-ized by the presence of laws that are legislatively enacted and implemented to ensure accountability and administrative efficiency of the bureaus. The second rational type of legitimate authority is traditional leadership which exercises personal rule. Examples of these include hereditary monarchs, papal personages and in some ways, patriarchal caliphs and chiefs. Since the procedures for their social mobility are either hereditary or reflections of well testable or tested cul-ture, they rise to power. Third, charismatic leadership is so magnetic that it can lead to instability and failure. Hitler's Nazi Germany and Mussolini's fascist Italy are classic examples of regimes, which had charismatic leaders. Of these three types of authority, the charismatic and the traditional leadership forms are more monocratic or autocratic systems whose authoritarian regimes lack formu-las for democratic efficacy. The monocratic variety of the bureaucracies "is so technical and efficient that it develops the capability for "attaining the highest degree of efficiency and is in this sense formally the most rational known means of carrying out imperative control over human beings. It is superior to any other form in precision, in stability, in the stringency of its discipline and it reliability" (Weber 1947, 24). The evolution of modern corporate organizations are off-shoot reflections of bureaucratic machinery. Churches, states, armies, political parties, economic organizations and clubs, etc. trace their normative administra-tive structure and morphology in bureaucratic systems. These bureaucratic or-ganizations do not exactly look like the "bureaucracies" of the academy, parliamentary or congressional committees, Soviets in former USSR, honorary officers and lay judges. Relative to these latter bodies, the bureaucratic administration is a formal, technical and rational type whose indispensability and massification are essentially paramount. Both the capitalistic and socialistic economic systems have structured, rational and technical bureaucracies.

Weber argued that, "When those subject to bureaucratic control seek to escape the influence of the existing bureaucratic apparatus, this is normally possible only by creating an organization of their own which is equally subject to the process of bureaucratization. Similarly the existing bureaucratic apparatus is driven to continue functioning by the most powerful interests which are material and objective, but also in character" (25). Without the use of bureaucracy, Western, Eastern, and Southern societies would not function. The societies would experience entropy and falter. Under normal circumstances, the permanent secretaries who have experience, technical knowledge and social clout are better able to control the bureaucratic machinery than the normal ministers who may be less informed than their counterparts. Though both capitalism and bureaucracy are dichotomous and concomitant systems, the roots of their evolutionary and historical development are radically different. The former is a product of medieval feudalism and the Protestant Ethic. The latter is a byproduct of the state, empire, and public and private administration.

As a rational machinery, the bureaucracy is very "stable, strict, intensive and calculable administration" (25). It is a central and crucial element of any large-scale administration. Its political, religious, and economic elements have been improved by the historical development of the capitalist and socialist systems whose ideological and philosophical orientations are perpetually antagonistic to each other. Though bureaucratic administration, has in the recent past, relied on the services of railways, telephone, and telegraph for transportation and communication, postmodern society has started to rely on these same services and the new ones provided by the use of computer, fax and automobile, telephone, cell phone, and aircraft. These services are not only massively consumed, but their consumption is associated with bureaucratic evolution and advancement in terms of their structural technostructure. Within the socialist camp, and due to lack of discipline and creative innovation, absence of historic precedent and moral rational philosophical consciousness, the Soviet bureaucracy lost the vitality of its essence – the rationality of its irrationality. With the eventual development of a massive presence of its ideological bankruptcy, the Soviet bureaucratic machinery lost its important theological rhetoric for power which was used for cementing and organizing the social weaknesses of the Soviet Empire. This contributed to its collapse, the bankruptcy of its ideological theology, which was initially, when it was strong, used to create it, was responsible for its collapse. The ideological bureaucracy lost its religious zeal for creating mew, dynamic and universal zealots who could have extended and strengthened, through management, the mission and value, the glorious and universal beauty and contributions of the empire. This collapse shows how formal or instrumental and substantive rationality could be conflictual. Apart from Weber who had descriptively prescribed rational procedures and structures, Taylor, Gulick, Urwick and other great thinkers have ratified the rational theory of scientific management and scientific administration (Gortner et al. 1997). These minds argue that all modern organizations must and should seek to use rationality. Rationality is the "quality or state of having or being based on reason" (61). Rationality is important to all organizations in our modern, technological, interdependent world" (61).

There are two levels of rationality. The first level is substantive rationality which is concerned with goals or ends. The second is instrumental rationality that is concerned with personal security and survival. Though both levels are imperative, the logic and analytic tools involving the use of each are radically different.

According to Paul Diesing (1962), the five types of rationality that exist in modern society include the "technical, economic, social, legal, and political" (Gortner et al. 1997, 61). The bureaucracy is superior in technological and global interdependence, superior in calculation because it is knowledgeable, technical, and legal, and superior in efficiency because the bureaucracy gets things down with a sense of accountability. When a rational bureaucracy is superior in predictability, discipline, technostructure, interdependence, predictability and calculable lawfulness, the consequences of its performance are instrumental – hence instrumental rationality (Weber 1947). The classical, Western and Taylorist school of thought assumed that such bureaucratic and rationalized instrumental superiority with respect to the use of rationality was the "only one best way" (Gortner et al. 1997, 61: Scott 1981; and Pugh 1987).

The rational bureaucracy's weaknesses may include waste, incompetence, red tape, and mediocrity (McKenna 1994). Its meritocracy enables it to establish and maintain high standards of performance. For example, the bureaucracy has ability to make decisions and control abstract, concrete and "official secrets" (Pugh 1981, 26). There are three consequences of bureaucratic control. These include:

1. The general tendency to hire or recruit on the basis of technical competence.
2. The bureaucracy is a Plutocracy (government by wealthy people only) that has technical training (30 years).
3. The bureaucracy is dominated by the spirit of "formalistic impersonality, sine ira et studio which has neither hatred nor passion, which lacks affection and enthusiasm." Its norms are "duty and formal equality of treatment" (27).

These characteristics produce an ideal official who is capable of managing his/her office. The leveling of social classes in the capitalistic world is suitable for the evolutionary climate conductive to the elimination of its class privileges of which "the appropriation of means of administration and the appropriation of authority as well as the occupation of offices on an honorary basis or as an avocation by virtue of wealth. This combination everywhere inevitably foreshadows the development of mass democracy" (Pugh 1987, 27). In terms of how it operates, the rational bureaucracy is formalistic because it is interested in its own "personal" security and survival. Contrary to its formalism, the bureaucracy substantively functions in a utilitarian way in order to articulate the interest and welfare of those they serve. This is a form of substantive rationality that is supportive of democracy.

In the private sector, rationality and efficiency can be determined by observing "how successful the organization is achieving the goals of profit, size and growth" (Gortner et al. 1997, 62). The strategic success of the whole market is assessed in the context of long term business cycles and in terms of TQM" (63) though most of the goals are not, for obvious reasons, implementable in the public sector.

Rago (1994) argues that unlike the business world, successful public agencies pay the price without expanding their revenue base. For instance:

> Many companies in the industrial sector undertake TQM to improve their bottom lines by increasing the market share by improving quality. Increase in market share means new customers and mew revenues. Conceivably, increased revenue enables companies to hire employees and purchase equipment as necessary to ensure that supply keeps up with demand. In many government service organizations, the order of business is opposite that of industry. That is, the more customers the organization has the less money available to provide the service.
>
> As the government service organization gains efficiency in the delivery of services as a result of TQM, it expands its customer base by providing services to those citizens who needed the services but who were too far down on the waiting list to obtain them typically, this expansion occurs without a correlated expansion in revenue (66-64, and Gortner et al. 1997, 63).

According to Gortner et al. (1997) "TQM assumes top management support but political officials operate under a different concept of rationality than do business officials...TQM focuses ultimately, on economic factors – in the long term, businesses increase profits or gain a larger segment of the market. Public officials focus on the short term – next election" (63). They must be reelected. If not, their closest supports must be elected. Public officials have fewer incentives for management. For example, the fact that a mayor, a governor, a senator or minister, or president has been elected and has been successful during his, her reelection does not mean that they have many incentives.

Second, substantive rationality (efficiency) is different from instrumental rationality. As normally it is the case, total quality management looks for "efficiency in procedures and uses scientific methods to achieve the one current best way of production." Other theorists such as Weber, Taylor, Gulick, and others value only instrumental level of rationality. They definitely theorize that rationality and efficiency are identical. They argue that "efficient achievement of a single goal is technical rationality" (Taylor 1911 and Gortner et al. 1997, 64). The maximum achievement of many goals is economic rationality (Gulick and Urwick 1937, and Weber 1947). Gulick and Urwick argue that rationality, which is efficiency, is an effective principle of departmentalization and departmentalism which is comparable to, in the eyes of the alchemists, "the philosopher's stone" (Gulick and Urwick 1937, 31). Like Weber, they assert that all formal organizations have structural commonalties or similarities with which they are characteristically defined.

In the context of rationality or efficiency, substantive rationality could be irrelevant since the goals with which it is associated are externally constructed. In Taylorist perspective, technical rationality was intended to increase "output for the same amount of input. Inefficient scientific administration and organizational structures that maximized managerial functions were convinced that good organizational or bureaucratic management "guaranteed efficiency in operation and maximum return for tax dollars spent" (64). Weber interchangeably uses technical efficiency to mean rationality. Rationality is "the major benefit to be gained from bureaucracy and the reason that bureaucracy developed in the first place" (64).

In accordance with Flew's (1979) perspective, rationality is the opposite of irrationality or non-rationality or arationality. Humans are both rational and irrational. Taylor and his management contemporaries may have been influenced by Descartes, Spinoza and Leibniz who were 17th and 18th centuries' philosophers from the school of rationalism. The rationalist intellectual tradition was and is characterized by four logical assumptions: (a) "the belief that it is possible to obtain by reason alone a knowledge of the nature of what exists; (b) the view that knowledge forms a single system, which (c) is deductive in character; and (d) the belief that everything is explicable, that is, that everything can in principle be brought under the single system" (299). The rationalist school of thought rejects religious belief for being irrational and unscientific. Also, because it is committed to using reason and reason alone, it is analytically antagonistic to faith, prejudice, habit and all sources of irrationality. In other words, contemporary intellectual analysts agree that communism, as opposed to capitalism and democracy, came to an end in the former USSR because the foundations upon which it rested were more irrational and religious than the foundations of its capitalistic counterpart.

In general, in his interest for the study of organizations, Weber, unlike other scholars, was able to "(1) identify the characteristics of an entity he labeled bureaucracy; (2) to describe its growth and the reasons for its growth; (3) isolated the concomitant social changes; (4) to discover the consequences of bureaucratic organization can solve decision making problems, some of which are computational, by overcoming individual limitations with alternative forms of the organization in terms of labor. Though Weber's bureaucratic model is similar to that of Urwick and Gulick, it differs radically from mechanistic Taylorism and other models. Details related to these differences will are not the subject of this text.

Weber's model is more complex and elaborate because he analyzes the relationship between the official and the office. He views the bureaucracy to be an adaptive or strategic device whose specialization is instrumental to the solution of organizational problems in spite of human limitations.

Merton's model

More recent students of the bureaucracy – particularly Merton (1940), Selznick (1949) and Gouldner (1954) agree with Weber that bureaucracies are more efficient with respect to the operationalization of goals of bureaucratic (formal) hierarchy than alternative forms of organization. The major contribution of these organizational scholars is their recognition that the bureaucratic organization is characterized by important dysfunctional consequences. Together, they theoretically agree that there are anticipated and unanticipated consequences that leaders think result from the treatment of human beings as machines. When the machine model of human behavior is used for control, this usage encourages not only the continued use of the machine model, but, the resulting consequences are undesired by the organization. Merton assertively concluded that "change in the personality of individual members of the organization stem from factors in the organizational structure" (Pugh 1987, 29). The term personality refers to an externally observed consistent and persisting behavioral phenomenon which individuals display.

Merton elaborates that the system demands control to be the prerogative of the top leaders of the organizational hierarchy. The demand is characterized with an "increased emphasis on the reliability of behavior" (30) in the organization. In the light of the organizational echelons, reliability of behavior reinforces the need for accountability and predictability. Strict adherence to these behaviors results in the "machine model of human behavior" (30). The three consequences resulting from mechanistic human behavior include but are not limited to: (1) a reduction in the amount of personalized instrumental or expressive relationship; (2) internalization of the rules of the organization by the participants is increased for instrumental purposes in spite of their unanticipated consequences of which goal displacement is one; overspecialization and internalization of subgoals leads to goal displacement because specialists cannot communicate with people outside their specialty. (3) Increased use of categorization as a decision-making strategy decreases the search for usable alternatives by making use of the first ones. "The reduction in personalized relationships, the increased internalization of rules, and the decreased search for alternatives combine to make the behavior of members of the organization highly predictable; i.e. they result in an increase in the rigidity of behavior of participants. At the same time, the reduction in personalized relations" (31), including those of a competitive nature, helps to facilitate the development of an esprit de corps, i.e. increases the degree with which goals are shared with group members. Such sharing of common purpose, goals, and interest "increase the propensity of organization members to defend each other against outside pressures" (31). While such behavior intensely solidifies rigidity, the behavior is reminiscent of innovativeless "group think" with which the CIA has been characterized in the last 60 years.

Rigidity of behavior is characterized by three main consequences. First, rigid behavior satisfies the initial demand of reliability, maintenance need of the system, and strengthening of in-group identification. Second, it increases the defensibility of individual action at all levels of the bureaucratic pyramid. Finally, "the rigidity of behavior increases the amount of difficulty with clients of the organization and complicates the achievement of client satisfaction – a near-universal organizational goal" (31). Subordinate and defensive in-group members like to subject clients to the "trappings of authority" (31). Also, rigidity of behavior which needfully has the tendency to increase defensibility of individual action, prevents discrimination by resolving conflict between service and impartiality related to the implementation of public organizational learning in the structure of organizations.

Selznick's Model

Merton's model puts emphasis on rules as a response to the demand for control. Selznick's (1949) model stresses delegation of authority (Figure 2.4). Like Merton and unlike no one else, Selznick wants to show how delegation as (a control technique) is responsible for provoking a variety of unanticipated consequences. In addition, and unlike Merton as well, Selznick points out that the consequences emanate from the "problem of maintaining intensive and expressive interpersonal relations."

In this model, the demand for control is made by the hierarchy. As a result of the demand, increase in delegation of authority is instituted and on the one hand, ratified. Delegation of authority increases the chances for training in specialized competencies. Such competence improves an employee's ability or capacity to deal with more sophisticated problems. As a result, 'delegation tends to decrease the difference between organizational goals and achievement, and thus to stimulate more delegation" (33). On the other hand, delegation stimulates the creation of "departmentalization and increased bifurcation of interests among the subunits in the organization" (33). The maintenance needs of the subunits

Figure 2.4. The Simplified Selznick Model

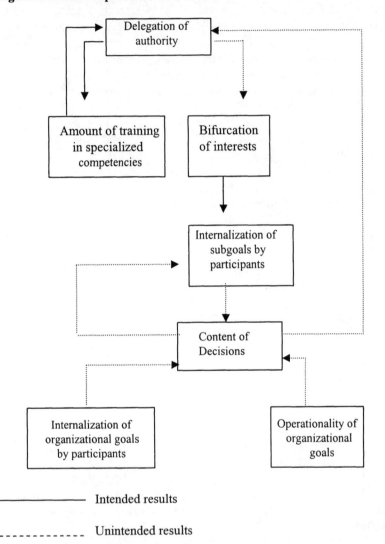

_____ Intended results

_ _ _ _ _ _ _ _ _ _ _ _ _ Unintended results

Source: Pugh, D.S. 1984. *Organization Theory: Selected Readings.* London: Penguin Books, p. 35.

dictate a commitment to the goals over and above their contribution to the total organizational program. Many individuals' needs depend on the continued success and expansion of the subunit.

Bifurcation of interest is stimulated by the specialized training which delegation produces. Training results in increased competence, increase in costs of changing personnel, and in further differentiation of subunit goals. The "bifurcation within the organization leads to increased conflict among organizational subunits" (33). Consequently, the content of organizational decisions depends increasingly on the nature of internal strategic options especially if there is "little internalization of organizational goals by participants" (33). Consequently, there is an increase in the difference between organizational goals and achievement. This difference results in an increase in delegation. This influences daily decisions. First, the struggle for internal control not only affects directly the content of decisions, but, it also causes greater elaboration of ideologies that are used to legitimize subunits. Second, each subunit struggles to succeed in fitting its policy in consonant with the official doctrine of the larger organization for the legitimization of its demands. This tactic increases the internalization of subgoals by participants of the subunits.

Internalization of subgoals is reinforced by a feedback from the daily decisions it influences. Making daily decisions is necessarily a process of precedent setting. Decisions that become precedential are organizationally operational in terms of the applicability of their subunit goals. Precedents are habitually relevant because they consistently reinforce the internalization of subunit goals. Since internalization of subgoals is relatively dependent on the operationality of organizational goals, it is more likely than otherwise, to observe and test how effectively goals are achieved. "Variations in the operationality of organizational goals affect the content of daily decisions" (34) and the extent to which subunit goal decisions are internalized daily.

Evidently, it is clear, based on this analysis, that delegation of authority or responsibility has both functional and dysfunctional consequences in relation to the achievement of organizational goals. Delegation contributes to the "realization and deflection" (34) of the goals in question. Theoretically, it is hypothesizable that both increases and decreases in goal achievement cause an increase in delegation. In other words, even when goals are not attainable, bureaucratic authority tends to delegate responsibility in spite of the expectations to the contrary. This happens because within the framework of the "machine model" (34) delegation is the correct and the only alternative response. Figure 2.4 illustrates the highly simplified Selznickian model.

Gouldner's Model

Gouldner's model or paradigm (1954) is simpler than Mertonian and Sel-znickian models though they all have certain similarities. Like Merton, Gould-ner is concerned with the consequences of bureaucratic rules for the mainte-nance of organizational structure. He, like Merton, tries to portray how "control technique designed to maintain the equilibrium of a subsystem disturbs the equi-librium of a subsystem disturbs the equilibrium of a larger system, with subse-quent feedback on the subsystem" (Pugh 1987, 36).

Due to the demand for control created by the hierarchical structure, gen-eral and impersonal rules are used to regulate organizational norms, procedures and precedents. One consequence of such rules is to decrease the visibility of power with the group. The visibility of authority differences in the context of the work groups interacts with the extent to which equality norms are held to affect the legitimacy of the supervisory role. Subsequently, it affects the degree of impersonal tension within the work group. Sociologically, because American culture is egalitarian, the power and visibility of the worker decreases with the legitimate increase in supervisory role. Such a relationship helps to decrease tension within the group. According to Gouldner, the above-mentioned antici-pated consequences of rule-making take place in order to allow the survival of the work group unit. The unit uses rules that are reinforced. The work rules pro-vide cues for organizational members beyond those intended by the authority figures in the organization. The rules enable the organizational members to know what acceptable and unacceptable behavior means. Oversupervision and closeness of supervision may cause organizational disequilibrium. Organiza-tional disequilibrium may take place due to the mechanistic nature of Gould-nerianism. If performance is low or poor, more detailed inspection and control of the "machine model" may be required. It should be made clear that close su-pervision, which may cause disequilibrium, may stimulate that element of or-ganizational dysfuntionalism due to the fact that the nature of supervision tends to increase visibility of power relations within the organizations. This tends to raise tension level within the work group – resulting in disequilibrium. Gould-ner's model is graphically illustrated in Figure 2.5. Intense supervision is per-ceived to be either authoritarian or punitive. Authoritarianism and punitivity are inconsistent with stimulated motivation for higher performance.

Other comparable bureaucratic models worthy of mention include Bendix (1947) who has analyzed the limitations of technical rationality in organiza-tional and other settings. Bendix has shown the intriguing problems that arise with the use of spy systems of control. Dubin's (1949) model is similar to that of Merton, Blau (1955) evaluated the changes in operating procedures that take place at the lower levels of the bureaucratic pyramid. Such an examined evalua-tion is carried out due to the pressure exerted by work groups needs.

Figure 2.5. The Simplified Gouldner Model

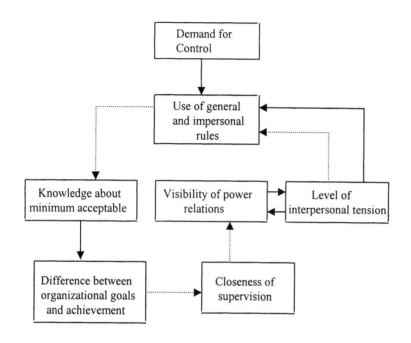

_____ Intended results

- - - - - - - - - - - Unintended results

Source: Pugh, D.S. 1984. *Organization Theory: selected Readings.* London: Penguin Books: 37.

In all these three and other previous models, the elaboration of evoking their connections, the inherent unintended cues, and the organizationally evolved dysfunctional learning associated with these models tend to be responsible for a large part of the unanticipated consequences which these theories or models articulate.

T. Burns Model

Burns has shown that the history of modern Western industrialization is about two centuries old. Within this period, industrialization, just like other institutions (family, church, government, military force) has undergone and continues to undergo dynamic change. The two technologies of industrialization are material and social forms of engineering. The third successful technology was the creation of the first factory by Strutt and Arkwright. Factory means "the combined operation of many work people, adult and young, in tending with assiduous skill system of productive machines continuously impelled by a central power. It is the constant aim and tendency of every improvement in machinery to supersede human labor altogether" (Pugh 1987, 41).

Karl Marx, in his *Das Kapital,* has described the factory in the following manner:

> A collection of machines in a building all driven by one prime mover, and prefera-
> bly, of the same type and engaged on the same process. Attending the machines
> were men and women who themselves were attended by 'feeders', most of them
> children, who fetched ad carried away materials. There was also a 'superior, but
> numerically unimportant' class of maintenance and repair workers. All of these
> worked under a master, with perhaps a chief workman or foreman. The primitive
> social technology of the factory system still confined it, even by the 1850s, largely
> to the mass production of textiles (Pugh 1987, 41).

With the technical advancements in transportation and communication, with the influence of cultural, political and commercial centers like London and Paris, with the coming of the free trade and the introduction of the manufacture, distribution and consumption of military hardware, these new technical advances were used to produce and revolutionize industrial development. Machine tools of iron and steel boomed in the market. Advancement in chemical technology evolved first in Germany and later in other countries. These evolutionary and infantile industrial beginnings (1850-1860s) became the base or springboard from which more advanced and historically evolutionary methods and forms of industrialization developed. In essence, the gradual improvement of material technology and the attendant social techniques of industrial organization had been established. "With the extension of the factory system into engineering, chemical, iron and steel processing, food manufacture and clothing, an organizational development took place which provided for the conduct and control of many complex series of production process within the same plant" (41). One positive development which came as a result of the evolution of the factory system was the increase in the number of "salaried officials employed in industry" (41). Comparatively speaking, the number of factory managers and supervisors (administrative employees) as compared to that of like workers (production employees) in England had risen from 8.6% in 1907 to 20% in 1948. In general, similar increases were repeated in Western Europe and the U.S.A.

The fact that industrial managers (administrative officials) were so many may be a reflection of the growth of the organizational structure which was characterized by a variety of "department managers, sales managers, accountants, cashiers, inspectors, training officers, publicity managers, and the rest emerged as specialized parts of the general management function as industrial concerns increased in size" (42). Chester Barnard has emphasized that loyalty, which is the acceptance that the organizational man- employee is essentially important cannot be overemphasized.

The second phase of industrialization was stimulated by the growth of bureaucratic structure, bureaucratic rationality and the development of material technology. Industrial development was marked by a major breakthrough in technological advancement. Initially, rapid technological advances accompanied by immense industrial production led to a significant death rate of the smaller and in some cases, larger enterprises. Industrial growth occurred when the rate of technical development slowed down because less capital and labor intensive techniques, industrialists and entrepreneurs had saved or invested in profit-making business climates and "consumer demands" that tended to become more "standardized through publicity and price reductions, and the technical progress" become consequently restrained (42). These happenings enabled companies to remain stable while "large-scale production was built up by converting manufacturing processes and routine cycles of activity for machines or semi-skilled assembly hands" (42-43).

Under these conditions specific industrial companies grew in size and manufacturing. Processes became permanently routinized, mechanized and quickened. Consequently, various management functions became not only routinized, but they also became technologically specialized. These functions for which the attendant bureaucracy was supervisorily charged with included "specialized management task: those of ensuring employee cooperation, of coordinating different departments, of planning and monitoring" (43). In recent years, the second phase of industrialism has continued to dominate the institutional and organizational life of Western and other societies. Its bureaucratic character, however, belongs to the first phase of the industrial organization.

The third industrial phase, which J.K. Galbraith has called the *Affluent Society*, is about 30 or 40 years old. This industrial phase is new and has "more insecure relationship with the consumer who appears wary as production catches up and overtakes spontaneous domestic demand. The 'propensity to consume' has had to be simulated by advertising, by styling, and by marketing promotions guided by research into the habits, motives, and potential needs of consumers" (43). Industrial expansion and governmental spending on the military industrial complex may have enhanced elements of sizeable influx in industrial and information technology which constitute, because of malaise and competition from Europe and Asia, a "challenged technological leap" in the United States.

In brief, organizational strategic planning is not only a rational, scientific, and futuristic philosophy, but, the strategic philosophy of planning is also alive because if the impact of strategic forces on the institution. Strategic force is the process through which external and internal factors of the organization are integrated to produce strategic policy which can be implemented to result in definite responses (see Figure 2.6) which may also serve as a summary of this chapter.

Conclusion

Strategic planning provides a logical framework for budgeting, evaluating, organizing, staffing, leading, and controlling the work of the organization. In higher education, strategic planning helps the organization define its mission, its unique strengths and weaknesses, the nature of its clientele, and the methods through which it can accomplish its objectives. It also enables an organization to deal with environmental pressures and anticipate necessary organizational adaptations.

The strategic planning process, then, involves the analysis of an organization's desired future state and the policies and strategies necessary to bring that state about. Strategic planning deals with the futurity of current decisions through the identification of opportunities and threats in the environment. It is a continuous process that begins with the definition of organizational aims or missions, defines strategies and policies to achieve them, and develops detailed plans to make sure that the strategies and policies are effectively implemented. Strategic planning connotes a philosophy, which relates day-to-day organizational activity to a thorough contemplation of the future. In this sense, strategic planning is more of an intellectual exercise than a prescribed set of procedures or techniques or philosophical rhetoric. It seeks to link the long-range objectives of an organization with short-range programs, budgets, and operating plans. Strategic planning is effective planning which does not attempt to make future decisions or control the organization's environment. Rather, it involves the design of an overall organizational strategy to adaptively help an organization achieve a better match with its environment.

The prescribed decision-making process in bureaus and other organizations has undergone a good deal of change during the last three decades from classical rational model to incrementalism and satisficing to the reincarnation of rationalism as policy analysis, and now to the group method of expressive model. These changes are probably not due to more than shifts in theory and

Figure 2.6. Strategic Forces

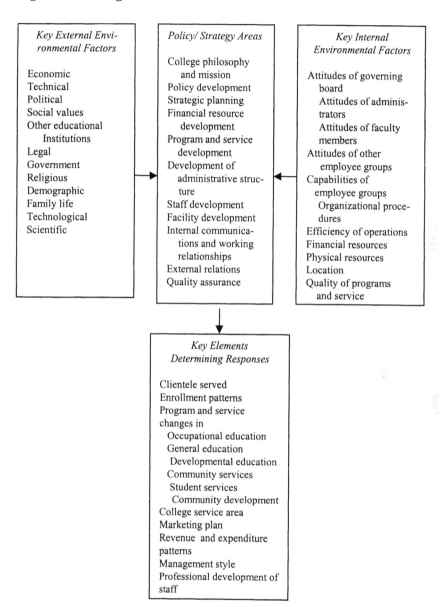

Key External Environmental Factors	*Policy/ Strategy Areas*	*Key Internal Environmental Factors*

Economic
Technical
Political
Social values
Other educational
  Institutions
Legal
Government
Religious
Demographic
Family life
Technological
Scientific
	College philosophy
	  and mission
	Policy development
	Strategic planning
	Financial resource
	  development
	Program and service
	  development
	Development of
	  administrative struc-
	  ture
	Staff development
	Facility development
	Internal communica-
	  tions and working
	  relationships
	External relations
	Quality assurance
		Attitudes of governing
		  board
		Attitudes of adminis-
		  trators
		Attitudes of faculty
		  members
		Attitudes of other
		  employee groups
		Capabilities of
		  employee groups
		Organizational proce-
		  dures
		Efficiency of operations
		Financial resources
		Physical resources
		Location
		Quality of programs
		  and service

*Key Elements
Determining Responses*

Clientele served
Enrollment patterns
Program and service
changes in
  Occupational education
  General education
  Developmental education
  Community services
  Student services
  Community development
College service area
Marketing plan
Revenue and expenditure
patterns
Management style
Professional development of
staff

Source: Myran A. Gunder. 1984. Strategic Management in the Community College. *New Directions for Community Colleges* 11: 1-20

new research findings. But rather, they reflect new popular and political views on what constitutes a legitimate process of choice. There appears to be a cyclical pattern in these changes in method as well, from the earlier view of bureau decision-making as a matter of deferring in hierarchical authority and expertise to the acknowledgement of an overtly political role for bureau decision makers to the recent efforts to erase politics from process, replacing it with analytic expertise and a leveling of power differences.

The reasons for the recent shifts to analytic and purportedly apolitical methods of decision-making in bureaus are not easily identified. One possibility may be that suspicion of the pluralist-bargaining method generally grows from disillusionment with interest group liberalism and pork barrel politics in an era of budgetary restraints. The move from acknowledging a political method to interest in the more technically deliberate may also be part of the larger recent interest in high technology and futurist thinking. Attempts in the past two decades to adopt more quantitative and analytic criteria of policy effectiveness may also be related to changes in decision processes.

The shifts in decision-making methods, in theory and practice, illustrate that the bureau's most fundamental processes are not static; they respond to a variety of internal and external, political and technological changes. The search for a single best decision-making process in bureaus may, therefore, be based on an unrealistic assumption about the stability of bureaus and the environment in which they operate. These bureaus are agencies or independent establishments and government corporations that are hierarchically structured policy or goal oriented and publicly accountable in their operations. Like public schools and colleges, which are accountable to their communities (states) and the boards of regents, these bureaus are accountable to Congress and the federal government. The incorporation of intelligent technological systems into organizational operations will enable these organizations to become more efficient and productive in respect to the visualization of their virtual reality and information processing capabilities.

Herbert Simon is a scientific pioneer in the study of organizational decision-making. He was one of the first social scientists to advance the science of administrative decision-making. His purpose was to make an attempt to reconcile the reactional choice model of economic theory with the emergent findings on human behavior in organizations. This approach was theoretically and implicitly classical rather than modern or contemporary. Simon invented the term satisficing. He emphasized that decision-making can maximize efficiency. When managerial leadership suboptimizes, the leaders do so because rationality is bounded in the context of time, monetary, ethnic or political environment. Bounded rationality is limited human capability which tends to satisfice rather than maximize or optimize. Hence, public bureaucracies refrain from carrying out effective performance evaluations, providing workload measures or evaluations. As a result, they tend to concentrate on routine work which stifles creativity and makes it difficult to innovate bureaucratic decision-making which is a form of documented public decisions.

These bureaucratic decision rules are standard operational procedures that are sanctioned by professional norms, procedures and processes for service delivery. Externally, Waldo and Appleby view administration as organizational politics characterized by open systems, organic, natural systems and cybernetic elements of behavior. In other words, both Waldo and Appleby normatively deviated from the classical and mechanistic approach to organizational decision-making in the public arena and placed emphasis in natural or behavioral and cybernetic systems.

Katz and Kahn (1978) who reinterpreted Parsonian systems theory, argue that it is impossible to separate politics from public administration. Politics is not only "who gets what, when and how," but it is also the authoritative allocation of values. Public administration, in which decision-making models are used, is different from corporate or private administration because the former operates in the political millieux. This difference between the two systems raised the possibility of separating facts and values. The fact-value dichotomy is a demonstration that there is a true science of administration. Most of what goes on in politics is more artistic than scientific although both art and science are elements of the political. There is no one best way.

The academic fields from which the literary ideas on Chapter 2 were drawn include but are not limited to strategic planning and management, organizational theory and organization behavior. Many of these ideas have been selectively identified, analyzed, paraphrased, and restructured with the use of Professor Sagini's *Organizational Behavior* (2001) and from other theorists. Specifically, decision making models, theories and processes rather than structures are central analytic concepts whose theoretical gamut provides the conceptual resume for the text's evolution and intellectual analysis.

Theoretically, the Chapter addresses five major components. First, it highlights the history, philosophy and governance of community colleges. Second, it comprehensively defines and rationalizes the theory of strategic planning in society. Third, the Chapter identifies various decision making techniques and tries to show how they are applied in public and corporate culture. Fourth, the Chapter shows how, when and why a variety of rationally constructed decision making tools (styles of leadership) can be applied to solve management problems in contemporary society. Fifth, the chapter shows, by using historical, empirical, and contextual approach, that strategic planning and management is not only a socially constructed philosophy of institutional governance, but it is a classic form of managerial human behavior, whose evolution is consistent with the organization's needs, struggles, and challenges that predate its survival and success. You, he, she, and I are the people who are directly, consciously, and unfictitiously involved in making their social reality to become a living testament.

Chapter 3

Methodology and Instrumentation

Introduction

Chapter 3 is a description of data collection methods and instrumentation. In essence, the chapter is a reflective analysis of how survey, ethnographic methodology and descriptive statistics were empirically applied for the purpose of collecting data from amidst challenging and rewarding experiences of the field (Colleges A, B, C, and D). Data were collected by conducting on-site interviews and selectively tape recording some of them. A survey instrument was designed to obtain basic information (data) from planning participants of each college. The data were collected by examining available institutional planning documents and by interviewing planners about institutional demographics, formalized planning, strategic planning and decision making, and the degree of effectiveness of their planning systems.

Methodology

Methodology is a set of principles and procedures that were used in this inquiry. The principles and procedures include:

1. Purpose of the study
2. Assertions
3. Population and sample design
4. Advantages of using the interview
5. Unit of analysis
6. The role and tasks of the interviewer

1. Purpose of the Study

The purposes of the study are fourfold:

1. To determine whether goals and objectives of the colleges were clearly identified and effectively implemented in keeping with institutional missions;
2. To determine whether programs were developed to achieve institutional goals and objectives;
3. To observe, analyze, and reflect on the role of institutional research to the planning process; and
4. To determine whether goals, objectives, and research were rationalized in the context of a formal planning model.

2. Assertions

A paramount theme, which underlies the study, suggests that educational institutions changeably use planning model(s) for the purpose of improving organizational planning operations. On the basis of such an understanding, organizations which use planning model(s) do so in order to manage their own affairs more efficiently and effectively. The research question, which the study intends to answer then, is "What planning model(s) did planners use for planning the activities of their colleges?" The answer for this question is an assertion, which states that:

1. Planners who display authoritarian leadership styles in their colleges are more likely to use rational planning than other planning models. A subsidiary research question states that: "What other planning model(s) did the planners use for planning in their colleges?" The answer to the question is likely to result in two researchable or observable assertions. The assertions state that

2. Planners who successfully use any one of the other commonly known planning models are less likely to use the rational planning model in their colleges.
3. Planners who neither use the rational model, nor any one of the more commonly known planning models tend to use more than two of them.

These assertions were theoretical statements, which were analytically, substantively, or inductively used to confirm or disconfirm empirical evidence. In other words, confirming or disconfirming their essence was an attempt to analytically break them asunder and see what they mean, imply, and reflect.

3. Population and Sample Design

A sample of 42 top and middle level planners was identified and selected from a population of 60 college administrators. The sampling units (elements) were chosen on the basis of informed opinion "expert sampling" (Warwick and Lininger 1975, 74).

A survey-interview was designed and administered for data collection of planning perceptions in one junior college and three community colleges in Michigan. The four colleges are among the twenty-nine public two-year institutions in the state. An interview-survey was designed to obtain basic planning information on strategic planning and management from each of the four colleges. Each of the planners was contacted in advance and was willing to respond and provide information on college administrative structure, principal tenets of the planning participants, planning parameters, planning procedures, planning products, and strategic planning.

In addition, each interviewee (respondent or informant) was provided with a copy of the interview-survey. These interviews were unstructured and scheduled. The interviews were conducted during daytime, either in each respondent's office or in the main administrative committee room. The interviewees were composed of top and middle-level management administrators who participate in planning and decision-making activities of each college. Such management teams were called "Administrative Councils" in College A, "Presidents' Cabinet" in Colleges A and B, and "Administrative Committee" in College C. Each of these teams of college planners was composed of people from both sexes whose age ranged between 30 and 60 years. These predominantly white, middle-class, and middle-aged administrators, of whom males were numerically and administratively dominant in three colleges, were composed of three presidents, eight vice-presidents, fifteen deans, two comptrollers, and fourteen directors. Their numerical distribution in each college, except for the presidents, was uneven. These college planners also differed in planning and administrative experience and in academic levels and specialties. Above all, thirty were males and twelve were females. Only one of the females was an African American. For further details, see Table 3.1.

4. Advantages of Using the Survey Interview

The interview instrument was in a form of both open and close-ended questionnaire. The interview permitted greater depth of exploration; it permitted probing to obtain more complete data; it made it possible to establish and maintain rapport with the respondents, or at least helped to determine when rapport had not been established; and it provided a means of checking and assuring the effectiveness of communication. Irrespective of these advantages, interviews were costly, time consuming, and at times emotionally and psychologically inconvenient.

Table 3.1.
Population and Sample

Category	Population	Sample	Males	Females	Presidents	Vice Presidents	Deans	Other*
A	13	12	9	3	1	4	3	4
B	13	11	6	5	1	2	4	4
C	10	10	8	2	1	1	3	5
D	24	9	7	2	-	1	5	3
Total	**60**	**42**	**30**	**12**	**3**	**8**	**15**	**16**

* Note: Other – Registrar, Director, or Comptroller.

The three main reasons for using the survey interview were:

1. To determine whether the interview could be an exploratory device for identifying variables and relations for suggesting the assertions and to guide other phases of the research.
2. To use it as an instrument for collecting research data.
3. To supplement the tape recorded method of the research study and delve more deeply into the feelings, attitudes, beliefs, and motivations of each chief planing official (respondent) in each of the four colleges.

5. Unit of Analysis

The unit of analysis was each individual planner (administrator). The responses of each planner in each college formed the data-corpus of each specific college. The collective responses from each college became the data-corpus used for comparative strategic planning perceptions which provided not only the means for testing the generality of relationships between and among institutional variables, but such an analysis was, oftentimes, a means for realizing new concepts, theoretical insights, and the generation of new assertions and subassertions about the phenomena involved in the study.

6. The Role and Tasks of the Interviewer

As explained above , the goal of the interviewer (researcher) was to maximize the collection of adequate, relevant, and valid information from interviewees. To collect the information effectively, the interviewer acted the role of an observer, a note taker, and analyst. The tasks, as Gorden (1980, Chapter 3) indicates, included (1) understanding the purpose of the interview, (2) communicating clearly and purposefully, (3) detecting and correcting misunderstandings and the questions by interviewees, (4) distinguishing the irrelevant from the relevant, (5) probing for the relevant, (6) motivating interviewees to respond willingly and uninhibitedly, (7) detecting and resisting inhibitive characteristics in the respondent (interviewee), and (8) refraining from putting pressure on the interviewee to give information before he/she was ready to do so.

Instrumentation

Instrumentation is the application of instruments (survey and tape recorders) for observation, measurement, control, and data analysis. In this study, the instruments were used in accordance with a variety of procedures, principles and steps that are explained below as follows:

1. Setting
2. Preliminary preparation for entry
3. Interview sites
4. Pretesting and the interviews
5. Interviewing techniques
6. Data recording procedures
7. The tape recording

1. Setting

The named colleges are A, B, C, and D. They are located in central and southern Michigan. Two are rural institutions and two are urban. For either of the two pairs, one is big and the other is small. Essentially, all the colleges serve the needs of a majority of the disadvantaged communities.

2. Preliminary preparation for Entry

A contact person was identified and he laid the groundwork for the researcher's role-negotiation and entry into each college. Three presidents in the colleges and one dean in the fourth college became the intermediaries for establishing the structure and format of the interviews. To play their intermediary roles effectively, each participant was supplied with samples of interview-surveys, human subjects document and an abstract of the doctoral dissertation proposal. Through telephone communication, the interviewer did not only discuss with the contact person for attempts to seek support and cooperation from them and their planning teams, but, they also accepted scheduled and unscheduled interviews.

3. Interview Sites

The interview sites for colleges A, B, and D were the offices of each planning official (administrator). An administrative council committee room was the common interview site for college C interviews. The sites were selected on the basis of maintaining privacy, convenience, confidentiality, and control. Control was a system of checks and balances for operational efficiency and empirical accountability.

4. Pretesting and the Interviews

With the recommendation of and in consultation with one of the senior master planners of each of the four colleges, four administrators were selected and pretested on the survey and item suitability, relevance, and understandability. The four administrators were preinterviewed and supervised by divisional (departmental) deans. Each pretested interview took one hour. The pretestees suggested a few survey corrections, modifications, and gave some positive comments about the instrument. They individually mailed their pretest responses to the researcher who used the suggested opinions, comments, and corrections to refine the original survey-interview instrument.

The researcher visited each interview site as scheduled. He was either introduced by the contact person or introduced himself to his potential respondent, shook hands with and thanked the potential respondent, and supplied him/her with the human subjects document, survey-interview (instrument), and abstract. The purpose of each visit was examined. Each introduction was brief, data collection-purpose oriented, and geared to making the interviewees feel comfortable, friendly and uninhibited. In addition, the interviewer made it clear to each interviewee that he/she was free to express or not to express information at his/her convenience. An attempt was made to direct the discourse into desirable channels by motivating each respondent to reveal information and facts that could be drawn from their experiences and knowledge.

5. Interviewing Techniques

The objective of using interviewing techniques were to obtain relevant, reliable, and valid information. The main goal was to create a positive climate for obtaining maximum and relevant information through the process of maintaining optimum interpersonal relations. The aim was to maximize the flow, quality, and quantity of information with optimal rather than maximum interpersonal relations per se. To gather the information more effectively, and in light of pressing demands for meeting institutional and personal time schedules, four types of interviews were used: personal, group, telephone, and tape recording.

First, face-to-face meetings between an interviewee and the interviewer (researcher) were convened in each administrator's office, except for institution C in which the personal interviews were conducted in an administrative council's committee room.

Secondly, ten of the eleven administrators in Institution B and two of the eight administrators of Institution D convened for group interviews. Each group was composed of three people – the two interviewees (respondents) and the interviewer (researcher). There were six group interviews. Like the personal interviews, and with the exception of the group interview held at College D where the interview was conducted while one of the interviewees was driving around the city getting his child from school and taking him home, between 3:30 and 4:30 p.m., the five group interviews were held in private settings. Since each of the three people in the group had a copy of the instrument, and since each could fill it in respectively, each interviewee could express himself/herself fully and truthfully.

The group interviews were composed of eight men and four women: four directors, one comptroller, five deans, and two vice presidents. With their apparent divergence in backgrounds, these administrators explored problems, raised issues, and meticulously evaluated propositions. The information they gave varied considerably. However, they helped one another to recall, verify, and rectify. They moderated the trilogue to enable the other participant to express himself/herself freely and thoroughly.

Thirdly, only one telephone interview was conducted between the researcher and one of the deans at College C. Although the researcher did not directly interact with the interviewee, the conversation was private, convenient, thematically relevant, and fruitful.

Fourthly, a tape recorder was used selectively to gather crucial information and analyze its transcription.

6. Data Recording Procedures

The survey instrument, sample, and the interviews were designed and structured to selectively make systematic, sharp, and discriminating, but objective, observations. The observations were made in light of a relevant universe of discourse. These observations or responses were recorded on the survey instrument during interactive and reflective field experiences.

7. The Tape Recorder

The second method of collecting data was using the tape recorder. The two most experienced planners in each college were selectively tape recorded on the basis of seniority and ability to provide needed data. The purpose of selectively recording some interviews was to explore complex issues perceived to contain, as well as further explore latent feelings, attitudes, inconsistencies, interruptions, and tenseness. After every tape-recorded interview, the entire tape was replayed, transcribed, and material was inserted in the survey instrument. Analytic interpretations of the study were given in light of social structure and culture of the institutions and society in general, immediate interviewing situations, and the demands posed by the questions and the ultimate requirements for data.

Summary

Chapter 3 is a brief description on how ethnographic (substantive) and non-parametric methodologies and techniques were used to generate data from 42 planners of four post-secondary institutions in the state of Michigan. A ten-page survey instrument was constructed and used for observation and measurement of the responses from the members of the sample. Data pertaining to institutional demographics, formal planning, long-range and strategic planning, decision-making, and institutional research were collected. The analytic integration of ethnographic and histogramatic theories and practice formed the basis for data analysis. The integrative process and the review of the literature in Chapter 2 were viewed as dynamic intellectual processes without which this study would have lacked satisfactory evidentiary warrant for analysis, reflection and credible documentation.

Chapter 4

Data Analysis

Introduction

Chapter 4 is based on a comprehensive and comparative analysis of data. The data were analyzed with the use of tables (histograms) and theoretically grounded interpretive commentary.

Interactively, the major problem of the study was based on the assumption that the rational planning model was the ideal model suitable for institutional and management operations in higher institutions of learning. Since it was not clear whether the model was widely used or not used in such organizational settings, the study was designed to investigate the veracity, reliability and validity of the assumption. Because the rational model (according to Chaffee, 1983) is the best planning model in higher education circles, the research employed strategic planning theory and ethnographic and nonparametric measures to investigate the problem in four Michigan Community Colleges (A, B, C and D).

The problem was extended to refer to three major *assertions* of which the first one, according to the rational model is authoritarian (Rutherford and Fleming, 1985). The three research assertions include:

1. Planners who display authoritarian decision-making styles in their colleges are more likely to use rational planning than other planning models.
2. Planners who successfully use any one of the other commonly known decision-making styles (anarchy, bureaucratic, political, consensus, and compromise) are less likely to use the rational planning model in their colleges.
3. Planners who neither use the rational nor any one of the more commonly known planning models tend to use more than two of them.

The result of these three research assertions, Table 4.35 and the interpretive commentary, were, in a sense, partly used for comparative analysis. In addition, two *analytic questions* were derived from the assertions. Those analytic questions, on which some of the conclusions of the study were based were:

1. What planning model(s) did planners of Colleges A, B, C, and D use in planning activities of their colleges?
2. What other planning model(s) did the planners use for planning in their colleges?

Purpose of the Study

The purposes of the study are four:

1. To determine whether goals and objectives of the colleges were clearly identified and effectively implemented in consonant with institutional missions.
2. To determine whether programs were developed in achieve institutional goals and objectives.
3. To observe, analyze, and reflect on the role of institutional research to the planning model and process.
4. To determine whether goals, objectives, and research were articulated in the context of a formal planning model.

To make the analysis clearer and structurally objective, Chapter 4 is divided in five sections. Section one is a display of tables containing descriptive comments about observed phenomena. Section two is composed of findings of the section. Section three contains a brief interpretive commentary based on tables, and most importantly, tape recorded data. Section four is a brief analysis of goals and objectives. The last section is a summary of Chapter 4.

Display of Tables

Table 4.1 displays relevant demographics. In all four colleges, resources used for institutional research and other programs corresponded with the size of the institution; however, College B's board used the least time (10 hours) yearly for planning.

Table 4.2 shows that all respondents indicated that their colleges planned formally.

Table 4.3 illustrates that most of the college planners believed that formulized planning was an excellent, rather than a good way to plan.

Table 4.4 demonstrates that most respondents did not believe that MBO was used for management

Table 4.1
College Demographics

Categories	A	B	C	D
Total annual budget used (in millions of $'s)	15	8	4.25	25
Total institutional funds used for Instruction (in millions of $'s)	12	5.6	4	16
Total maintenance budget (in millions of $'s)	1.8	.25	.25	--
Total budget for Institutional Research	.12	0.005	0.005	.15
Total full time equivalent Enrollment	3,600	1,600	1,000	10,500
Total head count enrollment	8,000	5,500	2,200	35,000
Number of campuses of the colleges	1	1	1	1
Number of students in transfer program	2,000	675	521	6,000
Number of students in vocational And tech programs	1,500	300	554	4,500
Number of hours planners use to make a decision in a year	100	100	100	100
Number of hours board used to make a decision in a year	75	10	20	500
Number of locations in which the college offered classes	2	6	1	--

-- Not reported

Table 4.2
Use of Formal Planning in College

Categories	President P	Vice President P	Dean P	Other P	Totals P	Totals T	Percentages P	Percentages T
A	1	4	3	4	12	12	100	100
B	1	2	4	4	11	11	100	100
C	1	1	3	5	10	10	100	100
D	B	1	5	3	9	9	100	100
Total by Rank	3	8	15	16	42	42	100	
Percentages by Rank	100	100	100	100	100	100		

Note: Other means Registrar, Director, or Comptroller
B = Did not respond
P = Positive
T = Total

Table 4.3
Formalized Planning

Categories	President		Vice President		Dean		Other		Totals			Percentages		
	E	G	E	G	E	G	E	G	E	G	T	E	G	T
A	1		3	1	3		4	1	11	1	12	91.7	8.3	100
B		1	2		2	2	3	1	7	4	11	63.6	36.4	100
C	1		1		2	1	2	3	6	4	10	60	40	100
D			1			5	1	2	7	2	9	77.8	22.2	100
Total by Rank	2	1	7	1	7	8	10	6	31	11	42	73.8	26.2	100
Percentages by Rank	66.7	33.3	87.5	12.5	46.7	53.3	62.5	37.5	73.8	26.2	100			

Other means Registrar, Director or Comptroller
E = an excellent way to plan
G = a good way to plan
T = Total

Table 4.4
Whether or Not MBO was Used by College Planners

Categories	President		Vice President		Dean		Other		Totals			Percentages		
	P	N	P	N	P	N	P	N	P	N	T	P	N	T
A	--	1	2	2	--	3	2	2	4	8	12	33.3	66.7	100
B	--	1	2	--	2	2	1	3	5	6	11	45.5	54.5	100
C	1	--	1	--	--	3	4	1	6	4	10	60	40	100
D	--	--	1	--	1	4	1	2	3	6	9	33.3	66.7	100
Total by Rank	1	2	6	7	3	12	8	8	18	24	42	42.9	57.1	100
Percentages by Rank	33.3	66.7	75	25	20	80	50	50	42.9	57.1	100			

Other means Registrar, Director or Controller
P = Positive, N = Negative, T = Total
Percentages were approximated because of the rounding of numbers

Colleges A, C, and D had developed according to their stated goals and objectives as Table 4.5 shows. In college B, 63.6 percent of the measured perceptions indicated, it had not.

In relation to the person(s) who control(s) formalized planning, College A's president used a participatory approach in the cabinet meetings, rather than in instructional settings. The budget planning committee controlled it too. Operational decisions were reviewed quarterly.

In College B, only cabinet members and hardly any other groups, could participate in formalized planning. The four deans who acted as members of the expanded cabinet were invited to the cabinet only on an occasional basis.

In College C, the administrative council and the Committee of 2001, which was concerned with planning, controlled the formalized planning process. The board of trustees acted in an advisory capacity only. The committee for the year 2001 was composed of five committees (campus development, community development, curricular development, marketing development, and student development).

In College D, college-planning councils, deans, vice presidents, and the president were involved in planning. The college did not have a planning officer or planning office per se, except a planning task force. The trustees of College D had a long-range planning committee of 40 people whose special committees were given the responsibility to plan for a variety of specific needs within the public school district, which controlled the institution's governance and operational matters.

In relation to persons who set college goals, in College A, the board, chief administrators, cabinet, faculty, administrative council (president, vice president, dean, directors, and divisional chairpersons and staff) assessed goals quarterly, annually, and tri-annually.

In College B the cabinet and the expanded cabinet set college goals. Divisional heads and the board of trustees were occasionally invited for consultation or briefing retreats. Goals and objectives were assessed regularly.

In College D, administrative councils, faculty, students' long-range planning committees, and board of trustees of the public school district set goals. Goals were assessed annually for effectiveness or failure and adjustment. Table 4.5 describes how colleges were perceived to have developed according to their stated goals.

In Table 4.6 describes how the colleges analyzed their external environment and became informed to make more intelligent decisions.

Table 4.7 indicates how the college studies were internally prepared and used to monitor trends.

Table 4.8 shows the perceptions which influenced the attitude of planners to manage the colleges according to established academic standards for all colleges; these perceptional influences included: for College A students and government; for B, economic trends; for C, economic trends and students; for D, policies and economic trends.

Institutional research is the gathering, analysis, integration, (synthesis) interpretation, and dissemination of data and information suitable for improvement

Table 4.5
Whether or Not Each College Had Developed According to its Goals and Objectives

Categories	President		Vice President		Dean		Other		Totals			Percentages		
	P	N	P	N	P	N	P	N	P	N	T	P	N	T
A	1	--	3	1	3	--	2	--	9	3	12	75	25	100
B	--	1	2	--	1	3	1	3	4	7	11	36.4	63.6	100
C	1	--		1	3	--	4	1	8	2	10	80	20	100
D			1	--	5	--	2	1	8	1	9	88.9	11.1	100
Total by Rank	1	2	6	2	12	3	9	7	29	13	42	69	31	100
Percentages by Rank	66.7	33.3	75	25	80	20	56.25	43.75	69	31	100			

Other means Registrar, Director or Controller
P = Positive, N = Negative, T = Total
Percentages were approximated because of the rounding of numbers

Table 4.6

Whether Planning Officials Analyzed the External Environment

Categories	President	Vice President		Dean			Other			Totals				Percentages			
	P	P	NR	P	N	NR	P	N	NR	P	N	NR	T	P	N	NR	T
A	1	3	1	3			4		1	11	1	12	24	91.7	--	8.3	100
B	1	2		3		1	4		1	10	1	11	22	90.9	--	9.1	100
C	1	1	--	1	2		4		1	7	2	1	10	70	20	10	100
D		1		5			1	1	1	7	1	1	9	77.8	11.1	11.1	100
Total by Rank	3	7	1	12	2	1	13	1	2	35	3	4	42	83.3	7.1	9.5	100
Percentages by Rank	100	87.5	12.5	80	13.3	6.7	81.3	6.25	12.5	83.3	7.1	9.5	100				

Other means Registrar, Director or Controller

P = Positive, N = Negative, NR = No Response, T = Total

Percentages were approximated because of the rounding of numbers

Table 4.7
How Environmental Studies Were Prepared for Analyzing

Categories	President	Vice President		Dean		Other			Totals				Percentages			
	I	I	C	I	C	I	C	MN	I	C	MN	T	I	C	MN	T
A	1	4	--	3	--	--	3	--	11	--	--	11	100	--	--	100
B	1	2	--	2	--	1	3	1	8	1	1	10	80	10	10	100
C	1	1	--	2	--	1	4	--	8	--	1	9	88.9	--	11.1	100
D	--	--	1	3	1	1	1	--	4	2	1	7	57.1	28.6	14.3	100
Total by Rank	3	7	1	10	1	3	11	1	31	3	3	37				
Percentage by Rank	100	87.5	12.5	71.4	7.1	91.7	8.3		83.8	8.1	8.1	100				

Other means Registrar, Director or Controller
I = Internal way of monitoring trends, C = College research task, MN = Other and written minutes and newsletters,
T = Total
Percentages were approximated because of the rounding of numbers

Table 4.8
What Influenced Attitudes of Planners To Manage the College

Categories	College							
	A		B		C		D	
	No.	%	No.	%	No.	%	No.	%
Politics	8	12.3	4	11.4	4	7.1	9	13.6
Students	8	12.3	8	22.8	8	14.3	5	7.6
Government	11	16.9	3	8.6	4	7.1	7	10.6
Political Elite	2	3.1	--	--	3	5.4	3	4.5
Economic Trends	12	18.5	5	14.3	10	17.9	8	12.1
Ethnicity	2	3.1	--	--	2	3.6	7	10.6
Faculty	5	7.7	5	14.3	5	8.9	7	10.6
External Agency	3	4.6	4	11.4	5	8.9	5	7.6
Superintendent of Education	1	1.5	--	--	2	3.6	6	9.1
Academic Goals and Standards	12	18.5	6	17.1	8	14.3	8	12.1
Other	1	1.5	--	--	3	5.4	1	1.5
Total Number of Responses	65	100	35	100	56	100	66	100

Note: Percentages were approximated due to the rounding of numbers.

of administrative decision making. Table Nos. 4.9 – 4.12 concern institutional research.

Table 4.9 describes the perceptions concerning persons responsible for analytically sensitizing the reality of the external environment and integrating that reality with internal institutional planning dynamics.

The respondents indicated the persons responsible were president's and vice presidents' office in College A, the office of director of institutional research and public relations in College B, the offices of the president, vice president, and student affairs in College C, and the offices of director of institutional research in College D.

According to Table 4.10, each college tried to analyze data from its environment, the sources of information used for analysis included local government studies and occasionally directed College research for A. Occasionally directed college research for College B, independent external agencies for College C, and local government studies and professional groups for D.

College planners relatively analyzed their educational, social, economic, political, and cultural environments in order to develop better goals and objectives (Table 4.11 and 4.12)

Tables 4.13 and 4.14 show that planners in all four colleges responded that they had criteria for appointing people for specific administrative and instructional positions.

Table 4.15 shows the process of recruiting administrative and instructional personnel to the colleges. Of the nine terms employed in the process, three (recruitment, selection, and hiring) were more commonly applied than the other six (see Table 4.15).

Tables 4.16 and 4.17 indicates that planners said that each of the colleges had specific budget goals and objectives and that they (planners) prioritized fund allocations.

None of the four colleges reported using PPBS, MBO, ZBB, MIS, IB, and EDUCOM planning techniques; although college planners were familiar with the techniques as Table 4.18 illustrates.

Table 4.19 addresses the question, whether the colleges made faculty and staff changes. Planners in all colleges made faculty and staff changes in order to make adjustments consistent with the level of enrollments, funding ability, program demand, and student interests.

Whether the college eliminated academic courses and departments was illustrated in Table 4.20. The colleges could discontinue academic courses and departments on the basis of the same reason given in Table 4.19.

Table 4.21 shows that planners in the four colleges said that their departments had clear course goals and objectives.

Table 4.22 indicates that faculty applied and used course goals priorities. According to Table 4.23, planners in Colleges A, B, and C said that they did not consolidated (join courses together into whole units). College D planners said that their institution eliminated classes that were underenrolled, understaffed, or both. The research did not indicate that these conditions were necessarily influenced by the quality of instruction.

Table 4.9
Person(s) Who Prepare(s) Environmental Studies for Analysis

Categories	College A No.	%	B No.	%	C No.	%	D No.	%
President	5	17.2	1	3.2	4	26.7	3	9.7
Vice President	9	31	1	3.2	6	40	4	12.9
Senior Academic Officer	2	6.9	2	6.4	1	6.7	4	12.9
Senior Financial Officer	2	6.9	1	3.2	--	--	3	9.7
Office of Student Affairs	2	6.9	5	16.1	3	20	2	6.5
Director of Institutional Research	--	--	10	32.2	--	--	7	22.6
Public Relations Office	2	6.9	6	19.4	--	--	1	3.2
College Planning and Management Office	1	3.4	1	3.2	--	--	--	--
Registrar	1	3.4	2	6.4	--	--	3	9.7
Other	5	17.2	2	6.4	1	6.7	4	12.9
Total by College	29	100	31	100	15	100	31	100

Note: Percentages of responses were approximated due to the rounding of numbers.

Table 4.10

Source of Information for Analyzing Studies of the Environment

	College							
	A		B		C		D	
	No.	%	No.	%	No.	%	No.	%
Teacher's Union or Association	4	69	1	2.7	3	10	6	11.8
Occasionally Directed College Research	9	15.5	9	2.43	5	16.7	5	9.8
Expertise of Consultants	8	13.8	6	16.2	4	13.3	6	11.8
Superintendents of Education	2	3.4	--	--	--	--	5	9.8
Local Government Studies	11	19	6	16.2	5	16.7	7	13.7
Independent External Agencies	8	13.8	5	13.5	6	20	5	9.8
Professional Groups	6	10.3	5	13.5	2	6.7	7	13.7
Institutes of Ed. (UM or MSU)	4	6.9	4	10.8	4	13.3	6	11.8
Other	6	10.3	1	2.7	1	3.3	4	7.8
Total Number of Responses	58	100	37	100	30	100	51	100

Note: Percentages were approximated due to the rounding of numbers.
       UM = University of Michigan, MSU = Michigan State University

Table 4.11
Environmental Analysis and the Validity and Reliability of College Goals

Categories	President	Vice President		Dean		Other		Totals			Percentages		
	P	P	N	P	N	P	N	P	N	T	P	N	T
A	1	3	1	3	--	4	--	11	1	12	91.7	8.3	100
B	1	2	--	3	1	4	1	10	1	11	90.9	9.1	100
C	1	1	--	3	--	4	1	9	1	10	90	10	100
D	--	1	--	3	2	1	2	5	4	9	55.8	44.4	100
Total by Rank	3	7	1	12	3	13	3	35	7	42	83.3	16.7	100
Percentage by Rank	100	87.5	12.5	80	20	81.25	18.75	83.3	16.7	100			

Other means Registrar, Director or Controller
P = Positive, N = Negative, T = Total
Percentages were approximated because of the rounding of numbers

Table 4.12
Trends Evaluated by a College Unit

Categories	President			Vice President				Dean				Other				Totals					Percentages				
	E	P	S	E	P	S	C	E	P	S	C	E	P	S	C	E	P	S	C	T	E	P	S	C	T
A	1	1	1	4	2	3	1	3	3	3	3	3	1	3	1	11	7	10	5	33	33.8	21.2	30.3	15.2	100
B	1	1	–	2	2	2	2	1	2	1	–	4	–	4	–	8	5	7	2	22	36.4	22.7	31.8	9.1	100
C	1	–	–	1	–	1	1	3	3	1	–	4	2	3	3	9	5	5	4	23	39.1	21.7	21.7	17.4	100
D	–	–	–	1	1	1	–	3	2	2	1	2	2	2	1	6	5	5	2	18	55.9	32.3	27.8	11.1	100
Total by Rank	3	2	1	8	5	7	4	10	10	7	4	13	5	12	5	34	22	27	13	96					
Percentage by Rank	50	33.3	6.7	33.3	20.8	29.2	16.7	32.3	32.3	22.6	12.6	39.1	14.3	34.3	14.3	35.4	22.9	28	13.5	??	35.4	22.9	28	13.5	100

Other means Registrar, Director or Controller
E = Economic, P = Political, S = Social, C = Cultural, T = Total
Percentages were approximated because of the rounding of numbers

Table 4.13
Does Your College Have a Criterion for Appointing Administrative Personnel?

Categories	President	Vice President	Dean		Other			Totals			Percentages		
	P	P	P	N	P	N	T	P	N	T	P	N	T
A	1	4	3	--	3	1	--	11	1	12	91.7	8.3	100
B	1	2	3	1	3	1	--	9	2	11	81.8	18.2	100
C	1	1	3	--	--	5	--	10	--	10	100	--	100
D	--	1	2	3	--	2	1	5	4	9	55.6	44.4	100
Total by Rank	3	8	11	4	6	9	1	35	7	42	83.3	16.7	100
Percentages by Rank	100	100	73.3	26.7	37.5	56.25	6.3	83.3	16.7	100			

Other means Registrar, Director or Controller
P = Positive, N = Negative, T = Total
Percentages were approximated because of the rounding of numbers

Table 4.14
Does Your College Have a Criterion for Appointing Instructional Personnel?

Categories	President		Vice President		Dean		Other		Totals			Percentages		
	P	N	P	N	P	N	P	N	P	N	T	P	N	T
A	1	0	4	0	0	3	4	0	12	0	12	100	0	100
B	1	0	2	0	4	0	4	0	11	0	11	100	0	100
C	1	0	1	0	3	0	5	0	10	0	10	100	0	100
D			1	0	5	0	1	2	7	2	9	77.8	22.2	100
Total by Rank	3	0	8	0	15	0	14	2	40	2	42	95.24	4.76	100
Percentage by Rank	100	0	100	0	100	0	87.5	12.5	95.24	4.76	100			

Other means Registrar, Director or Controller
P = Positive, N = Negative, T = Total
Percentages were approximated because of the rounding of numbers

Table 4.15
Terms Used in the Processes of Appointment of Administrative and Instructional Personnel

	College							
	A		B		C		D	
Categories	No.	%	No.	%	No.	%	No.	%
Recruitment	11	16.9	10	17.2	8	14.8	8	17.4
Selection	11	16.9	10	17.2	10	18.5	7	15.2
Hired (Employed)	10	15.4	7	12.1	8	14.8	7	15.2
Training, Retraining, and Faculty Development	9	13.8	9	15.5	6	11.1	8	17.4
Promotion on Merit	5	7.7	5	8.6	5	9.3	5	10.9
Promotion on Academic Performance	7	10.8	4	5.9	3	5.5	2	4.3
Promotion on Other Grounds	4	6.2	5	8.6	1	1.9	1	2.2
Security of Tenure (Faculty only)	3	4.6	2	3.4	6	11.1	4	8.7
Salary Increases	5	7.7	6	10.3	7	13	4	8.7
Total	65	100.0	58	100	54	100	46	100

Note: Percentages of responses were approximated due to the rounding of numbers.

Table 4.16
Whether College Had Specific Budget Goals and Objectives

Categories	President		Vice President		Dean		Other		Totals			Percentages		
	P	N	P	N	P	N	P	N	P	N	T	P	N	T
A	1	0	3	1	3		2	2	9	3	12	75	25	100
B	1	0	2	0	2	2	4	0	9	2	11	81.1	18.2	100
C	1	0	1	0	2	1	5	0	9	1	10	90	10	100
D	0	0	1	0	4	1	3	0	8	1	9	88.9	11.1	100
Total by Rank	3	0	7	1	11	4	14	2	35	7	42	83.3	16.7	100
Percentages by Rank	100	0	87.5	12.5	73.3	26.7	87.5	12.5	83.3	16.7	100			

Other means Registrar, Director or Controller
P = Positive, N = Negative, T = Total
Percentages were approximated because of the rounding of numbers

Table 4.17
Whether College Had Priorities to Allocate Funds

Categories	President		Vice President		Dean		Other		Totals			Percentages		
	P	N	P	N	P	N	P	N	P	N	T	P	N	T
A	1	0	3	1	3	0	3	1	10	2	12	83.3	16.7	100
B	1	0	2	--	4	0	3	1	10	1	11	90.9	9.1	100
C	1	0	1	--	3	0	5	--	10	--	10	100	--	100
D	--	--	1	--	5	0	3	--	9	--	9	100	--	100
Total by Rank	3	0	7	1	15	0	14	2	39	3	42	92.9	7.14	100
Percentage by Rank	100	0	87.5	12.5	100	0	87.5	12.5	95.24	7.14	100			

Other means Registrar, Director or Controller
P = Positive, N = Negative, T = Total
Percentages were approximated because of the rounding of numbers

Table 4.18
College Familiarity with PPBS, MBO, ZBB, MLS, IB, and EDUCOM

Categories	President		Vice President		Dean			Other			Totals				Percentages			
	P	N	P	N	P	N	NR	P	N	NR	P	N	NR	T	P	N	NR	T
A	0	1	1	3	1	1	1	2	--	2	9	--	3	12	75	--	25	100
B	0	1	2	--	1	3	--	1	3	--	4	7	--	11	36.4	63.6	--	100
C	0	1	1	--		3	--	1	3	1	2	7	1	10	20	70	10	100
D	--	--	1	--	1	4	--	3	--	--	5	4	--	9	55.6	44.4	--	100
Total by Rank	--	3	5	3	3	11	1	7	6	3	20	18	4	42	47.6	42.8	9.6	100
Percentages by Rank	0	100	62.5	37.5	20	73.3	6.7	43.8 37.5 18.8			47.6	42.8	9.6	100				

Other means Registrar, Director or Controller

P = Positive, N = Negative, NR = No Response, T = Total

Percentages were approximated because of the rounding of numbers

Table 4.19
Whether College Made Faculty/ Staff Changes

Categories	President		Vice President		Dean		Other		Totals			Percentages		
	P	N	P	N	P	N	P	N	P	N	T	P	N	T
A	1	0	2	2	2	1	3	1	8	4	12	66.7	33.3	100
B	1	0	2	--	2	2	3	1	8	3	11	72.7	27.3	100
C	1	0	1	--	3	--	5	--	10	--	10	100	--	100
D	--	0	1	--	4	1	3	--	8	1	9	88.9	19.05	100
Total by Rank	3	0	6	2	11	4	14	2	34	8	42	80.95	19.05	100
Percentage by Rank	100	0	75	25	73.3	26.7	87.5	12.5	80.95	19.1	100			

Other means Registrar, Director or Controller
P = Positive, N = Negative, T = Total
Percentages were approximated because of the rounding of numbers

Table 4.20
Whether College Eliminated Academic Courses and Departments

Categories	President		Vice President		Dean		Other		Totals			Percentages		
	P	N	P	N	P	N	P	N	P	N	T	P	N	T
A	1	0	4	0	3	0	3	1	11	1	12	91.7	8.3	100
B	1	0	2	0	4	0	3	1	10	1	11	90.9	9.1	100
C	1	0	1	0	3	0	5	--	10	--	10	100	--	100
D	--	0	1	0	5	0	3	--	9	--	9	100	--	100
Total by Rank	3	0	8	0	15	0	14	2	40	2	42	95.24	4.8	100
Percentage by Rank	100	0	100	0	100	0	87.5	12.5	95.24	4.76	100			

Other means Registrar, Director or Controller
P = Positive, N = Negative, T = Total
Percentages were approximated because of the rounding of numbers

Table 4.21

Whether Each Department Had Clear Course Goals and Objectives

Categories	President		Vice President			Dean			Other			Totals				Percentages			
	P	N	P	N	NR	P	N	NR	P	N	NR	P	N	NR	T	P	N	NR	T
A	--	1	2	1	1	3	--	-	2	--	2	7	1	4	12	58.3	8.3	33.3	100
B	1	--	2	--	-	2	1	1	3	1	--	8	2	1	11	72.7	18.2	9.1	100
C	1	--	1	--	-	2	1	--	5	--	--	8	1	1	10	80	10	10	100
D	--	--	1	--	-	5	--	-	3	--	--	9	--	--	9	90	--	--	100
Total by Rank	2	1	6	1	1	12	2	1	13	1	2	32	4	6	42	76.2	9.5	14.3	100
Percentage by Rank	66.7	33.3	75	12.5	12.5	80	13.3	6.7	81.3	6.3	12.5	76.2	95.3	14.3	100				

Other means Registrar, Director or Controller

P = Positive; N = Negative; NR = No Response

Percentages were approximated because of the rounding of numbers

Table 4.22
Whether Faculty Applied and Used Course Priorities

Categories	President P	President N	Vice President P	Vice President N	Dean P	Dean N	Dean NR	Other P	Other N	Other NR	Totals P	Totals N	Totals NR	Totals T	Percentages P	Percentages N	Percentages NR	Percentages T
A	--	1	2	2	3	--	-	1	--	3	6	0	6	12	50	--	50	100
B	1	--	2	--	2	1	1	1	3	--	6	4	1	11	54.5	36.4	9.1	100
C	--	1	1	--	2	1	--	--	4	1	7	1	2	10	70	10	20	100
D	--	--	1	--	4	1	--	2	--	1	7	1	1	9	77.8	11.1	11.1	100
Total by Rank	1	2	6	2	11	3	1	4	7	5	26	6	10	42	95.24	4.76		100
Percentage by Rank	33.3	66.7	75	25	73.3	20	6.7	25	43.8	31.3	61.9	14.8	23.8	100				

Other means Registrar, Director or Controller
P = Positive, N = Negative, NR = No Response, T = Total
Percentages were approximated because of the rounding of numbers

Table 4.23
Whether Your College Faculty Consolidated Courses

Categories	President		Vice President			Dean			Other			Totals				Percentages			
	P	N	P	N	NR	P	N	NR	P	N	NR	P	N	NR	T	P	N	NR	T
A	--	1	2	--	2	3	--	--	--	1	3	5	1	6	12	41.7	8.3	50	100
B	1	--	--	2	--	1	2	1	1	3	--	3	7	1	11	27.3	63.6	9.1	100
C	--	1	1	--	--	1	1	1	2	2	1	4	3	3	10	40	30	30	100
D	--	--	--	1	--	4	1	--	1	1	1	5	3	1	9	55.5	33.3	11.1	100
Total by Rank	1	2	3	3	2	9	4	2	4	7	5	17	14	11	42	40.5	33.3	26.2	100
Percentage by Rank	33.3	66.7	37.5	37.5	25	60	26.7	13.3	25	43.8	31.3	40.5	33.3	26.2	100				

Other means Registrar, Director or Controller
P = Positive, N = Negative, NR = No Response, T = Total
Percentages were approximated because of the rounding of numbers

Table 4.24 illustrates responses to the question, do faculties eliminate courses? The faculties of Colleges A, C, and D eliminated (discontinued) courses which were not in demand. Those of B said that they both eliminated and retained courses.

Table 4.25 demonstrates that faculty reorganized courses to make adjustments on full-time equivalent, underenrollments, teaching loads, and student interest.

According to Table 4.26, faculty did not have criteria for measuring and maintaining course quality; according to Table 4.27, those in College C and D had their criteria. The criteria were based on grade point average, student evaluation of faculty, faculty evaluation of students, and observation results of the North Central Accreditation requirements.

In Table 4.28, planners of Colleges A, C, and D said that their college goals and objectives had changed in 10 – 15 years. The goals and objectives had not changed in College B – it appeared that no change had taken place in it in all these years.

College planners were asked how internal priorities were identified (Table 4.29). Colleges A, B, and C identified them by consultation. College D applied analytic approaches.

Table 4.30 demonstrates that College A also used planners who could analyze, were experienced, and sensitive to institutional action effects, to determine crucially factual relationships. Colleges B and D determined institutionally related facts and relationships by using experienced individuals.

Data in Table 4.31 demonstrates that planners in all colleges said that they were selected for decision making because of their expertise rather than statesmanship or position.

The locus (center of power or consultation) of consultation for all colleges was wide rather than narrow, according to Table 4.32.

While planners in College D felt that the degree at which they used analytical information was high (Table 4.23), those in Colleges A, B, and C said that analytical information was used moderately. In Table 4.33, only presidents show that the degree of analysis of information used for management is high. Other planners in all the four colleges think that information is moderately analyzed.

Planners of Colleges A and C said that priorities were ranked for decision making, as indicated in Table 4.34. This meant that priorities which were considered superior in importance or rank took the place in the process of prioritization. In Colleges B and D, decision-making priorities were developed by top administrators. Obviously, planners in the latter colleges which did not broaden the base for decision making were likely to be less democratic and participatory than those in Colleges A and C.

The consensus model displayed in Table 4.35 was used in Colleges A, B, and C and rational model was used in College D. The table has been described fully in several places in the text.

According to Table 4.36 planners in Colleges A, B, and C said that decision making style of central administration had changed in three years. The planners of College D disagreed that any change had occurred.

Table 4.24
Whether Faculty Eliminated Courses

Categories	President		Vice President			Dean			Other			Totals				Percentages			
	P	N	P	N	NR	P	N	NR	P	N	NR	P	N	NR	T	P	N	NR	T
A	--	1	2	--	2	3	--	--	1	--	3	6	--	6	12	50	--	50	100
B	1	--	--	2	--	2	1	1	2	2	--	5	5	1	11	45.4	45.4	9.1	100
C	--	1	1	--	--	2	--	1	3	1	1	6	1	3	10	60	10	30	100
D	--	--	1	--	--	4	1	--	3	--	--	8	1	--	9	88.9	11.1	--	100
Total by Rank	1	2	4	2	2	11	2	2	9	3	4	25	7	10	42	59.5	16.7	23.8	100
Percentage by Rank	33.3	66.7	50	25	25	73.3	13.3	13.3	56.3	18.8	25	59.3	16.7	23.8	100				

Other means Registrar, Director or Controller
P = Positive: N = Negative; NR = No Response, T = Total
Percentages were approximated because of the rounding of numbers

Table 4.25
Whether Faculty Reorganized Courses

Categories	President		Vice President		Dean		Other		Totals			Percentages		
	P	N	P	N	P	N	P	N	P	N	T	P	N	T
A	--	1	3	1	3	--	2	2	8	4	12	67.7	33.3	100
B	1	--	1	1	3	1	4	--	9	2	11	81.8	18.2	100
C	--	1	1	--	2	1	4	1	7	3	10	70	30	100
D	--	--	1	--	5	--	3	--	9	--	9	100	--	100
Total by Rank	1	2	6	2	13	2	13	3	33	9	42	78.6	21.4	100
Percentage by Rank	33.3	66.7	75	25	86.7	13.3	81.25	8.75	78.57	21.43	100			

Other means Registrar, Director or Controller
P = Positive, N = Negative, T = Total
Percentages were approximated because of the rounding of numbers

Table 4.26
Whether Faculty Had a Limited Number of Courses and Objectives

Categories	President		Vice President			Dean			Other			Totals				Percentages			
	P	N	P	N	NR	P	N	NR	P	N	NR	P	N	NR	T	P	N	NR	T
A	--	1	1	1	2	1	2	--	1	--	3	3	3	6	12	25	25	50	100
B	1	--	2	--	--	1	2	1	--	4	--	4	6	2	11	36.4	54.4	9.1	100
C	--	1	--	1	--	1	1	2	2	2	1	3	4	4	10	30	40	30	100
D	--	--	2	--	--	2	3	--	--	2	1	3	5	2	9	33.3	55.5	11.1	100
Total by Rank	1	2	4	2	2	5	8	2	3	8	5	13	18	11	42	30.9	42.9	26.2	100
Percentage by Rank	33.3	66.7	50	25	25	33.3	53.3	13.3	18.8	50	31.3	30.9	42.9	26.2	100				

Other means Registrar, Director or Controller
P = Positive, N = Negative, NR = No Response, T = Total
Percentages were approximated because of the rounding of numbers

Table 4.27
Whether Faculty Had a Criteria for Measuring and Maintaining Course Quality

Categories	President		Vice President			Dean			Other			Totals				Percentages			
	P	N	P	N	NR	P	N	NR	P	N	NR	P	N	NR	T	P	N	NR	T
A	1	--	2	--	2	1	2	--	--	1	3	3	3	6	12	25	25	50	100
B	1	--	--	2	--	1	2	1	--	4	--	1	8	2	11	9.1	73.7	18.2	100
C	1	--	--	1	-	1	1	1	4	1	--	5	3	2	10	50	30	20	100
D	--	--	--	1	-	4	1	--	1	1	1	6	2	1	9	66.7	22.2	11.1	100
Total by Rank	3	--	2	4	2	7	6	2	5	7	4	15	16	11	42	35.7	38.1	26.2	100
Percentage by Rank	100	0	25	50	25	46.7	40	13.3	31.3	43.8	25	35.7	38.1	26.2	100				

Other means Registrar, Director or Controller
P = Positive, N = Negative, NR = No Response, T = Total
Percentages were approximated because of the rounding of numbers

Table 4.28

Whether College Goals and Objectives Have Changed in 10 – 15 Years

Categories	President	Vice President		Dean		Other		Totals			Percentages		
	N	P	NR	P	NR	P	NR	P	NR	T	P	NR	T
A	1	2	2	3	--	1	3	6	6	12	50	50	100
B	1	1	1	2	2	2	2	5	6	11	45.4	54.6	100
C	1	1	--	2	1	4	1	7	3	10	70	30	100
D		1	--	5	--	1	2	7	2	9	77.8	22.2	100
Total by Rank	3	5	3	12	3	8	8	25	17	42	59.5	40.5	100
Percentage by Rank	100	62.5	37.5	80	20	50	50	59.9	38.1	100			

Other means Registrar, Director or Controller

P = Positive, N = Negative, NR = No Response, T = Total

Percentages were approximated because of the rounding of numbers

Table 4.29
How Internal Problems and Issues Were Identified

Categories	President	Vice President			Dean			Other			Totals				Percentages			
	C	A	C	I	A	C	I	A	C	I	A	C	I	T	A	C	I	T
A	1	1	2	1	1	3	1	1	2	3	3	8	5	16	18.8	50	31.3	100
B	1	--	2	--	1	1	2	--	2	2	1	6	4	11	9.1	54.5	36.4	100
C	1	--	1	--	--	1	2	2	2	2	2	5	4	11	18.2	45.4	36.4	100
D	--	1	--	--	2	4	1	2	1	--	5	4	2	11	45.4	36.4	18.2	100
Total by Rank	3	2	5	1	4	9	6	5	7	7	11	23	15	49	22.4	47	30.6	100
Percentage by Rank	100	25	62.5	12.5	21	47.4	31.6	26.3	36.8	36.8	22.4	47	30.6	100				

Other means Registrar, Director or Controller
A = Analysis, C = Consultation, I = Individual reaction, T = Total
Percentages were approximated because of the rounding of numbers

Table 4.30
Determination of Crucial Facts and Relationships

Categories	President			Vice President			Dean			Other			Totals				Percentages			
	A	E	AC	A	E	AC	A	E	AC	A	E	AC	A	E	AC	T	A	E	AC	T
A	--	1	--	3	3	1	2	1	2	1	1	3	6	6	6	18	33.3	33.3	33.3	100
B	--	--	1	--	--	2	2	2	--	2	2	--	4	4	3	11	36.4	36.4	27.2	100
C	1	--	--	1	1	--	1	2	--	2	3	--	5	6	--	11	45.4	54.6	--	100
D	--	--	--	--	1	3	3	2	2	1	1	1	4	4	3	11	36.4	36.4	27.2	100
Total by Rank	1	1	1	3	5	3	8	9	4	6	7	4	19	20	12	51	37.3	39.2	23.5	100
Percentage by Rank	33.3	33.3	33.3	33.3	41.7	25	38.1	42.9	19.1	35.3	41.2	23.6	37.3	39.2	23.5	100				

Other means Registrar, Director or Controller
A = Analysis, E = Experience, AC = Action effects, T = Total
Percentages were approximated because of the rounding of numbers

Table 4.31
Why Planners Were Selected for Decision Making

Categories	President	Vice President		Dean			Other			Totals				Percentages			
	E	E	S	E	S	P	E	S	P	E	S	P	T	E	S	P	T
A	1	3	1	3	--	--	2	2	--	9	3	--	12	75	25	--	100
B	1	2	--	1	1	2	2	2	--	6	3	2	11	54.5	27.3	18.2	100
C	1	--	--	3	--	--	5	--	--	9	--	--	9	100	--	--	100
D	--	1	--	3	1	1	1	1	1	5	2	2	9	55.6	22.2	22.2	100
Total by Rank	3	6	1	10	2	3	10	5	1	29	8	4	41	70.7	19.5	9.8	100
Percentage by Rank	100	85.7	14.3	66.7	13.3	20	62.5	31.3	6.25	70.7	19.5	9.8	100				

Other means Registrar, Director or Controller
E = Expertise, S = Statesmanship, P = Position, T = Total
Percentages were approximated because of the rounding of numbers

Table 4.32
Locus of Consultation

Categories	President N	President W	Vice President N	Dean N	Dean W	Other N	Other W	Totals N	Totals W	Totals T	Percentages N	Percentages W	Percentages T
A	--	1	4	--	3	1	3	1	11	12	8.3	91.7	100
B	--	1	2	2	2	1	3	4	7	11	36.4	63.6	100
C	1	--	1	--	3	3	2	3	7	10	30	70	100
D			1	2	3	3	--	2	7	9	22.2	77.8	100
Total by Rank	1	2	8	4	11	8	8	10	32	42	23.81	76.19	100
Percentage by Rank	33.3	66.7	100	26.7	73.3	50	50	23.81	76.19	100			

Other means Registrar, Director or Controller
N = Narrow, W = Wide, T = Total
Percentages were approximated because of the rounding of numbers

Table 4.33
To What Degree of Analytical Information Used in College

Categories	President	Vice President		Dean		Other		Totals			Percentages		
	H	H	M	H	M	H	M	H	M	T	H	M	T
A	1	1	3	1	2	--	4	2	10	12	16.7	83.3	100
B	1	--	2	--	4	--	4	--	11	11	--	100	100
C	1	1	--	--	3	--	5	1	9	10	10	90	100
D	--	1	--	2	3	2	1	5	4	9	55.5	44.4	100
Total by Rank	3	3	5	3	12	2	14	8	34	42	19.9	80.1	100
Percentage by Rank	100	37.5	62.5	20	80	12.5	87.5	19	81	100			

Other means Registrar, Director or Controller
H = High, M = Medium, T = Total
Percentages were approximated because of the rounding of numbers

Table 4.34
How/ By Whom Priorities Were Developed for Decision Making

Categories	President		Vice President			Dean			Other			Totals				Percentages			
	A	F	G	A	F	G	A	F	G	A	F	G	A	F	T	G	A	F	T
A	1	--	1	3	1	9	1	1	1	3	1	11	8	3	22	50	36.4	13.6	100
B	1	--	1	1	--	2	3	--	2	2	--	5	7	--	12	41.7	58.3	--	100
C	--	1	1	--	--	1	2	1	2	1	2	4	3	4	11	36.4	27.2	36.4	100
D	--	--	--	1	--	1	4	1	3	1	1	4	6	2	12	33.3	50	16.7	100
Total by Rank	2	1	5	5	1	13	10	3	8	7	4	24	24	9	57	42.1	42.1	15.8	100
Percentage by Rank	66.7	33.3	33.3	55.6	11.1	50	38.5	11.5	42.1	36.8	21.1	42.1	42.1	15.8	100				

Other means Registrar, Director or Controller
G = Goal Ranking, A = Top Administrators, F = with Faculty input, T = Total
Percentages were approximated because of the rounding of numbers

Table 4.35
The Most Typical Decision-Making Model (Responses)

Categories	President	Vice President		Dean		Other		Totals			Percentages			
	V	V	W	V	W	V	W	V	W	T	V	W		T
A	1	1	3	2	1	1	3	5	7	12	41.7	58.3	--	100
B	1	--	2	--	4	--	4	1	10	11	--	90.0	9.1	100
C	1	1	--	2	1	2	3	6	4	10	60	40	--	100
D	--	--	1	--	5	--	2	--	8	9	100	--	--	100
Total by Rank	3	2	6	4	11	3	13	12	30	42	28.6	71.4	--	100
Percentage by Rank	100	25	75	26.7	73.3	18.8	81.3	28.6	71.4	100				

Other means Registrar, Director or Controller
V = Very well, W = Well, T = Total
Percentages were approximated because of the rounding of numbers

Table 4.36
If Decision-Making Style of Central Administration Had Changed in Five Years

Categories	President		Vice President		Dean		Other		Totals			Percentages		
	P	N	P	N	P	N	P	N	P	N	T	P	N	T
A	1	--	2	2	2	1	3	1	8	4	12	66.7	33.3	100
B	1	--	2	--	4	--	4	--	11	--	11	100	--	100
C	--	1	--	1	2	1	4	1	6	4	10	60	40	100
D	--	--	--	1	3	2	1	2	4	5	9	44.4	55.6	100
Total by Rank	2	1	4	4	11	4	12	4	29	13	42	69.05	30.95	100
Percentage by Rank	66.6	33.3	50	50	73.3	26.7	75	25	69	31	100			

Other means Registrar, Director or Controller
P = Positive, N = Negative, T = Total
Percentages were approximated because of the rounding of numbers

Overall, college goals were realized well in Colleges A and B, and very well in College C and D, according to Table 4.37.

Of the eight conditions rank-ordered for their contribution to the evolution of college master plans in the 1960's, "interdisciplinary nature of many courses" was ranked first (Table 4.38).

Three out of ten goals (teaching, economic, and academic standards) were ranked highest in the three sets of Community College goals (Table 4.39).

Findings of the Study

The findings of the study have been extrapolated from the analysis of data and interpretive commentary. These findings can be divided into five sections or categories consistent with the structure of the survey instrument and perceptions of the respondents. The five sections into which the findings are categorized include:

1. Demographics
2. Formal planning
3. Strategic planning
4. College goals
5. Decision making

Findings Related to Demographics

Table 4.1 shows the demographics of the colleges. According to the table, the Board of Trustees of College B spent the least time (10 hours) a year in planning for the college. In addition, the expenditure of resources by each college depends on its size and mission. By inference, the fact that College B used the least resources for planning annually indicated that its mission is either different and unique compared with the other three.

1. Findings Related to Formal Planning

a. All respondents (100%) in the four colleges indicated that their institutions used formal planning procedures (Table 4.2) for managing these institutions

b. For all colleges, 91.7% of College A planners, 63.3% of College B, 60% of College C, and 77.8%of College D believed that formalized planning was an excellent rather than good way of planning (Table 4.3).

c. With the exception of College C, Colleges A, B, and D did not formally (officially) use Management by Objectives (MBO) for planning (Table 4.4). On individual basis, some college planners of these four colleges tried to use MBO.

Table 4.37
How Well College Goals Were Realized

Categories	President	Vice President		Dean		Other		Totals			Percentages			
	V	V	W	V	W	V	W	V	W	T	V	W		
A	1	1	3	2	1	1	3	5	7	12	41.7	58.3	--	100
B	1	--	2	--	4	--	4	1	10	11	--	90.0	9.1	100
C	1	1	--	2	1	2	3	6	4	10	60	40	--	100
D	--	--	1	--	5	--	2	--	8	9	100	--	--	100
Total by Rank	3	2	6	4	11	3	13	12	30	42	28.6	71.4	--	100
Percentage by Rank	100	25	75	26.7	73.3	18.8	81.3	28.6	71.4	100				

Other means Registrar, Director or Controller
V = Very well, W = Well
Percentages were approximated because of the rounding of numbers

Table 4.38
Condition Rankings by College and Position – Master Plan

College	Number of Respondents	Position	Mean	Standard Deviation
Overwhelming Knowledge Explosion After 1960's				
Entire Sample = 36			3.6	2.2
A	1	President	4.0	0.0
	2	Vice President	4.8	1.5
	3	Dean	4.5	2.1
	4	Other	3.8	3.1
B	1	President	2.4	2.4
	2	Vice President	1.0	0.0
	3	Dean	4.7	3.1
	4	Other	1.5	1.0
C	1	President	5.0	0.0
	2	Vice President	8.0	0.0
	3	Dean	4.3	2.1
	4	Other	3.4	1.8
D	1	President	3.0	1.9
	3	Dean	2.0	1.4
	4	Other	5.0	0.0
Increasing Costs and Reducing Budget				
Entire sample = 37			6.1	2.0
A	1	President	8.0	0.0
	2	Vice President	7.0	0.82
	3	Dean	5.5	3.5
	4	Other	5.3	2.1
B	1	President	7.1	1.3
	2	Vice President	5.0	0.0
	3	Dean	7.7	0.50
	4	Other	7.6	0.50

Table 4.38. Continued

College	Number of Respondents	Position	Mean	Standard Deviation
C	1	President	3.0	0.0
	2	Vice President	5.0	0.0
	3	Dean	5.0	3.5
	4	Other	4.4	2.5
D	1	President	7.0	1.2
	2	Vice President	7.0	0.0
	3	Dean	6.5	1.3
	4	Other	8.0	0.0

Size of Campus Enrollment

Entire Sample = 37			5.5	2.1
A	1	President	7.0	0.0
	2	Vice President	7.0	1.4
	3	Dean	6.0	1.4
	4	Other	3.8	3.1
B	2	Vice President	7.0	0.0
	3	Dean	6.0	1.0
	4	Other	3.4	1.8
C	1	President	8.0	0.0
	2	Vice President	7.0	0.0
	3	Dean	6.3	2.1
	4	Other	3.4	1.8
D	2	Vice President	6.0	0.0
	3	Dean	5.5	1.7
	4	Other	5.5	2.1

External Support Organization

Entire Sample = 37			5.2	1.7
A	1	President	2.0	0.0
	2	Vice President	3.8	1.3
	3	Dean	3.5	2.1

Table 4.38. Continued

College	Number of Respondents	Position	Mean	Standard Deviation
	4	Other	6.2	0.50
B	2	Vice President	6.0	0.0
	3	Dean	5.3	1.2
	4	Other	5.5	1.3
C	1	President	2.0	0.0
	2	Vice President	4.0	0.0
	3	Dean	4.7	1.5
	4	Other	5.6	1.5
D	2	Vice President	8.0	0.0
	3	Dean	7.5	0.58
	4	Other	4.5	2.1

Student Interest in Programmatic Areas

Entire Sample = 36			5.5	1.9
A	1	President	6.0	2.2
	2	Vice President	6.0	2.2
	3	Dean	4.0	4.2
	4	Other	4.0	1.2
B	2	Vice President	4.0	0.0
	3	Dean	5.3	1.5
	4	Other	6.0	1.4
C	1	President	7.0	0.0
	2	Vice President	6.0	0.0
	3	Dean	5.7	2.1
	4	Other	7.4	1.3
D	3	Dean	5.3	1.3
	4	Other	4.0	4.2

Articulated National Planning

Entire Sample = 36			2.3	1.9

Table 4.38. Continued

College	Number of Respondents	Position	Mean	Standard Deviation
A	1	President	1.0	0.0
	2	Vice President	1.5	1.0
	3	Dean	1.5	0.7
	4	Other	3.3	3.2
B	2	Vice President	2.0	0.0
	3	Dean	2.0	1.0
	4	Other	2.5	1.0
C	1	President	21.0	0.0
	2	Vice President	1.0	0.0
	3	Dean	1.3	0.6
	4	Other	3.2	2.2
D	3	Dean	3.5	3.3
	4	Other	2.5	2.1

Interdisciplinary Nature of Many Courses

Entire Sample = 36			3.2	1.6
A	1	President	3.0	0.0
	2	Vice President	2.3	0.5
	3	Dean	4.0	0.0
	4	Other	3.8	2.2
B	2	Vice President	3.0	0.0
	3	Dean	2.3	1.2
	4	Other	4.0	1.4
C	1	President	6.0	0.0
	2	Vice President	2.0	0.0
	3	Dean	4.3	3.2
	4	Other	3.0	2.1
D	3	Dean	2.8	0.5
	4	Other	2.5	0.7

Table 4.38. Continued

College	Number of Respondents	Position	Mean	Standard Deviation

Development of Manpower of Michigan & U.S.A.

College	Number of Respondents	Position	Mean	Standard Deviation
Entire Sample = 36			4.8	2.1
A	1	President	5.0	0.0
	2	Vice President	4.3	2.5
	3	Dean	7.0	1.4
	4	Other	6.0	1.8
B	2	Vice President	8.0	0.0
	3	Dean	2.6	2.1
	4	Other	4.0	2.2
C	1	President	4.0	0.0
	2	Vice President	3.0	0.0
	3	Dean	4.3	1.5
	4	Other	5.6	2.2
D	3	Dean	4.0	1.6
	4	Other	4.0	2.8

Table 4.39
Condition Rankings by College and Position – College Goals

College	Number of Respondents	Position	Mean	Standard Deviation
Teaching				
Entire Sample = 40			2.7	0.65
A	1	President	3.0	0.0
	2	Vice President	2.5	1.0
	3	Dean	2.3	1.2
	4	Other	2.8	0.5
B	1	President	1.0	0.0
	2	Vice President	3.0	0.0
	3	Dean	2.5	1.0
	4	Other	3.0	0.0
C	1	President	3.0	0.0
	2	Vice President	2.0	0.0
	3	Dean	3.0	0.0
	4	Other	2.8	0.4
D	2	Vice President	3.0	0.0
	3	Dean	2.8	0.4
	4	Other	3.0	0.0
Community Service				
Entire Sample = 41			1.5	0.74
A	1	President	1.0	0.0
	2	Vice President	1.8	1.0
	3	Dean	1.7	1.2
	4	Other	1.3	0.5
B	1	President	3.0	0.0
	2	Vice President	1.0	0.0
	3	Dean	1.8	0.5
	4	Other	1.8	1.0

Table 4.39 – Continued

College	Number of Respondents	Position	Mean	Standard Deviation
C	1	President	1.0	0.0
	2	Vice President	3.0	0.0
	3	Dean	1.3	0.6
	4	Other	0.14	0.5
D	2	Vice President	3.0	0.0
	3	Dean	1.2	0.4
	4	Other	1.0	0.0

Training Manpower

Entire Sample = 40			1.9	0.61
A	1	President	2.0	0.0
	2	Vice President	1.8	0.5
	3	Dean	2.0	0.0
	4	Other	2.0	0.8
B	1	President	2.0	0.0
	2	Vice President	2.0	0.0
	3	Dean	1.8	1.0
	4	Other	1.7	0.6
C	1	President	2.0	0.0
	2	Vice President	1.0	0.0
	3	Dean	1.7	0.8
	4	Other	1.8	0.8
D	2	Vice President	3.0	0.0
	3	Dean	2.0	0.7
	4	Other	2.0	0.0

Politically Inclined

Entire Sample = 39			2.1	1.0
A	1	President	2.0	0.0
	2	Vice President	1.3	0.5
	3	Dean	2.3	0.6

Table 4.39 – Continued

College	Number of Respondents	Position	Mean	Standard Deviation
	4	Other	2.5	1.0
B	1	President	4.0	0.0
	2	Vice President	2.0	0.0
	3	Dean	2.3	1.0
	4	Other	2.0	1.0
C	1	President	1.0	0.0
	2	Vice President	1.0	0.0
	3	Dean	2.3	1.2
	4	Other	1.2	0.4
D	3	Dean	2.4	1.2
	4	Other	4.0	0.0

Culturally Oriented

Entire Sample = 39			1.8	0.96
A	1	President	1.0	0.0
	2	Vice President	1.8	0.5
	3	Dean	1.0	0.0
	4	Other	2.09	1.4
B	1	President	2.0	0.0
	2	Vice President	1.0	0.0
	3	Dean	1.3	0.5
	4	Other	1.7	1.2
C	1	President	3.0	0.0
	2	Vice President	2.0	0.0
	3	Dean	1.7	0.6
	4	Other	2.4	1.1
D	3	Dean	2.4	1.3
	4	Other	1.0	0.0

Table 4.39 – Continued

College	Number of Respondents	Position	Mean	Standard Deviation

Economically Attuned

Entire Sample = 41			3.7	0.57
A	1	President	4.0	0.0
	2	Vice President	4.0	0.0
	3	Dean	3.7	0.6
	4	Other	3.8	0.5
B	1	President	3.0	0.0
	2	Vice President	4.0	0.0
	3	Dean	3.5	1.0
	4	Other	4.0	0.0
C	1	President	4.0	0.0
	2	Vice President	3.0	0.0
	3	Dean	3.7	0.6
	4	Other	3.6	0.9
D	2	Vice President	4.0	0.0
	3	Dean	3.6	0.5
	4	Other	3.0	0.0

Socially Geared

Entire Sample = 40			2.5	0.88
A	1	President	3.0	0.0
	2	Vice President	3.0	0.0
	3	Dean	3.0	0.0
	4	Other	1.8	0.5
B	1	President	1.0	0.0
	2	Vice President	3.0	0.0
	3	Dean	3.0	0.8
	4	Other	2.3	0.6
C	1	President	2.0	0.0
	2	Vice President	4.0	0.0
	3	Dean	2.3	1.5

Table 4.39 – Continued

College	Number of Respondents	Position	Mean	Standard Deviation
	4	Other	2.8	0.4
D	2	Vice President	4.0	0.0
	3	Dean	1.6	0.5
	4	Other	2.0	0.0

To Maintain Academic Standards

College	Number of Respondents	Position	Mean	Standard Deviation
Entire Sample = 40			2.9	0.33
A	1	President	3.0	0.00
	2	Vice President	3.0	0.0
	3	Dean	3.0	0.0
	4	Other	3.0	0.0
B	1	President	3.0	0.0
	2	Vice President	3.0	0.0
	3	Dean	2.8	0.5
	4	Other	2.8	0.5
C	1	President	3.0	0.0
	2	Vice President	2.0	0.0
	3	Dean	2.7	0.6
	4	Other	3.0	0.0
D	2	Vice President	2.0	0.0
	3	Dean	3.0	0.0
	4	Other	3.0	0.0

To Produce Elite

College	Number of Respondents	Position	Mean	Standard Deviation
Entire Sample			1.2	0.50
A	1	President	1.3	0.5
	2	Vice President	1.3	0.6
	3	Dean	1.0	0.0
	4	Other	1.5	0.6
B	1	President	1.0	0.0
	2	Vice President	1.0	0.0
	3	Dean	1.3	0.5

Table 4.39 – Continued

College	Number of Respondents	Position	Mean	Standard Deviation
	4	Other	1.7	1.2
C	1	President	1.0	0.0
	2	Vice President	1.0	0.0
	3	Dean	1.0	0.0
	4	Other	1.0	0.0
D	3	Dean	1.3	0.5
	4	Other	1.5	0.7

To Liberate the Poor

College	Number of Respondents	Position	Mean	Standard Deviation
Entire Sample = 36			1.9	0.53
A	1	President	1.7	0.5
	2	Vice President	1.8	0.5
	3	Dean	2.0	0.0
	4	Other	1.5	0.6
B	1	President	2.0	0.0
	2	Vice President	2.0	0.0
	3	Dean	2.0	0.8
	4	Other	1.7	0.6
C	1	President	2.0	0.0
	2	Vice President	3.0	0.0
	3	Dean	2.3	0.0
	4	Other	2.0	0.0
D	2	Vice President	3.0	0.0
	3	Dean	2.0	0.0
	4	Other	1.5	0.7

2.   **Findings Related to Strategic Planning**

a.   Although planners in all the four colleges evaluatively monitored environmental trends, they were more sensitive to monitoring economic than political, social, cultural, and technological trends. This showed that people were more sensitive to economic trends because the trends greatly influenced their lives more than other trends (Table 4.12).

b.   Specific individuals in institutional units were assigned the responsibility of preparing studies of the environment for articulation and analysis (Table 4.9).

c.   When the colleges' environment was scanned, it made it easier for the planners of the four colleges to formulate more valid and reliable goals for institutional planning and operations (Table 4.9).

d.   Each college used different sources for generating information on environmental analysis (Table 4.10).

e.   With the exception of College A, which had initiated a few institutionally designed procedures for the articulation of strategic concerns, the other colleges used long-range rather than strategic planning systems.

f.   A large number of college planners in all colleges, except College A, as it was observed, did not know who or which office was responsible for research matters of their institutions.

g.   Institutional research offices were not independent units. The offices were incorporated into the administrative responsibilities of either the president's office or the vice president's or registrar's or the director's office.

h.   Particular processes for monitoring environmental trends existed in each college. The main processes for monitoring the trends included assessments conducted by specific faculty members, local government studies, studies of professional consultants, and summaries given through presidential briefings.

i.   Whenever the external environment had been relatively analyzed, it became easier for planners to make more informed institutional decisions (Table 4.6).

3.   **Findings Related to College Goals**

a.   Various divisions and departments had clear goals and objectives

b.   The goals and objectives were integrated in institutional missions and programs.

c.   Planners in all colleges applied and used course priorities.

d.   Faculty were not limited by the number of courses and objectives they taught.

e.   Colleges A, C, and D had developed according to their stated goals and objectives. College B had not because 63.6% of its planners (respondents) believed so.

f.   The community college faculties were tenured; administrators were not.

g. Planners in each college had an unwritten criterion for appointing personnel into administrative positions.

h. The same planners had an unwritten criterion for appointing people into instructional positions.

i. The planners in these colleges had specific budget goals and objectives

j. They all used priorities to allocate funds.

k. The managers of the four colleges made faculty and staff changes on the basis of changes in enrollments, student interest, and program demands.

l. Also, administrators reorganized courses on the basis of changes in enrollments, student interest, and program demands.

m. Planners in all four colleges discontinued academic courses and departments when funding and enrollment opportunities dwindled.

n. Of the eight conditions that were rank ordered for their influence on the institutional master-plans during the 1960's, "interdisciplinary nature of many courses" was rank ordered first (Table 4.38).

o. When ten academic and strategic goals of community colleges were also rank-ordered in three sets for their priorities, the three goals that were ranked highest were related to teaching, economic, and academic standards (Table 4.39).

4. Findings Related to Decision Making

a. In all the four colleges, a majority of planners indicated that they were selected for decision making due to their expertise rather than statesmanship or position.

b. Based on the perceptions of the planners, the best planning model was consensual rationality (consensus-rational).

c. Planners in College A and C were more democratic in decision-making approaches than planners in Colleges B and D. Several explanations have been conclusively advanced to explain this phenomenon.

d. The locus of consultation in the colleges was wide rather than narrow.

The unique characteristics of College B and D were as follows.

College B

1. Its Board of Trustees spent the least amount of time (10 hours a year) in planning

2. Only cabinet members (top policy makers), excluding deans, for most of the time, made all decisions regarding institutional management.

3. Had no criteria for measuring and maintaining course quality

4. College goals and objectives had not changed in 10-15 years.

5. Decisions were made by top administrators only.

College D

1. Top administrators made decisions
2. Used rational model
3. Decision-making style had not changed in three years

Chapter 5

Summary, Conclusions, Implications, and Recommendations

Chapter 5 is a summary of the purposes, review of the literature, research design, and findings of the study. Conclusions which resulted from data analysis were displayed and followed by implications for planning, and further research. Also, recommendations were identified and prescribed.

Summary

Purpose of the Study

With the current demand for managerial efficiency and effectiveness, the need to establish the degree to which effective college planning, or the absence of it, made it necessary to investigate the merits and demerits of institutional and managerial efficiency and effectiveness. In a sense, this research was experimentally an implementation evaluation of institutional policy called policy analysis. The major purposes of the empirical study are fourfold:

1. To determine whether or not institutional goals and objectives were clearly implemented in accordance with institutional missions,
2. To determine if programs were developed to achieve institutional goals and objectives,
3. To ascertain the role of institutional research in the planning process and
4. To determine whether goals, objectives, and research were articulated in the context of a formal planning model.

Review of the Literature

The review of the literature, as related to four major categories, (A, B, C, and D) was in keeping with the purposes of the study. The reviewed areas and their findings were summarized as:

1. History, philosophy, governance, and planning structures of community colleges
2. Planning and strategic planning
3. Organizational structure
4. Rational and consensual decision making

Design of the Study

For the purpose of conducting the study, it was imperative for the researcher to develop a survey instrument which was used to measure perceptions of rational, strategic and structural planning and decision making in the four community colleges categorized as A, B, C, and D.

A sample of 42 college planners (administrators) was selected from the population of 60. Its composition was made of three presidents, eight vice-presidents, fifteen deans, and sixteen directors. These planners were selected on the basis of informed opinion (expert sampling) and the measuring instrument was administered through the processes of personal and group interviews and tape recording of respondents. The instrument was pre-tested in one college (A). Since the comments, observations, and recommendations of those tested were consistent with the study's design, and because its structure and format had evolved from studying several similar instruments, the interviewer decided, on face value, largely, and with the advice of two institutional research consultants, to use it for data collection.

Summary of the Findings of the Study

The findings of this research were a product of data analysis and interpretation. Their analytic and interpretable uniqueness was consistent with the purposes of the study.

The findings addressed planning and management concerns in the areas of institutional demographics, formal planning, strategic planning, decision making, and the degree of success or failure of goal implementation. One of the most interesting findings was that urban institutions use different planning models from those used by rural institutions.

Conclusion

With regard to the findings of this study, and in reference to the named population, the following conclusions were empirically arrived at and offered.

On the basis of the first research question, it was clear that the rational model was perceived as a good planning tool by planners of College D only. College D was the largest of the four institutions and its planners (those who were interviewed) were academically and experientially highly qualified persons. Both their experience, qualifications, and the complexity of their metropolitan political, socioeconomic, and technological environment would have influenced institutional planners to select rationality for institutional planning. It was not distinctly clear whether the planners use of the rational model made them authoritarian. Although arguments for the existence of authoritarianism could be advanced, more scientific evidence on the subject could be provided through ethnographic and sociological methodology.

In relation to the second question, planners of Colleges A, B, and C used the consensus or democratic approach in decision making. Other planning models were less important in this regard. Therefore, it can be clearly asserted that planners who successfully used any one of the other commonly known planning models (anarchy, compromise, bureaucratic, consensus, political, and rational) were less likely to have used the rational planning model in their colleges.

With regard to the research question which was intended to articulate measured perceptions of other models, it was found that planners who used the rational and the consensus model did not decisively use other planning models.

Each college had achievable and written goals and objectives incorporated into institutional planning structures. Though the comprehensiveness of goal utilization and other planning perceptions affirmed that planning was not very simplistic in these colleges, the qualitative generality of their objectives necessitates the establishment of a machinery that could quantify, specify, and make them measurable. That the degree of goal realization, and with the exception of College B, was generally quite good, testified the tempo of seriousness with which the goals were implemented and operationalized.

Interpretation

Within the college environments, college planners, at intervals rather than continuously, attempted to design, conduct, synthesize and apply institutional research for the purpose of improving academic management. Institutional research was applied for the purpose of utilizing the accuracy and validity of institutional data, and for orchestrating the usefulness of a centralized, controlled, and monitored reporting system.

Although traditionally oriented managerial planners underutilize, due to lack of funds and research methodology, the role and the office of the institutional researcher, his/her responsibility is to educate the president and his/her cabinet on institutional strategic concerns without whose understanding, institutional operations would stall, became disarrayed or crisis prone and unmanageable.

As a whole, based on the evidence at hand, the four community colleges were tuned to using long-range plans rather than strategic ones. The essence of strategic planning is visionary, scientific, and philosophical involvement which leads to dynamic change. Conversely, the essence of long-range planning is the modified duplication of the past planning traditions and institutionalized perpetual craving for cosmetic improvements aimed at maintaining the status quo. Strategic planning is dialectical intellectual culture and synergistic management while long-range planning is static cultivation of complacence and comfortable routine.

Implications for Research and Administrative Practice

If all institutions are to succeed in their academic management, they have to design and utilize suitable (good) management models. A good model is an effective model because it shows what is important for the institution, its constituents, clientele, etc., and the existing relations between organizational means and ends, i.e., inputs and outputs.

Models may be quantitative or qualitative. Some may be static or dynamic, efficient or in effective, and explicit or implicit. Regardless of the mode of a model, it involves subjective judgments and institutional values. A model, is designed to assist management officials (planners) and policymakers to make more informed decisions about the allocation of resources and the translation of the mission of the organization into tangible outputs.

With reference to the purposes of the study, therefore, the following five implications are instructive:

1. Colleges, and especially College B, need to develop internal communicative working relationships. This network of contacts should involve and enable people to be involved in activities that are participatory of all administrators, faculty, staff, and student groups in the governance structures of the college. Such activities need to be designed both quantitatively and qualitatively in order to have maximum effect.
2. The communication network of activities needs to be designed and structured to include program evaluation, evaluation of administrative functions, staff evaluation, and the evaluation of general and specified accreditation and the functions of institutional research.
3. Activities designed to ensure the effective functioning of the Board of Trustees and major college policies need to be evaluated too.
4. A participatory decision-making model needs to be designed and implemented to involve all groups which benefit the colleges and from which the colleges benefit.

5. Other local, national, and international institutions and organizations which have not become strategically sensitive in their operations need to make relevant and appropriate strategic adjustments in order to enhance institutional adaptability to change.

Implications for Research

The purpose of designing a model is not only for improving the strategic concerns of academic management (decision makers), but, it is also to increase one's understanding of some phenomena in order to advance scientific knowledge, to aid teaching, learning, management, or even to satisfy intellectual creativity and curiosity.

In relation to the research problem, ethnographically and quantitatively oriented scholars need to pursue this study further and discover valid conclusions on the effects of the concept of the "administrative iron curtain" which was empirically observed as one of the decision making strategies top management uses.

The concept of the administrative iron-curtain evolved with the interviewer's interpretive integration of the review of the literature and data analysis. The interviewer conceptualized three reasons why senior academic managers behave that way. First, senior academic managers influence or determine the agenda, policy, and goals of the institution. Determination of agenda, policy, and goals, etc. may take place at the level of the president, or inner cabinet, or vice president's council. When this kind of planning has been done, it becomes the strategic policy (decisions) which is collegially further shared in the administrative cabinet or in the administrative council. The four or five or more administrative power groups or governance structures in which decisions are shared do not allow those making them to clearly identify the decision-making model (style) of the senior administrator. This argument is based on the observations made in College A. The reason for using this politically oriented administrative model was to control power by manipulating the strongest institutional coalitions to legitimize authority.

In the case of College B, the senior administrator was an autocrat, yet the same person was still perceived by planners as one who articulated consensus. Autocracy was viewed to serve these functions:

1. To eliminate or exclude strong opposition from central (strategic) decision-making arena.
2. To consolidate support from those perceived to be loyal, trusted, and able but conservative elements of the institution.
3. To narrow the scope of participation in central decisions and make their implementability possible.

Finally, through the administrative iron-curtain phenomenon, senior planners can brilliantly distance themselves from unpopular decisions. The rational model which stifles creativity is rigid, and equally exclusive, but also legimizable. It is legitimizable because the privileged few who use it can justify their actions in the name of accountability and institutional responsibility. Comparatively speaking, the essence of autocracy is insecurity and doubt, while the essence of rationality is authoritarianism. The former relies on manipulative and political tactics; the latter depends on intellectual power of reasoning and scientific rationality and creativity.

Secondly, researchers need to find out what the positive and negative aspects of the administrative iron curtain are and provide an explanation for its causes and what could be done to alleviate its side effects if any.

Recommendations

From the analysis of data, it was learned that the best planning model in these settings was consensual rationality. The best model is a good and participatory model.

A good model has the following criteria:

1. A model should be simple
2. A model should be complete on important issues
3. A model should be easy to control
4. A model should be stable
5. A model should be adaptive
6. A model should be easy to communicate
7. A model should be technologically rationalizable

In respect to the entire study, consensual rationality can explicitly be used to develop a plan or make a decision. It can also be used to produce a better result than intuition and judgment. Intuition and judgment are implicit models. Their implicitness, though mostly useful in legal and other circles, makes them less objective in scientific scholarship and organizational operations.

Consensual rationality is simple because its users can be taught or guided how to use it. It is complete because it is democratic and rational. It is controllable by the users (planners or model) who will decide on which aspect of its consensual rationality they will use to articulate circumstantial issues, concerns, problems, and needs. It is stable because of its capability to be used rationally and with flexibility. It is adaptive because of its immense potentialities in strategic theory and practice. It is easy to communicate if its users understand when, why, how, and where to use it. In the technological age, it is rationalizable because we use the internet and a variety of computer languages. Because of its flexibility, its use enables institutions, organizations, and agencies to become more open, functionally efficient, and objectively effective.

1. Five guidelines are recommended for utilizers of models. First, decision makers who use models should be involved in their development. Data used

for model construction must be representative and reliable. Each model should have an executive godfather. All models should be comfortable to their users. Analytical models and their results should be communicated with care.

2. Since model construction is a strategic and intellectual process, decision makers should know their models so they can practically control and change them to suit rising demands, needs, and situations. Model builders should share their assumptions in order to increase communicative competence and constructive creativity. Their creativity can be used to challenge the validity of computer models and increase their ability to deal with the model. To be effective, model building should be an open and participatory process of organizational development and evolution.

3. Based on the interpretation of data analysis and literature review, there are seven major advantages of using consensual rationality for planning and decision making.

    i.   Organizational goals and values are known and responsibility for activating them is equally shared.

   ii.   Solutions to problems are not only viewed from a means to ends continuum, but the search for solutions is determined by participatory and iterative practices.

  iii.   Decisions are made by maximizing deliberative alternatives, yet maintaining the shared power, authority, and solidarity of the group.

  iv.   Choices are made by selecting best alternatives which satisfy most of all participants.

   v.   The results of implemented choices are based on intended consequences characterized by transitional change; detailed choices may be delegated or enacted by each person concerned.

  vi.   Feedback is given on the basis of information related to understanding casual relations and the nature of the problem which can be analytically and openly examined before conclusions are informally shared.

 vii.   To use the model successfully requires unity of commitment to organizational purposes, application of appropriate technology, unanimity on major functions and assumptions, time and opportunity for discussion, and mutual respect.

Substantive Interpretation

This research is based on comparative perceptions of planners in college planning and the study's observational fieldwork results that were computationally analyzed. Since administrators used the mission, goals, and objectives to plan, and because institutional planning was conducted on the basis of relevant, observable, and measurable data, the research was in a sense, a form of institutional policy analysis and evaluation whose major objective was to make useful and analytical observations on the strengths and weaknesses of institutional planning and provide viable recommendations for reforming the four institutional planning systems. Institutional policy analysis focused on the utilization of variables and changeable aspects of institutional governance. The boards, presidents, vice presidents, deans, faculty, students, and others (directors, comptrollers, etc.) are some of the governance and power-group structures in the community colleges.

In this study, the researcher used procedural values to investigate the processes and structures of internal institutional governance. The criteria which was used in this investigation included such terms as participation, administrative efficiency, expertise, rationality, formality, planning model, effectiveness, mission, goals, roles (positions or ranks) etc. Such terms formed a logical substantive structure and criteria which was applied to study the problem(s) of institutional and research design as viewed from a strategic viewpoint.

Substantively, the criteria of data collection and analysis were used to assess the functions of planners (college administrators), norms or parameters and values of institutions (e.g., standards, planning models, goals, objectives, and missions) and institutional procedures which included planning techniques such as MBO, MBBS, etc. The utilization of institutional (planning) functions and norms were viewed as values which reflected institutional culture whose maintenance was regulated by those who played various planning roles in light of prescribed institutional rules defined as rights and obligations. The planning processes were conducted through established institutional governance structures. The structures used a variety of planning models to make institutional decisions. The consensus and the rational models were more commonly used than the organized anarchy, compromise, conflict resolution, and bureaucratic models. The fact that all these models were used reflected not only the degree of freedom with which planners expressed by using them, but, these expressions were reflections of institutional willingness to accommodate flexible variability in decision-making processes.

Although the consensus and rational models were more dominantly used than other models, the decision-making styles of the four colleges were amenable to eclectic consensual rationality. The institutional governance structures which flexibly utilized a variety of decision-making models were viewed as a form of educational architecture.

The institutional existence and utilization of a variety, rather than a uniformity of governance structure(s) and planning model(s) did not only show the presence of class struggle (conflict of interests) latent in hierarchical institutional settings, but that conflict of interest was reminiscent of situations which arose from institutional desire for career and professional paths, technological advancement, social class, the ideology of individual self-determination (autonomy), and the status of the community colleges themselves. Because the conflict of interests were, inevitably, indirectly or directly, impacted on by strategic forces, what happened daily in these institutions, was impacted on by strategic forces. Also, what happened daily in these institutions, and perhaps in many other higher education institutions, mirrored the wider dynamics of the cultural, social, and economic fabric from which these institutions have evolved.

In relation to students, and their station in life, and even as (Clark 1976 and Brint and Karabel 1989) had also observed in theory and practice, a democratic society tries to limit and block culturally instilled goals and the approaches needed to "deflect the resentment and modify the disappointment of those whom opportunity is denied" (Clark 1976, 151) to subject them to bad jobs. Looked at from this perspective, the major function of the community college then was to cool the aspirations of students and temper their frustrations through gradual accumulation of evidence based on tests, course grades, teacher recommendations, and the advice of counselors. Cumulative evidence from these sources convinced students to make decisions which influenced them to get two-year vocational /technical and terminal degrees instead of making decisions on transfer to four-year institutions. This implies that society limits and blocks culturally instilled goals of the majority of students whose social mobility may have been considered ipso facto, undesirable.

Each of the four institutions was viewed as a formal and rationally organized subsystem in the social structure. The subsystem's structure involved an element of clearly defined patterns of activity in which a series of actions were functionally related to the purposes of each institution. There were a series of integrated offices(positions), characterized by a hierarchy of statuses which had obligations and privileges. The obligations and privileges (rights) were defined by limited and specific rules. Each position was awarded on the basis of proven competence and responsibility. Each planner in each office had authority which was a form of power used for planning, controlling, directing, and programming. The authority was derived from acknowledged status. In other words, authoritative power, used for strategic management, did not rest in the person, it rested with the office. Planning actions occurred within the framework of pre-existing institutional rules.

Planning actions were related to the purposes (mission, goals, and objectives) of each institution. The purposes (parameters) were defined, implemented, and subjected to periodic evaluations. The offices were arranged in a hierarchical order and circumscribed by regulations, and procedures.

The structure of each institution largely rested on the bureaucratic organizational theory rather than on the human relations and matrix theories. Within that kind of pyramidal order, management (planning) activities were instituted scientifically. Responsibility for designing and formulating institutional goals and objectives, determining the scope of each worker's/employee's job description, place of work, and job specification, evaluating performance, distributing rewards and penalties, and hiring and dismissing rested with the chief planning officers of each institution within the central administration.

On the basis of each governance structure in the four colleges, the control system was a set of processes and techniques designed to increase the probability that people would behave in ways that led to the achievement of institutional goals. The intent of the control system was not to control people's behavior per se, but to influence them to act and make decisions which influenced the effective application of institutional goals. The factors which influenced the effective application of institutional goals were size and structure of each college, technology, environment, and dominant coalitions. With respect to colleges, and in reference to Table 4.35, college planners indicated that their dominant decision-making model was consensus for A, B, and C. Ironically, these observations of the colleges were not consistent with the testimony of the chief planning officials of Colleges A and B. The chief planning official in College A very brilliantly used the political model to orchestrate the decision-making mechanisms in his institution whose decision-making structure was based on four power groups (the inner cabinet, the president's cabinet, vice president's council, and the administrative council). College A's senior planning officer, influenced the structural design of these power groups and used the political model to influence the strongest coalitions to support his policies (institutional policies) and make, implement, and evaluate decisions and performance.

The reasons which appeared to account for his success in using the political model (conflict resolution) were largely based on his thorough understanding of the American political process, the lot of community college education, and the gamut of the strategic environment. In addition, this chief planning officer's ability to remain open rather that closed, enabled the power groups or resultant coalitions to perceive institutional reality, as interpreted by the chief planning official, to be open, free, democratic, and therefore, beneficial and acceptable to them.

The inner cabinet was made of the president and some loyal and trusted members of the cabinet. The vice president's council was made up of the vice presidents only: the cabinet was made of the president, vice presidents, three deans, and four directors; and the administrative council which was composed of 35 people, was comprised of the cabinet and divisional chairpersons. It was evidently clear that most decisions made at the higher levels of administrative authority were not certain to those in lower echelons of the administrative structure. What this implied was that planners at College A's lower ranks were not seriously involved in participatory decision-making forums of the college's power groups.

Unlike College A, College B's senior planning official used the autocratic decision-making model. The structure of internal-governance power groups in College B was composed of the inner cabinet (made up of the president, three women, and one man who was invited occasionally) and finally, the annual off-campus retreat in which all planners and faculty informally met for the articulation of long-range goals and policy decisions of the college.

The senior planning official in College B succeeded in making Decisions for the college by utilizing several coalitions of interests reminiscent of the internal institutional governance structures (power groups). Ironically, although 41.2 percent of the respondents (largest percentage) indicated that the planning model for College B was consensus, the chief planning officer believed that it was autocratic (tape No. 5; 3-16-87). Autocracy is a "government in which one person possesses unlimited power" (*Webster's New Collegiate Dictionary* 1979, 75). This autocratic decision-making model, as it was perceived, may have been used to eliminate faculty and deans from the decision-making processes of the college. If the issue of elimination was true, then College B's management strategy was less participatory, less healthy for institutional operations, and unhealthy for strategic planning purposes.

For both Colleges A and B, and as it was implied earlier, large percentages of responses from planners showed that the consensus planning model was dominantly used. However, evidence based on close scrutiny of the chief institutional planners in the two colleges argue to the contrary. College A's chief planner used the political model (conflict resolution) while his College B's contemporary was an autocrat. Paradoxically, other senior and middle level planners were not able to determine the nature of models they used in their governance structures. The chief planning officials of institution A and B were so acute in political acumen that they designed governance structures that worked for their own interests and concerns to the detriment of the majority of fellow planning officials. They also were able to do so because their authoritative power sanctioned the loyalty and support of their followers who, hopefully, may have found it difficult to question the malaise of administrative inefficiency. The ability of senior administrators to design decision-making mechanisms that mean one thing, yet are perceived to be different by different people, is a form of "administrative iron curtain." While the essence of the political model is to keep the senior planning official in power indefinitely, the essence of autocracy is insecurity. The power base of the former is in the ability to brilliantly control planning participants through the processes of dominant coalitions (within the governance structures) while that of the latter is in the ability to systematically eliminate the influence, regardless of its creativity and foresight, of the person(s) and coalitions viewed as detrimental to the dominance of the regime. The major goal of the college of the former chief planner was to teach student's, that of the latter was to serve the community. How each college applied the goals in question shows where they put their emphasis in terms of accountability.

Lall and Lall (1979) have argued that autocratic leadership is poor human relations. The leader uses rewards to motivate subordinates. Members of the organization do not have the opportunity to participate and exchange ideas. Expertise and all potential are subdued. Workers are manipulated to accomplish the goals of the leader.

The two authors continue to say that autocracy is a defense mechanism which arises with feelings of insecurity, inferiority, incompetence, uncertainty, and indecision. The authors summarized Kimball Wiles and John Lovell and said that a group led by an autocratic leader is characterized by

Intense competition, lack of acceptance of all members, buck passing, avoidance of responsibility, unwillingness to cooperate, aggression among members and toward persons outside the group, irritability, and a decrease in work when the supervisor is absent. A group with a benevolent autocrat

*for an official leader loses initiative, shows regression, to childlike depend-
ence, becomes increasingly submissive, does not continue individual development, cannot accept added responsibility easily* (96).

In reference to autocratic leadership in community college governance
structures, Zoglin (1976, vii) asserts that the leader's insecurity and arrogance is
viewed with "suspicion, disdain, and tolerance by collegiate and university
power groups."

Contrary to autocratic behavior, the behaviors nurtured by the consensual
and democratic leader develop power within the group for participation in planning, goal setting, and group opinion or decision making. Because the power
base of the democratic and consensual leader, as viewed in Colleges A and C, is
broader than that of the insecure autocrat in College B, consensual and democratic leadership enhances worker morale, motivation, productivity, and goal
achievement (Lall and Lall 1979, 96).

With the progressive development of community colleges from the periods
of evolution to those of expansion, community college leaders who were initially parochial, developed and advanced in management too. During the period
of their crystallized consolidation (comprehensiveness), a new generation of
their managers (planners) emerged. These were entitled "minority services,
community services, public relations, business and industry services, and
women's resources" (Editor, *New Directions for Community Colleges* 1983, 2).
Through the planning processes of their institutions, these minority managers
(planners) have managed to considerably assert their leadership on the institutions and their respective communities. Although the impact of their leadership
has largely been perceived to be educational, its influence on the strategic forces
has had far reaching political, economic, social, technological, and cultural implications. By so doing, community colleges play a constructive role of mobilizing forces with the disadvantaged classes of society, which collectively develop
strength and power for articulating their needs at the higher echelons of more
powerful societal structures. When their needs are effectively orchestrated, the
governance structure of the more powerful and higher levels of authority liberal-
ize the mechanisms for the reverse flow of information and resources which the
colleges and communities utilize for empowerment, adaptability and change.

Rationality and Change

Rationality, is a philosophy of life which cannot be limited to mere argumentative reasoning, but by extension, can be viewed as a value-laden process
of intellectual autonomy, and existentialist philosophy that is governed by moral
conceptions of a cosmopolitan, technological, industrial, bureaucratic, and democratic order. Characteristic of western culture, and other cultures, whether
rationality is formal or substantive, value-oriented or purposive, rational action
is ethically based on principles of conviction and responsibility. In other words,
to act or plan rationally does not necessarily underrate relationally and philoso-

phically oriented economic, political, ethical, erotic, or aesthetic ideals, all of which emanate from ideas about human nature. These ideas are empirical and normative extensions of rationality.

The use of rationality (reason) per se should not be restricted to its anthropological sense. Rationality's utility should be extended to include its moral, logical, and scientific perspectives. When rationality is carried on in such philosophically and scientifically interpretive and practical ways, it becomes a form of education which can be used to preserve the real humanity, independence, dignity and integrity of life.

Within the community college setting of the four colleges, responses, observations, and interpretations of rational planning approaches were reminiscent of the decision-making activities of the wider rational and democratic social fabric in the West and other societies. In other words, rationality is not a monopoly of the planning leadership in the four institutions alone, it is a cultural, scientific and philosophical rationale deeply embedded in people's lives, thoughts, values, and norms.

Rationality is reflective critical thinking. Consistent reflective and critical thought does not only empower the rational thinker, but such thinking and reflective power liberates the thinker. If the thinker expresses himself/herself critically and powerfully, critical thinking or rationality may be interpreted as a form of revolutionary thought. Rational, critical, and revolutionary thought is a form of elite cultural imperialism. Since community colleges are not elitist institutions, their leaders (planners) could not largely afford to encourage the utilization of critical and reflective rational thought commonly used in universities with which, Chaffee, the chief proponent of rationality, was familiar. The less emphasis placed on the use of rationality in community colleges is, therefore, justifiable and self-explanatory.

Although 37.5 percent of the planners in College D formed the largest group which (see Table 4.35) used the rational model, 78.75 percent of the planners in the same college indicated that they used other models bureaucratic = 18.75 percent; compromise = 13.5 percent; consensus = 25 percent; and conflict resolution (debate) = 12.5 percent). What this meant was that the majority of planners in College D used different models other than the rational model alone. Then, since the rational model was not, in totality, the most popular, it was unlikely to be the most suitable planning model in College D. Therefore, it is evidently clear that five, rather than one planning model(s) were perceived to be individually and collectively used to make management decisions in College D.

Again, in the context of Table 4.35, the majority of planners in Colleges A, B, and C indicated that they planned consensually. Percentage-wise, College A had 10 percent for rational, 45 percent for consensus, 10 percent for conflict resolution, and 5 percent for the bureaucratic model. Consensus was dominantly used in College A. But it was not the only decision-making model used by the planners in College A. Other models, though less frequently used, were also used anyway. Together, their total percentage was 55 percent. Individually they were less dominant. Collectively, the models were eclectically useful in their contributions to decision making in the college. The same argument could be applicable to Colleges B and C in which consensus was thought or perceived to be the dominant decision–making model.

Consensus was collective opinion of the planners in Colleges A, B, and C. The planners in each college formed a planning system. Each member within the planning system (group) participated in the discussions related to suggestions, arguments, issues, values, policies, procedures, and resources of planning the community colleges. The discussions were ratified by a vote, or a collective yes, or general common feeling of accord. The purpose of such collective agreement was to effect given purposes, goals, or objectives. In this case, consensus was not only collective affirmation of responsibility, but it was also purposive in nature. Collective and purposive affirmation of responsibility in decision making was participatory management and collective wisdom. Such collective and consensual wisdom was not the monopoly of the four community colleges alone, but consensus is inherently superior, and democratic human behavior which makes it possible for human beings to solve crucial administrative and management problems in organizational and institutional settings. In other words, within the context of the four colleges, the utilization of consensus was a miniature reflection of its wider use in the political and socioeconomic fabric at large.

Both the rational and consensus models were perceived to be the best decision-making models in the four community colleges. Even though the two models are not the only ones used in a diverse, pluralistic, and class-conscious capitalistic environment. Of the six models, consensus was perceived to be predominantly best in College A, B, and C and second best in College D; while the rational model was the best in College D only and the second best in Colleges C and B.

Goals and Objectives

Goals of the Colleges A, B, and D were relatively comprehensive, well structured, and integrated into the planning system of each institution and its policy (mission statement). The goals and objectives articulated matters related to fiscal and physical management, human resources, image of the institutions, student, curricula and instructional development, community and marketing issues, and long-range rather than strategic planning. In spite of their general similarities in composition, the goals of these three colleges differ radically in organization, content, and morphology.

The goals of College C were uniquely different from those of Colleges A, B, and D. First, the mission statement was composed of one sentence, printed on one and one-half lines, and contained only 17 words. Unlike the mission statements of Colleges A, B, and D. College C's mission statement was too brief to be clear. It did not explain the reason for the existence of the college. The reason for its being and the place of its history were not explained. The mission was vague, unsatisfactory and unwarranted.

The general goals of College C were observed. They articulated curricula, instruction, and community service matters. The college's more specific goals were related to admissions, financial aid, receptionist secretary, director of student services, campus programs and activities/visitations, student records, veterans, registration supervisor of staff, work study, nursing, liberal arts, counseling and academic advisement, testing, business, secretarial and cosmetology, professional development, vocational and technical education C.O.P.E., placement and career library.

These goals for College C were formulated by deans and directors of the college and formed part and parcel of the three management reports and plans or data-corpus which were used to give direction for institutional operations. Because they looked like general objectives, rather than goals, per se, they needed to be reconstructed and made more general, strategic, and diverse, rather than tactical and operational per se. The college was the only one which did not have objectives in the major planning documents of the institution's structure of its mission and goals, and/or management plans and reports. The objectives of Colleges A, B, an D were general and qualitative rather than specifically quantitative and measurable.

In Colleges A and B, total goals were realized well. The degree with which they were realized in C and D was very well (Table 4.39). The terms well and very well represent Likert Scale at the median score as shown in the instrument. Goals were realized either well or very well because of three reasons. In the socialization process, individual planners were made more knowledgeable and accepting of the institutional goals and values through formal and informal socialization processes during campus business meeting times or during retreats respectively. The purposive result of such familiarization of goals to planners was to shift each individual's personal goals toward those of the organization.

Secondly, the process of accommodation of common goals was used. The accommodation process occurred when management adjusted organizational goals to be consistent with individual (personal) goals. This approach enabled planners to match or integrate personal and institutional goals.

Third, in each institutional system, individual planners and their respective institutions, compromised on goals so that the more important goals of both parties could be attained. To make the goal integration process more achievable, institutions needed to incorporate the concepts of institutional compliance and control into their management systems.

Since goals were, and are, generally arranged in the context of a means-ends basis, they required decisions about the means (resources) with which they would be attained. An attempt was made to provide the means which were also subgoals of each management system. Through this process, the structure of goals was tabulated. As with institutional climate, decision-making style, and decision-making process and structures, the goal structure could vary from one hierarchical level to another in each institution; hence, the basis for compliance. Of the ten goals that were ranked for their importance in the four community colleges, three (teaching, maintaining academic standards, and economic) were ranked first in each of the three subsets into which they were categorized in all the four colleges.

In chapter 4, the and analysis of data was described with the use of tables and interpretive commentary both of which were useful for drawing conclusions. The major reason for data analysis was in accordance with the purpose of the study. Implicit in the purpose was an attempt to articulate the need for planning in the community colleges. The need for planning in colleges had arisen with the public outcry that the colleges had lost their identity and purposes. Since the identity and purposes are the raison detre of the colleges, and since the colleges' loss of that raison detre will mean that they have no existence, the analysis displayed evidences of planning characteristics whose long-term and apparent strategic manifestations proved the authenticity of the colleges' purposes. However, since each of the four colleges exists in a different environment, the purposes of each college were slightly different from those of other colleges; and similarly, the planning structures and styles of each were also different.

Because the institutions operated during the period of decline rather than one of growth, and since the turbulence (demographic changes, unstable economic growth, intense and variable competition for faculty, students, funds, acquisition of high-tech skills in areas of technology transfer, robotics, computer literacy etc.) of the environment was a menace, the need for planning more realistically (strategically) was essentially imperative.

The planning procedures and processes of each college were formalized and their planning environments were periodically monitored with institutionally designed offices, groups of persons, or committees, which analytically sensitized the threatening reality of the internal and external environments of the institutions. Once the nature of the strategic environment was understood, college planners became more informed to make instrumental decisions. Decisions were made by senior planning officials and delegated to lower officials for implementation and evaluation. The structure of governance and style of leadership of each institution determined who the decision makers would be, what kind of decisions were to be made, and who their implementers and evaluators would be. Overall, the quality of the social and academic atmosphere reflected the manner in which decisions were made and implemented.

Reflections

Comparison Between Business Management and Management of Public Organizations

In the industrialized world, business, labor, industry, and government collaborate in making decisions regarding the invention, use and transfer of technology. In the U.S., business and industry, which are successful models of industrial capitalism in the West, have become classic examples for emulation by other institutions including government and education. In this scenario, community colleges and higher education in general have dramatically been forced by strategic and global forces to translate and reform their missions in order to be molded by the whims of businessmen and industrialists who influence institutional decision-makers regarding which technological commodity they can buy and use for training people to master the skills which the commodity is marketable for.

This relationship between government, business, and industry on the one hand, and education on the other, has influenced the four institutions to productively plan, while keeping the needs of each other in mind. This type of planning is a form of institutional psychological reciprocity. Since business, industrial, and educational institutions are economically viewed as large-scale and interconnected/interrelated organizations, "certain operational similarities are transferable. These include defining purposes and objectives, organizing a work force, selecting managers, motivating the work force, and contributing and measuring work results" (Millett 1975, 221). The three institutional sectors are also dramatically opposed to each other in their character, quality, and quantity of the goals and objectives, the structure and roles of personnel, and the nature of motivation which not only impels the workers to produce and the students to learn, but it also shows how that motivation contributes to quantitatively and qualitatively measurable results in the economic-business versus the educational and learning environments.

The degree of similarities and differences between business/industrial versus public planners (managers) have their basic points of cleavages in the missions goals/objectives of production. In spite of these points of divergence, these different sectorial institutions are partners and stakeholders in education, public management, and economics. This relationship forces colleges and universities to design their curricula, facilities, and instructional methodologies and objectives for the purpose of accommodating the needs of business and industry. Hence education has become, and will continue to be a service and consumer industry which is heavily dependent on the genius of industrial capitalism. Such a heavily dependent institution can hardly find it reasonably convenient to be ethically and rationally accountable. Institutional accountability is jeopardized in areas of autonomy (relative institutional independence from unnecessary external influences), goals and objectives of learning, and collective bargaining (in which the academic community – faculty, behaves like organized labor in industrial and business settings).

Only well informed and highly cultivated academic managers will be able to identify the needs of learners versus those of business and industry, integrate and classify them, and plan more intelligently for their institutions. The institutions need to emphasize the paramountcy and essence of human and intellectual values over material culture. By doing so, they will encourage their students to integrate what is valuable and what is valueless in their academic, vocational, philosophical, professional, and life pursuits. Hence, institutions will be practically involved in teaching students how to learn and plan better for their future.

Consensually and rationally planned and managed institutions are organizations which change themselves and their environments. Institutions which change themselves and contribute to the change in their environment are dynamic because they contribute to institutional and societal growth and development. The fact that innovative solutions can be accepted for change, and since that change cannot be effected without a general consensus implies that consensual rationality is both individualized and collectivized.

If the political, bureaucratic, compromise, and anarchical models can be liberalized by being individually, collectively or consensually rationalized, the rationalization of the models would become the eclectic collectivization of consensual rationality or eclectic consensual rationality. Eclectic consensual rationality may sound or appear to be complex and sophisticated conceptually. In reality, eclectic consensual rationality could turn out to be strategically simple because it would be applied at any time or place for the purpose of meeting specific situations, needs, and circumstances. In this case, the model could not only be simple, but it would also be the ideal form of eclectic strategic and consensual rationality (strategic planning) whose empirical perceptions were disproportionately indicated in Table 4.35.

There are three advantages of using a model in an organization. First, a model is a verified and validated reference system. Second, a model achieves credibility when sufficient support emerges with respect to each area of evaluation. Third, a decision-making model can help to organize thinking and display it for systematic scrutiny or review. Any constructed and good model should be used in such a way that it can minimize the possibility of undesirable side effects. If the model has an executive godfather, it is adaptable, simple, stable, communicable and controllable. The model is particularly in public administrative arena, a suitable tool for policy analysis and implementation evaluation.

Policy Analysis and Implementation Evaluation

The motif of this study is policy analysis and implementation evaluation in public organizations. Public organizations can evaluatively and logically rationalize public administration.

Public administration is an activist and constructivist aspect of government that intervenes in society. Consequently, it is important to analyze and evaluate the implementation of public administration policies and programs in educational settings which mirror the public image. Policy analysis considers the extent to which a policy achieves its objectives and how the process through which the policy is implemented contributes to the achievement of objectives. In this research, implementation evaluation focused on whether appropriate educational values were maximized through strategic implementation. Under the Reagan and Bush II, the policies of tax cuts and "trickle down" economics were employed. Although Clinton emulated "Reaganomics", he influenced global measures to be employed to make the economy benefit the middle and working class families as opposed to the upper classes only.

In the public sector, perspectives vary on the desirability of administrative programs and activities. For instance, in the 1960s, President Johnson's Great Society programs sought to change fundamentally several aspects of social, political, and economic life. In the 1970s, the political mood shifted toward a more limited role for government and public administration in the society. Policy analysis gained impetus from the development of new research techniques, new budgetary approaches, such as PPBS and ZBB, congressional requirements, and from "sunshine" and "sunset" legislation.

There are three major types of policy analysis strategies in the public sector. First policy outputs are statements of governmental intent, delineations of powers and methods, and allocations of resources. They can involve tangible or symbolic activity. Policy impacts are the effect of policy implementation upon target groups, or social, educational, economic, or other phenomena. Second, impact analysis seeks to determine how the implementation of a policy affects a target. It is difficult to perform, due to limited opportunities for experimentation and the difficulty of ascertaining causality in complex social, educational, technological, and economic policy areas. Third, process analysis concerns the extent to which a policy is being implemented according to established guidelines. The process analysis recognizes that implementation or non-implementation may change the policy.

The traditional managerial perspective on evaluation emphasizes effectiveness about which this research was largely biased with. It favors predictability and clarity of objectives. This managerial approach tends to evaluate policy as being "good" when it is cost-effective and when its costs are kept to a minimum rather than maximum. The New Public Management favors "steering" rather than "rowing." In other words, wherever possible, the government should arrange for the provision of public administration. Results, not processes, are emphasized in the NPM approach. The introduction of business ideas into public administration is rooted in the political approach to the public administration. This approach evaluates policy based on its representativeness, opportunities for participation, and responsiveness to political officials or members of the public. The political approach also seeks accountability in policy implementation through sunshine and sunset legislation, general oversight, and legislative "casework." Federal implementation policies, theories, methods, and techniques are delegated to or reserved for the states which directly deal with colleges.

The legal approach to public administration will evaluate policies as "satisfactory" if they comport with constitutional values, precedents, and traditions. The consensus and conflicts among the approaches suggest the following conclusions with regard to policy evaluation: (1) overhead policy is best evaluated from the traditional managerial perspective; (2) sociotherapeutic policy is best evaluated from the political or NPM perspective and; and (3) regulatory policy is best evaluated from the legal perspective. All these perspectives are triadic reflections of how the principle of checks and balances is rationalized to legitimize the role of the three branches of government. The four colleges which this research analysis dealt with concerned the evaluation of overhead policy whose implementation was reminiscent of traditional and practice form of managerialism.

Community Colleges

The emphasis placed on opportunity and equity in terms of the role community colleges play appears to be a rhetorical rather than real and genuine commitment to the consumer's need for academic excellence. This rhetoric has instead put emphasis on the business model that emphasizes efficiency, outcomes and the needs of employers rather than community college students.

Enrollmentwise, and between 1965 and 1997, the number of community college students increased by 4.6 times while that of four-year colleges and universities increased 1.9 times. This is a radical transformation. Sociologically, it might be argued that the community college movement is a system of academic stratification whose remediation pacifies the dispossessed classes of society by cooling off their temper, resentment and frustration.

Federal policies enforced by Work-force Investment Act (WIA) and Temporary Aid to Needy Families (TANF) have reinforced non-degree community college education in two year rather than in degree programs and transfer to 4 year colleges and universities. Also, the market (business) driven philosophy that is becoming increasingly dominant emphasizes efficiency, profit, and strong ties with the business environment. Pell Grants have dwindled and students are subjected to loan systems that exploit them. Emphasis is placed on work rather than on long-term educational experience as a goal for self-sufficiency. "This shift in federal financial aid away from grants toward loans has also had a chilling effect on community college enrollment and completion and has further challenged the ability of Community Colleges to serve the underclass, the dispossessed, and the truly disadvantaged" (Wilson 1987 and Brint 2003).

Theoretically, the triangular relationships of the human capital, social contradiction and structuralism (Brint 2003) are schools of thought that help to explain the current plight of community college movement. Evidence shows that though these institutions are characterized by uniform class, intellectual and dropout conditions, their functionalist and traditional role does not enable them to accept the challenges associated with the alteration of the status quo. Such conditions have contributed to the deterioration of the climates in which their faculty work. In spite of these challenges, these institutions tend to appropriately respond to environmentally determined social needs on the basis of demand-supply curve that contributes to the unclear contradictions of their identity (Gumport 2003). That is why there is uncertainty concerning their raison detre not withstanding the pressures for adaptability.

For instance, the lack of uniform employee training by these colleges contributes to their misunderstanding of and contradictory application of public policy in the areas of transfer preparation, remedial education and general education. Community Colleges offer differential employee training based on the size of institution or industry. Employers in "health care, manufacturing, transportation, communications, utilities, and finance and insurance draw on community colleges much more than do employers in wholesale and retail trade, apparel making, and construction" (Dougherty 2003, 83-84).

The size, character, and composition of community college consumers experience the democratization processes in American higher education. Through these processes, these institutions are answerable to society's demands for accountability, productivity, efficiency and effectiveness. In recent memory, the demands for accountable, productive, efficient, and effective performance have not only assumed a capitalistic mentality and market stance, but this competitive, global, technologically and ideologically market-driven political environment is nonselective, low-cost, open door policy oriented system whose "enrollment has been eroded by the stratification of educational opportunity and declining college affordability" (Dowd, 2003, p. 92). Other obstacles which tend to marginalize their students' potential for success include but are not limited to bureaucratic red-tape, confusing obligations, lack of enlightenment models, limited counselor availability, poor advice from subordinate staff, inability to detect errors, and inefficiency in the dealing with conflicting obligations. For instance, "cross-state comparisons show that competing ideas about welfare recipients help structure and shape political debates, and policy outcomes" in several states (Mazzeo and Eachus 2003, 114). In addition, conclusive observations on the role of the Welfare Reform Act have indicated that there has been an overall reduction of the quality and quantity of educational experience available to welfare recipients. Further still, those who take no credit programs to ameliorate their station in life, like them for their lower cost, more open accessibility, flexibility and responsiveness. However, these non credit programs are not without their own challenges of which "inadequate funding, low status, inadequate support services, and inadequate articulation mechanisms" (Grubb, Badaway and Bell 2003, 218) are paramount.

To improve higher education in general and community colleges in particular, educational engineers should purposefully and intelligently restructure and reconstruct institutional governance and operations in such a way that the major changes of the global environment such as "globalization, immigration, rising socioeconomic inequality, centrality of the knowledge economy, and issues surrounding cultural identity" (Benjamin 2003, 8) will be transformatively articulated. These issues make the new and current education policy agenda. Given this reality, urban educational institutions should restructure their character and missions to address their needs and the needs of their surrounding communities. The context through which the social, economic, technological, demographic, and political forces which shape these needs evolve should be empowered with opportunities for access and outreach (McDowell and Riposa 2003). In these environments, the faculty should strengthen academic values by making the distinction between corporate culture and academic culture both of which have become the inextricable and transformational engines of American higher institutions of learning (Steck 2003). In such an environment, if managerialism dominates academicism, higher learning and faculty governance might be extinguished (Waugh 2003). Further still, if the role of public higher education in promoting equal opportunity declines, "a new generation of student aid programs will shift benefits away from the low-income and toward the middle and upper income students." Also, "increased competition will make admission to public colleges even more difficult" (Mumper 2003, 97). Creating new opportunities for low income students requires people who have the political will and courage to challenge the dominant middle class groups which control the resources for the articulation and provision of equal opportunity.

The loss of equal opportunity in American higher education is not the only major problem the colleges and universities experience. The fraternities and sororities of the Greek letter societies which dwell in student housing in residential colleges also cause difficulties such as "hazing, poor study habits, de facto segregation and alcoholism" (Los Reyes and Rich 2003, 118).

To compound the problems, American higher education is engineered with the use of three contradictory paradigms – [a professional paradigm characteristic of traditional higher education organization, a bureaucratic machine paradigm representative of traditional business organization, and an innovative or "adhocratic" paradigm defended by its proponents as a timely alternative to traditional bureaucratic] theory (Green 2003, 196). These contradictory paradigms are enforced without regard to existing designs. The adhocratic paradigm is advanced by theoretical high-tech theorists. This model causes personnel conflicts, managerial confusion and a variety of external pressures whose consequences are inconsistent with effective academicism. In addition, the fact that the bureaucratic and adhocratic models jointly reinforce parallel goals that juxtapose and reinforce each other may create conditions that strengthen and solidify their marriage to the exclusion and conflicting confusion of the professional paradigm. Such exclusionary problems, loss of equal opportunity, and market-driven educational purposes are the paradox of postmodernism within the community college movement and higher education in general.

Bibliography

Abell, F. Derek. 1984. Strategic windows. *Strategic Marketing: Planning, Implementation, and Control*. Boston: Kent Publishing Company: 395

Adachi, K. 1989. Problems and prospects of management development of female employees in Japan. *The Journal of Management Development* 8, 4: 32- 40.

Adams, R.J., R.B. Peterson, and H.F. Schwind. 1988. Personal value systems of the Japanese trainees and managers in a changing competitive system. *Asia Pacific Journal of Management* 5, 3: 169-179.

Agar, Michael H. 1980. *The Professional Stranger: An Informal Introduction to Ethnography*. Orlando, FL: Academic Press Inc.

Akira, E. 1987. Lost: Illusion about Japanese management. *Japan Quarterly* 34: 419-423.

Alston, J.P. 1989. Wa, guanxi, and inhwa: Managerial principles in Japan, China, and Korea. *Business Horizons* 32: 26-31.

Ambrose, S.E. 1985. *Encyclopedia of the American Presidency*. New York: Simon and Schuster.

Amsden, A.H. 1993. Asia's Industrial Revolution. *Dissent Summer*: 324-332.

Anderson, P. 1983. Decision making by objection and the Cuban missile crisis. *Administrative Science Quarterly* 28: 201-222.

Anderson, W.S. 1981. Meeting the Japanese economic challenge. *Business Horizons* 24, 2: 56-62.

Archibald, Sandra Orr, and Chester McCorkle. 1982. *Management and Leadership in Higher Education*. San Francisco: Jossey-Bass Limited.

Argyris, C., and D. Schon. 1978. *Organization Learning: A Theory of Action Perspective*. Reading, MA: Addison-Wesley.

Ashby, Erick.1960. *African Universities and Western Tradition.* Cambridge: Harvard University Press,

_____. 1964. *African Universities and Western Tradition*. Cambridge: Harvard University Press: 1-13, 96.

Atkinson, Norman. 1974. *Educational Cooperation in the Commonwealth: A Historical Study Series in Education—Occasional Paper No. 1.* Salisbury: 129.

Bamber, G.J., M.A. Shadur, and F. Howell. 1992. The international transferability of Japanese management strategies: An Australian perspective. *Employee Relations* 14, 3: 3-19.

Barnett, M.N. 1997. Bringing in the New World Order. Liberalism, legitimacy, and the United Nations. *World Politics* 49: 526-551.

Barnland, D.C. 1993. Public and private self in communicating with Japan. In *Japanese Business: Culture Perspectives,* edited by Subhash Durlabhji and Norton E. Marks. Albany, NY: State University of New York Press.

Basadur, M. 1992. Managing creativity: A Japanese model. *Academy of Management Executive* 6, 2: 29-42.

Beatty, J.R., J.T. McCune, and R.W. Beatty. 1988. A policy-capturing approach to the study of United States and Japanese managers compensation decisions. *Journal of Management* 14, 3: 465-474.

Becker, H. 1969. Problems of inference and proof in participant observation. In *Issues in Participant Observation,* edited by G. McCall and J. Simmons, 245-257. MA: Addison Wesley.

Beechler, J.R., and S. Taylor. 1993. The transfer of human resource management systems overseas: An exploratory study of Japanese and American *maquiladoras.* In *Japanese Multinationals: Strategies and Management in the Global Kaisha,* edited by Nigel Campbell and Nigel Holden. London: Routledge.

Beechler, J.R., and J.Z. Yang. 1993. The transfer of Japanese-style management overseas contingencies, constraints, and competencies in Japanese-owned firms in the United States. An Unpublished Paper Submitted to the *Journal of International Business Studies.*

Befu, H. 1989. A theory of social exchange as applied to Japan. In *Constructs for Understanding Japan,* edited by Yoshio Sugimoto and Rass E. Mouer. New York: Kegan Paul International.

Bendix, R. 1947. Bureaucracy: The problem and the setting. *American Sociological Review* 12: 493-507.

Benjamin, R. 2003. The environment of American higher education: A constellation of changes. *The Annals of the American Academy of Political and Social Science* 585: 8-30.

Benson, K. 1975. The interorganizational network as a political economy. *Administrative Science Quarterly* 20: 229-249.

Benveniste, G. 1994. *The Twenty-First Century Organization: Analyzing Current Trends-Imagining the Future.* San Francisco: Jossey-Bass.

Bergquist, W. 1993. *The Post-Modern: Mastering the Art of Irreversible Change.* San Francisco: Jossey-Bass.

Betts, R.K. 1997. Should strategic studies survive? *World Politics* 50: 7-33.

Birnbaum, R. 1989. The cybernetic institution: Toward an integration of governance theories. *Higher Education: The International Journal of Higher Education and Educational Planning* 18, 2.

Bittel, R. Lester. 1972. *The Nine Master Keys of Management.* New York: McGraw-Hill Book Company: v and iv.

Blake, R. Robert, and S. Jane Mouton. 1964. *The Managerial Grid III* (1985): ix.

Blau, P.M. 1955. *The Dynamics of Bureaucracy.* Chicago: Chicago University Press.

Boansi, K.O. 1997. *Africa in the Changing International Political Economy.* Paper presented at the New York State Political Science Association Conference, New York, April 1997.

Bogdan, R., and S. Biken. 1982. *Qualitative Research for Education: An Introduction to Theory and Methods.* Boston: Allyn and Bacon, Inc., Chapters 3 and 4.

Borrus, M. 1988. Chips wars: Can the U.S. regain its advantage in microelectronics? *California Management Review* 30, 40: 64-78.

Boyle, Deirone. 1977. *Expanding Media.* Bethesda, MD: Eric Document Reproduction Service, ED 148 370.

Boyle, Patrick G. 1981. *Planning Better Programs.* New York: McGraw-Hill Book Company.

Braunschweig, G.V. 1992. Order into chaos? How scientific knowledge shapes our world view. *Universitas: An Interdisciplinary Journal for the Social Sciences and Humanities* 34.

Brint, S. 2003. Few remaining dreams: Community colleges since 1985. *The Annals of the American Academy of Political and Social Science* 586: 16-37.

Brookfield, S. 1985. Community adult education. A comparative analysis of theory and practice. *Comparative Education Review* 29, 2: 232-239.

Brubacher, John. 1974. *On the Philosophy of Higher Education.*

Burns, T., and G. Stalker. 1994. *The Management of Innovation.* (Rev Ed.) Oxford: Oxford University Press.

Byers, Paul. Still photography in the systematic recording and analysis of behavioral data. *Human Organization* 23, 1: 78-84.

Callon, S. 1995. *Divided Sun: MITI and the Breakdown of Japanese High-Tech Industrial Policy,* 1975-1993. Stanford: Stanford University Press.

Caplovitz, David. 1983. *The Stages of Social Research.* New York: John Wiley & Sons,

Chaffee, Ellen Earle. 1983. *Rational Decision Making in Higher Education.* Boulder: National Center for Higher Education Management Systems.

Chang, H.J. and R. Rowthorn. 1995. *The Role of the State in Economic Change.* Oxford: Clarendon Press.

Chernoff, F. 1996. *After Bipolarity: The Vanishing Threat, Theories of Cooperation, and the Future of the Atlantic Alliance.* Ann Arbor. University of Michigan Press.

Choate, P. 1990. Political advantage: Japan's campaign for America. *Harvard Business Review* 68, 5: 87-103.

Circourel, V. Aaron. February 1982. Interviews, surveys, and the problem of ecological validity. *The American Sociologist* 17: 11-20.

Clark, K. 1979. Administration of higher education in our era of change and conflict. In *Conflict Retrenchment and Appraisal: The Administration of Higher Education,* edited by J. Monroe. Champaign, IL: University of Illinois Press.

Cohen, E. 1980. Systems paralysis. *The American Spectator*, November.

Cohen, M. Arthur, and Brawer, B. Florence, eds. 1986. Controversies and decision making in difficult economic times. *New Directions for Community Colleges* 53: Chapters 1-12.

Cohen, M., and J. Olsen. 1979. Organizational choice under ambiguity. In *Ambiguity and Choice in Organizations, 2ⁿᵈ Ed.,* edited by James March and Johan Olsen. Bergen, Norway: Universitetsforlaget.

Cohen, M, J. March, and J. Olsen. 1979. People, problems, solutions and the ambiguity of relevance. In *Ambiguity and Choice in Organizations, 2ⁿᵈ Ed.,* edited by James March and Johan Olsen. Norway: Universitetsforlaget.

Cole, R.E., and D.R. Deskins. 1988. Racial factors in site location and employment patterns of Japanese auto firms in America. *California Management Review* 31, 1: 9-22.

Collins, Martin. 1980. Interview variability: A review of the problem." *Journal of the Market Research Society* 11: 77-95.

Condon, J., and K. Kurata. 1987. *What's Japanese About Japan*: Tokyo: Shufunotomo Company, Ltd.

Contreras, N., and Rich, P. 2003. Review article: The literature of higher education. *The Annals of the American Academy of Political and Social Science* 585: 211-213.

Cope, Robert G. 1981. *Strategic Planning, Management, and Decision Making: Higher Education Research Report No. 9.*Washington, D.C.: American Association for Higher Education.

Court, David. 1975. The experience of higher education in East Africa: The University of Dar-es-Salaam as a new model? *Journal of Comparative Education* 11: 193-206.

_____. 1980. The development idea in higher education: The experience of Kenya and Tanzania. *Higher Education* 9: 643.

Crump, L. 1989. Japanese managers-western workers: Cross-cultural training and development issues. *The Journal of Management Review* 8, 4: 48-55.

Cusumano, M.A. 1988. Manufacturing innovation: Lessons from the Japanese auto industry. *Sloan Management Review* 30, 1: 29-39.

Cutts, R.L. 1988. The construction market: Japan slams the door. *California Management Review* 30, 4: 46-63.

_____. 1992. Capitalism in Japan: Cartels and keiretsu. *Harvard Business Review* 70, 4: 48-55.

Czinkota, M.R. 1985a. Distribution in Japan: Problems and changes. *Columbia Journal of World Business* 30, 3: 65-71.

_____. 1985b. Distribution of consumer products in Japan. *International Marketing Review* 2: 39-51.

Dalen, B. VanDeobold, and J. William Meyer. 1962. *Understanding Educational Research: An Introduction*. New York: McGraw-Hill Book Company, Inc.

Del-Amen, R. 2003. The social prerequisiter of success: Can college structure reduce the need for social know-how? *The Annals of the American Academy of Political and Social Science* 586: 120-143.

Demaree, E. William. 1986. Keeping the open door open. *New Directions for Community Colleges* 53: 41-46.

Deming, W.E. 1980. What can American manufacturers learn from the Japanese. *Iron Age* 6, 3: 51.

Dewey, John. 1966. *Democracy and Education*. New York: Macmillan Publishing Company, Inc.,

Diesing, P. 1962. *Five Types of Decisions and Their Social Conditions*. Urbana: University of Illinois Press.

Dillion, L.S. 1983. Adopting Japanese management: Some cultural stumbling blocks. *Personnel* 60, July: 73-77.

Dixon, James P., et al. 1977. Future Nigerian linkages in higher education. *American Council on Education*. Bethesda, MD.: Eric Document Reproduction Service, ED 138, 139.

Doucette, S. Donald, Richard C. Richardson, Jr., and Robert N. Fenske. 1985. Defining institutional mission. *The Journal of Higher Education*. Ohio State University Press: 191-192.

Dougherty, K.J. 1992. Community colleges and baccalaureate attainment. *Journal of Higher Education* 63, 2: 188-214.

_____. 2003. The uneven distribution of employee training by community colleges: Description and explanation. *The Annals of the American Academy of Political and Social Science* 586: 62 – 91.

Dowd, A.C. 2003. From access to outcome equity: Revitalizing the democratic mission of the community college. *The Annals of the American Academy of Political and Social Science* 586: 92-119.

Downs, A. 1967. *Inside Bureaucracy*. Boston: Little Brown, Revised in 1994 by Waveland Press in Illinois.

Drucker, P. F. 1981. Behind Japan's success. Harvard Business Review 49, 2: 83-90.

Drucker, Peter F. 1981. *Toward the Next Economics and Other Essays*. London: Heinemann.

Dubin, R. 1949. Decision-making by management in industrial relations. *American Journal of Sociology* 54: 292-297.

Duffield, J.S. 1995. *Power Rules: The Evolution of NATO's Conventional Force Posture*. Stanford: Stanford University Press.

Dunphy, D. 1987. Convergence/divergence: A temporal review of the Japanese enterprise and its management. *Academy of Management Review* 12, 3: 445-459.

Durlabhji, S. 1993. The influence of Confucianism and Zen on the Japanese organization. In *Japanese Business Cultural Perspectives,* edited by Subhash Durlabhji and Norton E. Marks. Albany, NY: State University of New York Press.

Dziech, W. Billie. 1986. Part-time faculty. *New Directions for Community Colleges*, No. 53: 1-6.

Dzierlenga, Donna. 1981. Sources and information: Research and planning. *New Direction for Community Colleges* 9: 105-116.

Educational Planning. 1970. UNESCO.

England, G.W. 1983. Japanese and American management: Theory Y and beyond. *Journal of International Business Studies* 14: 131-142.

Erickson, Frederick, and J. Wilson. Sights and sounds of life in schools: A resource guide to film and video for research and education. Research Series No. 125, IRT MSU: 39-62.

Erickson, Frederick, and J. Wilson. Audiovisual records as a primary data source. In Sociological Methods and *Research: Special Issue on Sound-Image Records in Social Interaction Methods,* edited by Grimshow, ed., II, 2: 213-232.

Esman, M.J., and S. Telhami. 1995. *International Organizations and Ethnic Conflict*. Ithaca: Cornell University Press.

Essid, Y. 1995. *A Critique of the Origins of Islamic Economic Thought*. Lieden and New York: E.J. Brill.

Etzioni, Amitai. 1964. *Modern Organization*. Englewood Cliffs, N. J.: Prentice Hall Inc. 1964: 5.

_____. 1967. Mixed scanning as a "Third" approach to decision making. *Public Administration Review* 27: 285-392.

Euben, R.L. 1997. Comparative political theory: Fundamentalist critique of rationalism. *The Journal of Politics* 59, 1: 28-55.

Farnsworth, L.W. 1995. Japan in political and economic change: Foundations for understanding. *Journal of Politics* 57, 4: 1169-1175.

Fasi, El. 1970. Address to the Association of African Universities. *Report of the Second General Conference of the Association of African Universities*. Kharatoum: p.27.

Fayol, H. 1949. *General Industrial Management*. London: Pitman.

Fegurson, C.H. 1990. Computers and the coming of U.S. keiretsu. *Harvard Business Review* 68, 4: 55-70.

Ferrarotti, Franco. 1985. Max Weber and the destiny of reason. *Theory Culture and Society: The Fate of Modernity* 2, 3: 182-84.

Field, H. 2003. Integrating tertiary education in Europe. *The Annals of the American Academy of Political and Social Science* 585: 182-195.

Fienberg, E. Stephen. 1977. Next steps in qualitative data collection. *Anthropology and Education Quarterly* 8, 2: 50-57.

Filley, A., R. House, and S. Kerr. 1996. *Managerial Process and Organizational Behavior. (2ⁿᵈ Ed.)* Glenview, IL: Scott Foresman.

Finn, Chester E. Jr., and Breneman, David W. 1978. *Public Policy and Private Higher Education: Studies in Higher Education.* Washington, D.C.: The Brookings Institution.

Fleur, A. 1974. *A Dictionary of Philosophy.* New York: St. Martin's Press.

Florio, Susan, and Clark Christopher. May 1982. The functions of writing in an elementary classroom. *National Council of Teachers of English.*

Floyd, Carol Everly. 1982. *State Planning, Budgeting, and Accountability: Approaches for Higher Education.* Higher Education Report No. 6. Washington, D.C.: American Association for Higher Education.

Frankel, Martin.1983. Sampling theory. In *Handbook of Survey Research,* edited by Rossi H. Peter, James D. Wright, and Andy B. Anderson, 21-67. Orlando FL: Academic Press.

Freire, P. 1993/1970. *Pedagogy of the Oppressed.* New York: Continuum Publishing.

Friedhoff, R.M., and W. Benson. 1989. *Visualization: The Second Computer Revolution.* New York: Abrams.

Galvin, J.R. 1991. *NATO Review: From Immediate Defense Towards Long-Term Stability.* Web Edition, No. 6.

Gannon, Philip J. 1983. World class colleges coming. *Community and Junior College Journal.*

Garvin, D.A. 1986. Quality problems, policies, and attitudes in the United States and Japan: An exploratory study. *Academy of Management Review* 30, 1: 126-142.

Geer, B. 1969. First days in the field: A chronicle of research in progress. In *Issues in Participant Observation,* edited by G. McCall, and J. Simmons, 144-162, MA: Addison-Wesley.

Giegold, C. William. 1978. *Management By Objectives: A Self-Instructional Approach.* New York: McGraw-Hill Book Company, Units 4 and 5.

Goetz, Judith Preissle, and Margaret Diane LeCompte. 1984. *Ethnography and Qualitative Design in Educational Research.* Orlando FL: Academic Press, Inc.

Gorden, R. 1980. *Interviewing Strategy, Techniques and Tactics.* Illinois: The Dorsey Press, Chapters 1 and 3.

Gormley, Jr., T. William. 1987. Institutional policy analysis: A critical review. *Journal of Policy Analysis and Management* 6, 2: 151-169.

Gortner, et al. 1997. *Organization theory: A Public Perspective.* Fort Worth, TX: Harcourt Brace College Publishers.

Gouldner, A. 1954. *Patterns of Industrial Bureaucracy.* Free Press.

Grandy, E. Richard, and Warner, Richard. 1986. *Philosophical Grounds for Rationality.* Oxford: Clarendon Press.

Green, L.H., and C. Wallat, eds. 1981. *Ethnography and Language.* New Jersey: Ablex Press, Chapter 7.

Green, R. 2003. Markets, management and "reengineering" higher education. *The Annals of the American Academy of Political and Social Science* 585: 196-210.

Green, R.T., and T.L. Larsen. 1987. Only retaliation will open up Japan. *Harvard Business Review* 65, 6: 22-28.

Griffths, R.C., 1980. Aid policy for universities in developing countries: a British view, *Higher Education* 9: 693.

Gross, Edward, and V. Paul Grambasch. 1968. *University Goals and Academic Power.* Washington, D.C.: American Council on Education.

Groves, Robert M., and Robert L. Khan. 1979. Sample designs for personal and telephone interview surveys. *Survey by Telephone.* Orlando FL: Academic Press: 15-37.

Grubb, W.N., N. Badway, and D. Bell. 2003. Community colleges and the equity agenda: The potential of noncredit education. *The Annals of the American Academy of Political and Social Science* 586, 218-240.

Gulick, L.H., and L. Urwick, eds. 1973. *Papers on the Science of Administration.* New York: Institute of Public Administration.

Gumport, P.J. 2003. The demand-response scenario: Perspectives of community college presidents. *The Annals of the American Academy of Political and Social Science* 586, 38-61.

Hackman, J.R., and R. Wagerman. 1995. Total quality management: Empirical, conceptual and practical issues. *Administrative Science Quarterly* 40: 309-342.

Hage, J., and A. Aiken. 1969. Routine technology, social structure and organizational goals. *Administrative Science Quarterly* 14: 366-376.

_____. 1970. *Social Change in Complex Organizations.* New York: Random House.

Halstead, D. Kent. 1974. *Statewide Planning in Higher Education.* Washington, D.C.: U.S. Government Printing Office.

Hankins, J.N. 1989. What makes the community college distinctive? *New Directions for Community Colleges* 65, 11-21.

Hanson, Jean Shirley. 1975. *The Principal and Accountability: A Study of the Relationships Among Elementary Principals' Ratings, Principal Autonomy, and Student Achievement.* Ph.D. dissertation, Michigan State University.

Harper, A. William, ed. 1981. *Community and Junior College Journal.* Washington, D.C.: 8 (51).

Harris, P.R., and R.T Moran. 1991. *Managing Cultural Differences.* Houston, TX. Gulf Publishing Company.

Hartleb, David, and William Vilter. 1986. The short-term cost effectiveness of part-time faculty creates long-term losses. *New Directions for Community Colleges* 53: 15-22.

Hayes, H. Robert. 1985. Strategic planning—forward in reverse? *Harvard Business Review* 6: 111.

Heads of State and Government. 1989. *Declaration. Treaty North Atlantic Council.* Brussels, May 29-30. Internet Address: www.nato.int/docu/comm/c890530a.htm.

Hearn, C. Hames, and B. Richard Heydings. 1985. Scanning the university's external environment. *Journal of Higher Education* 56, 4: 419-420.

Hedberg, B.P. Nystrom, and W. Starbuck. 1976. Camping on seesaws: Prescriptions for a self-designing organization. *Administrative Science Quarterly* 21: 41-65.

Hegel, G.W.F. 1997. Reason in history-classics. In *From Plato to Nietzsche: Philosophic Classics,* edited by Forrest E. Baird, and Walter Kaufmann. Upper Saddle River, N.J. Prentice Hall.

Hesburgh, Theodore M. 1985. *The Hesburgh Papers: Higher Values in Higher Education.* Kansas City: Andrews and McMell Inc.

Higher Education in East Africa: Report of the Working Party on Higher Education in East Africa. July-August, 1955, p. 28.

Higgins, M. Hames, and W. Jullian Vincze. 1983. *Strategic Management and Organizational Policy.* Text and Cases. 3rd ed. Chicago: The Dryden Press: 2.

Hines, E.R., ed. 1988. *Higher Education and State Governments.* ERIC: ASHE.

Hohne, K.H., et al. 1994. Medical volume visualization based on intelligent volumes. In *Scientific Visualization: Advances and Challenges,* edited by L. Rosenblum, R.A. Earnslow, J. Encarnacao, H. Hagan, A. Kaufman, S. Klimenko, G. Nielson, F. Post, and S. Thalmann, 21-35. San Diego, CA: IEEE Computer Society Press/Academic Press.

Hori, S. 1993. Firing Japan's white-collar economy a personal view. *Harvard Business Review* 71, 6: 157-172.

Hoverland, Hal, Pat McInturff, and Tapie C.E. Rohn. 1986. Editors' notes. *New Directions for Higher Education* 55: 1-3.

Hyslop, J.M. 1984. *The University of East Africa.* Minerva, Vol. II, No. 3: 286-301.

Ibe, M., and N. Sato. 1989. Educating Japanese leaders for a global age: The role of the international education center. *The Journal of Management Development* 8, 4: 41-47.

Ives, D. Edward. 1984. *The Tape-Recorded Interview: A Manual for Field Workers in Folklore and Oral History.* Knoxville: The University of Tennessee Press.

Ivory, M. 2003. The social context of applied science: Model undergraduate program. *The Annals of the American Academy of Political and Social Science* 585: 154-181.

Jacobs, J.A., and Winslow S. 2003. Welfare reform and enrollment in postsecondary education. *The Annals of the American Academy of Political and Social Science* 586: 194-217.

Jedamus, Paul, et al. 1981. *Improving Academic Management: A Handbook of Planning and Institutional Research.* San Francisco: Jossey-Bass Publishers.

Jefferson, E. Murphy. 1976. *Creative Philanthropy: Carnegie Corporation and Africa 1953-1973.* New York: Teachers College Press, Columbia University: 2.

Jensen, M.C. 1998. *Foundations of Organizational Strategy.* Cambridge, MA: Harvard University Press.

Johnson, B. Lamar. 1969. *Islands of Innovation Expanding: Changes in the Community College.* Los Angeles: Glencoe Press.

Johnson, C. 1986. *MITI and the Japanese Miracle: The Growth of Industrial Policy* 1925-1975. Tokyo: Charles E. Tuttle Co.

Johnson, Jerry Wright. 1975. *An Examination of the Management and Planning in Higher Education.* Ph.D. dissertation, University of Arkansas: 50.

Johnson, P. 1988. *The Flight of Reason. Intellectuals.* New York: Harper Perennial.

Kajubi, W. Denteza. 1984. Higher education and the dilemma of national building in Africa: A retrospective and prospective view. In *Insights into African Education,* edited by Andrew Taylor, 37. New York: Teacher's College Press.

Kappen, T.R. 1995. *Cooperation among Democracies: The European Influence on U.S. Foreign Policy.* Princeton: Princeton University Press.

Karabel, Jerome. 1986. Community colleges and social stratification in the 1980's. *New Directions for Community Colleges* 54: 13-30.

Karabel, J., and S. Brint. 1989. American education meritocratic ideology, and the legitimation of inequality: The community college and the problem of American exceptionalism. Higher Education: the International Journal of Higher Education and Educational Planning 18: 725-735.

Karabel, J., and S. Brint. 1989. The *Diverted Dream: Community Colleges and the Promise of Educational Opportunity in America, 1900-1985.* New York: Oxford University Press.

Katz, D., and R.L. Kahn. 1978. *The Social Psychology of Organizations.* New York: Wiley and Sons.

Kawesa, B. M. 1977. *Resource Sharing in Relation to Library Acquisition: A Case for East Africa.* Bethesda, MD: ERIC Document Reproduction Service, ED 176, 762.

Kearns, R.L. 1992. *Zaibatsu America: How Japanese Firms Are Colonizing Vital U.S. Industries.* New York: The Free Press.

Keddell, J.P. 1993. *The Politics of Defense in Japan.* Armonk, NY: M.E. Sharpe.

Keidel, R.W. 1995. *Seeing Organizational Patterns: A New Theory and Language of Organizational Design.* San Francisco: Berrett-Koehler.

Keller, George. 1983. *Academic Strategy: The Management Revolution in American Higher Education.* Baltimore: The John Hopkins University Press.

Kerr, Clark. 1980. Changes and for. *Community and Junior College Journal.*

Keys, J.B., et al. 1994. The Japanese management: Theory jungle – revisited. *Journal of Management* 20, 2: 373-402.

Kim, H.K., M. Muramatsu, and T.J. Pempel, eds. 1995. *The Japanese Civil Service and Economic Development. Catalysts of Change.*

King, Edmund J. 1979. *Other Schools and Ours: Comparative Studies for Today.* London: Holt, Rinehart, and Winston.

Kolodziej, E.A., and R.R. Kanet. 1996. *Coping with Conflict after the Cold War.* Baltimore, MD: Johns Hopkins University Press.

Korten, D. 1980. Community organization and rural development. *Public Administration Review* 40: 480-511.

Kottkamp, B. Robert. 1985. Review of in search of excellence. In Thomas J. Peters and Robert H. Waterman, Jr., eds., *Educational Administration Quarterly* 2:136.

Kuhn. 1962. *The Structure of Scientific Revolutions.* Chicago: The University of Chicago Press.

Kumar, D.D. 2003. Trends in postsecondary science in the United States. *The Annals of the American Academy of Political and Social Science* 585: 124-133.

Kumara, U.A.Y. Ha, and M. Yano. 1991. On understanding behavior characteristics of Japanese manufacturing workers: An analysis of Job climate. *International Journal of Intercultural Relations* 15: 129-148.

Lall, Geeta R., and Bernard M. Lall. 1979. *Dynamic Leadership.* Mountain View (Ca): Pacific Press Publishing Association.

Landau, M. 1973. On the concept of a self-correcting organization. *Public Administration Review* 40: 480-511.

Laurence, P.R., and W.L. Jay. 1986. *Organization and Environment: Managing Differentiation and Integration. Rev Ed.* Boston: Harvard University Press.

Lazer, W.S. Murata, and H. Kosaka. 1985. Japanese Marketing: Toward a Better Understanding. *Journal of Marketing* 49, 2: 69-81.

Legge, M. 1991. NATO Review: The Making of NATO's New Strategy. *Web Editions, No. 6.* Internet Address: www.nato.int/docu/review/article/9106-2.htm.

Leonardi, R. 1995. *Convergence, Cohesion and Integration in the European Union.* New York: St. Martin's Press.

Levin, J. 2001. *Globalizing the Community College: Strategies for Change in the Twenty-First Century.* New York: Palgrave.

Levine, C., R. Backoff, A. Calhoon, and W. Siffin. 1975. Organizational design: A post-Minnowbrook perspective for the new public administrative. *Public Administration Review* 35: 425-435.

Lewis, L.J. 1973. *Education and Political Independence in Africa.* Westport, CT: Greenwood Press Publishers.

Lincoln, J.R. 1989. Employee work attitudes and management practice in the U.S. and Japan: Evidence from a large competitive survey. *California Management Review* 32, 1: 89-106.

Lindblom, C. 1965. *The Intelligence of Democracy.* New York: Free Press.

Lindblom, C.E. 1959. The science of muddling through. *Public Administrative Review* 19: 79-99.

Litwak, E., and L. Hylton. 1962. Interorganizational analysis: A hypothesis on coordinating agencies. *Administrative Science Quarterly* 6: 397-420.

Lubbe, H. 1992. European unification is irreversible: Adelbert Reif in conversation with Herman Lubbe. *Universitas: An Interdisciplinary Journal for the Social Sciences and Humanities* 34.

Machyo, Chango. 1969. The University's Role in Africa. *East African Journal:* 25.

March, J.G. 1994. *A Primer on Decision Making: How Decision Happen.* New York: The Free Press.

March, J.G., and J.P. Olsen. 1976. *Ambiguity and Choice in Organizations.* Oslo: Universitetsforlaget.

March, J., and J. Olsen, eds. 1979. *Ambiguity and Choice in Organizations.* Bergen, Norway: Universitetsforlaget.

March, J.C., and H.A. Simon. 1993. *Organizations.* Cambridge, MA: Blackwell.

March, J.C., and H.A. Simon. 1993. *Organizations. 2nd Ed.* New York: John Wiley and Sons.

Markham, S.E. 1998. The scientific visualization of organizations: A rationale for a new approach to organizational modeling. *Decision Sciences* 29, 1.

Marlow-Ferguson, R, ed 2001. *World Education Encyclopedia: A Survey of Education Systems World Wide.* Detroit: Gale Group-Thomson Learning.

Maruyama, M. 1992. Lessons from Japanese Management Failures in Foreign Countries. *Human Systems Management* 11, 1: 41-48.

Master Plan Report for the University of Eastern Africa, (Kenya) for the General Conference of Seventh-Day Adventists Eastern African Division. 1981. Toronto: Matsui Baer Vanstone Freeman Architects, et al.

Matiru, Barbara, and Peter Sachesenmeier, eds. 1979. *Basic Training Course in Systematic Curriculum Development: Study Guide.* Institute of Education, Nairobi University, Bethesda MD. ERIC Document Reproduction Service, 196, 814. See also ED 196, 815.

Mazuri, Ali A. 1970. *The Role of the University in Political Development in Africa.* Bethesda, Md. ERIC Document Reproduction Service. ED 112, 741.

_____. 1978. *Values of the Educated Class in Africa.*

Mazzeo, C. 2003. Work-first or work-only: Welfare reform, state policy, and access to postsecondary education. *The Annals of the American Academy of Political and Social Science* 586: 144-171.

Mbirika, V.E., P. Abukuse. 1971. *The University of East Africa in Relation to the Needs of the People.* New York: p.169.

McCabe, Robert H. 1981. Now is the time to reform the American community college. *Community and Junior College Journal.*

McCraw, T.K. 1986. *America Versus Japan.* Boston: Harvard Business School Press.

McCune, J.C. 1990. Japan says sayonara to womb-to-womb management. *Management Review* November, 112-116.

McDowell, G.R. 2003. Engaged universities: Lessons from the land-grant universities and extension. *The Annals of the American Academy of Political and Social Science*, 585: 31-50.

McGrath, D., and Sear, M.B. 1991. *The Academic Crisis of the Community College*. Albany: Sunny Press.

McGuire, M. Hon, and Eldon Miller. 1986. Maintaining commitment to quality education. *New Directions for Community Colleges* 53: 57-63.

McKenna, G. 1998. *The Drama of Democracy: American Government and Politics*.

McKown, E. Roberta. 1975. *Kenya university students and politics*: 229.

McNeill, Barbara Lee. 1973. *A Critique of the Uses of the Rational Model in Educational Planning and Decision Making*. Ph.D. dissertation, Columbia University.

Mehallis, V. Martha. 1981. Improving decision making through institutional research. *New Directions for Community Colleges* 9: 95-102.

Mellander, A. Gustovo. 1986. Student enrollment: Ways to maintain the commitment. *New Directions for Community Colleges* 53: 47-56.

Merton, R.K. 1936. The unanticipated consequences of purposive social action. *American Sociological Review* 1: 894-904.

_____. 1940. Bureaucratic structure and personality. *Social Forces* 18: 560-568.

Millard, Richard M. 1976. *State Boards of Higher Education: Higher Education Research Report No. 4*. Washington, D.C. American Association for Higher Education.

Miller, Elden, and McQuire, M. John. 1986. Maintaining commitment to quality." *New Directions for Community Colleges* 53: 57-64.

Miller, T. George, and E. Clyde Learte,. *Strategic Planning in the Community College*.

Millett, John D. 1975. Higher education management versus business management. *Educational Record*: 221-225.

Mingle, James R., and Associates. 1981. *Challenges of Retrenchment*. San Francisco: Jossey-Bass Publishers.

Mlyn, E. 1995. *The State, Society, and Limited Nuclear War*. Albany: State University of New York Press.

Moore, M. Kay, and Baker III, A. George. 1983. The critical link: From plans to programs. *New Directions for Community Colleges* 11: 75-86.

Morgan, J.C., and J.J. Morgan. 1991. *Cracking the Japanese Market: Strategies for Success in the New Global Economy*. New York: The Free Press.

Morris-Suzuki, T. 1994. *The Technological Transformation of Japan: From the Seventeenth to the Twenty First Century*. New York: Cambridge University Press.

Mosher, F.C. 1982. *Democracy and the Public Service. 2nd Ed*. New York: Oxford University Press.

Mroczkowski, T. and M. Hanaoka. 1989. Continuity and change in Japanese management. *California Management Review* 31, 2: 39-53.

Mueller, B. 1987. Reflections of culture: An analysis of Japanese and American advertising appeals. *Journal of Advertising Research* 27, 3: 51-59.

Mulder, A. 1987. President of Lake Michigan College. *Tape-recorded Personal Interview Conducted on March* 16, 1987.

Mumer, M. 2003. The future of college access: The declining role of public higher education in promoting equal opportunity. *The Annals of the American Academy of Political and Social Science* 585: 97-117.

Munsey, R.C. William. 1986. Part-time faculty: The value of resource. *New Directions for Community Colleges* 53: 7-14.

Myran, A. Gunder. 1983.Strategic management in the community college. *New Directions for Community Colleges* 11: 1-20.

National Performance Review (U.S.) 1993. *Creating a Government that Works Better and Costs Less: The Report of the National Performance Review.* Vice President Al Gore. New York: Plume/Penguin.

Near, J.P., and R.W. Olshavisky. 1985. Japan's success: Luck of skill? *Business Horizons* 28, 6: 15-22.

Neelankavil, J.P. 1992. Management development and training programs in Japanese firms. *Journal of Management Development* 11, 3: 12-17.

Neufeldt, Harvey. 1991. The diverted dream: Community colleges and the promise of educational opportunity in America, 1900-1985. *Educational Studies* 22, 1: 60-65.

Ngiweno, Hilary, (ed.) 1985. The *Weekly* Review. Nairobi: 12-13.

Nigliazzo, A. Marc. 1986. The Fading Vision of the Open Door. *New Directions for Community Colleges* 53: 1-20.

Nishiguchi, T. 1994. *Strategic Industrial Sourcing: The Japanese Advantage.* New York: Oxford University Press.

North Atlantic Treaty Organization (NATO) 1998. *The North Atlantic Treaty.* Web-Archive. Internet Address: www.nato.int/docu/basictxt/treaty.htm.

Nzwilla, Philip Vamba. 1981. *The Development of Higher Education in East Africa from 1925 to 1981.* Ph.D. dissertation, University of Kansas: 13.

Oh, C.H. 2003. Information communication technology and the new university: A view of learning. *The Annals of the American Academy of Political and Social Science* 585: 134-135.

Ohio Board of Regents. 1974. *Planning Universities; Management Improvement Program.*

Ohmae, K. 1987. *Beyond National Borders: Reflections on Japan and the World.* Homewood, IL: Dow Jones-Irwin.

Olsen, J. 1979. Choice in an organizational anarchy. In *Ambiguity and Choice in Organizations, 2nd Ed.*, edited by James March and Johan Olsen. Bergen, Norway: Universitetsforlaget.

Orwig, Melvin, and J. Kent Caaruthers. 1979. *Budgeting in Higher Education: Higher Education Research Report No. 3.* Washington, D.C.: American Association for Higher Education.

Osbourne, D., and T. Gaebler. 1992. *Reinventing Government: How the Entrepreneurial Spirit Is Transforming the Public Sector.* Reading, MA: Addison-Wesley.

Oxenham, John. 1980. The university and higher level manpower. *Higher Education* 9: 643.

Paolillo, G. P., Joseph Jackson, and Peter Lorenzi. 1986. Fusing goal integration. *Human Relations: A Journal of Studies Toward the Integration of the Social Sciences* 39, 5.

Parekh, B. Satish. 1975. Long-range planning: An institution-wide approach to increasing academic vitality. *Change Magazine Press*: 13.

Parnell, Dale. 1987. A time for celebration. *Community, Technical and Junior College Journal*: 3.

Paulsen, B. Michael, and P. Edward John. 2002. Social class and college casts: Examining the financial nexus between college choice and persistence. *The Journal of Higher Education*, March/April: 189-236.

Pearce, A. John II, and Richard B. Robinson, Jr. 1982. *Strategic Management: Strategy Formulation and Implementation.* Homewood, IL; Richard D. Irwin, Inc.: 4.

Pearson, R.W. 2003. Editorial. A new look at the American Academy of Political and Social Science. *The Annals of the American Academy of Political and Social Science* 585: 6-7.

Pennings, M. Johannes. 1985. *Organizational Strategy and Change.* San Francisco: Jossey-Bass Publishers, Inc.: 1.

Perrow, C. 1967. A framework for the comparative analysis of organization. *American Sociological Review* 32: 194-208.

_____. 1970. *Organizational Analysis: A Sociological View.* Belmont, CA: Wasdworth.

Peters, Thomas J., and Robert H .Waterman, Jr.,. 1982. *In Search of Excellence: Lessons from America's Best Run Companies.* New York: Harper and Row Publishers.

Pinchot, G., and E. Pinchot. 1993. *The End of Bureaucracy and the Rise of the Intelligent Organization.* San Francisco: Berrett-Koehler.

Pincus, F.L. 1989. Contradictory effects of customized contract training in community colleges. *Critical Sociology* 16, 1: 77-93.

Porter, M.E. 1990. *The Competitive Advantage of Nations.* New York: Free Press.

Pressman, J. and A. Wildavsky. 1984. *Implementation: How Great Expectations in Washington Are Dashed in Oakland. 3rd Ed.* Berkley: University of California Press.

Pugh, D.S, ed 1987. Organizational theory: *Selected Readings.* London: Penguin Books.

Qubt, S. 1953. *Social Justice in Islam.* Translated by John B. Hardie. Washington, D.C: American Council of Learned Societies.

_____. 1991. *Ma'alim fi-Tariq* [Signposts Along the Road]. Beirut: Dar al-Shuruq [Originally published in 1961].

Rago, W.V. 1994. Adapting total quality management (TQM) to government: Another point of view. *Public Administration Review* 54: 61-64.

Ramsy, L William. 1981.Using research for planning. *New Directions for Community Colleges* 9: 25-34.

Rapoport, C. 1991. How the Japanese are changing. *Fortune* 122, 8: 15-22.

Redford, D.B. 1992. *Egypt, Canaan, and Israel in Ancient Times.* Princeton, N.J.: Princeton University Press.

Reed, S.R. 1993. *Making Common Sense of Japan.* Pittsburgh: University of Pittsburgh Press.

Research Committee. *The Impact of Community Colleges on Michigan and Its Economy.* Delta College.

Reys, G. de Los and Rich, P. 2003. Housing students: Fraternities and residential colleges. *The Annals of the American Academy of Political and Social Science* 585: 118-123.

Richardson, R.C. Jr., and L.W Bender. 1987. *Fostering Minority Access and Achievement in Higher Education.* San Francisco: Jossey-Bass.

Richardson, Richard C., Jr., Clyde E. Blocker, and Louis W. Bender. 1972. *Governance for the Two Year College.* Englewood Cliffs, N.J.: Prentice Hall, Inc.

Richman, Barry M., and Richard N. Farmer,. 1974. *Leadership, Goals, and Power in Higher Education.* San Francisco: Jossey-Bass Publishers.

Riposa, G. 2003. Urban universities: Meeting the needs of students. *The Annals of the American Academy of Political and Social Science,* 585: 51-65.

Ritter, J., ed. 1971. *Historiches Worterbuch der Philosophie* [Historical Dictionary of Philosophy]. Schwabe: Basel.

Rosenbloom, D.H. 1998. *Public Administration: Understanding Management, Politics and Law in the Public Sector.* New York: McGraw-Hill.

Rosenbloom, D.H., and R.S. Kravchuk. 2002. *Public Administration: Understanding Managements, Politics, and Law in the Public Sector.* Boston: McGraw-Hill.

Ross, R.S. 1995. *Negotiating Cooperation: The United States and China 1969-1989.* Stanford: Stanford University Press.

Roueche, E. John, and R. John Boggs. 1968. *Junior College Institutional Research: The State of the Art*: 2, 5, 6.

Rutherford, Desmond, and William Fleming. 1985. Strategies for change in higher education: Three political models. *Higher Education.* Amsterdam: Elsevier Science Publishers, V.B. Vol. 14: 433.

Rutter, S.D. Jr. 1998. NATO. Expansion fueled by U.S. capital. Internet Address: www.gl.umbc.edu/~sruttel/NATO.txt.

Ryan, J., and C. Sackrey, eds. 1984. *Strangers in Paradise.* Boston: South End Press.

Sagini, Meshack M.. 1983. *A Study to Analyze Kenya's Higher Education Between 1962 and 1982 and Their Implications for the University of Eastern Africa.* Master's Research Project, Berrien Springs: Andrews University: 23-24.

_____. 1985. *Organization of Community Education in Okemos, Michigan.* Unpublished paper. East Lansing, MI: Michigan State University.

_____. 1987. *Comparative Perceptions of Planners of Four Michigan Community Colleges.* Ph.D. dissertation, Michigan State University.

_____. 1996. *The African and the African-American University: A Historical and Sociological Analysis.* Lanham, MD: University Press of America.

_____. 2001. *Organizational Behavior: The Challenges of the New Millennium.* Lanham, MD: University Press of America, Inc.

Samuels, R.J. 1993. *Rich Nation, Strong Army.* Ithaca, NY: Cornell University Press.

Savage, D. Daniel (Ed.). 1987. *Community, Technical, and Junior College Journal.*

Scanlon, David C., ed. 1964. *Traditions of African Education: Education Classics No.16.* New York: Bureau of Publications, Teachers College, Columbia University Press.

Schatzman, L., and A. Strauss. *Field Research: Strategies for Natural Sociology.* New Jersey: Prentice Hall: Chapters 3 and 7.

Schwarz, B. 1997. Why Russians are worrying. Boston Globe, October 21. Internet Address: www.robust-east.net/NET/usa/russians.html.

Schwass, Rodger. 1986. The university and the concept of environmental education. *Universities and Environmental Education.* UNESCO: 33.

Scott, W.R. 1981. *Organizations Rational, Natural, and Open Systems.* Englewood Cliffs, N.J.: Prentice-Hall.

Selznick, P. 1949. *TVA and the Grass Roots.* Berkley: University of California Press.

Senge, P.M. 1990. *The Fifth Discipline: The Art and Practice of Learning Organization.* New York: Currency/Doubleday.

Shaw, K.M., and J.A. Jacobs. 2003. Preface: Community colleges: New environments, new directions. *The Annals of the American Academy of Political and Social Science* 586: 6-15.

Shaw, K.M., and S. Rab. 2003. Market rhetoric versus reality in policy and practice: The Workforce Investment Act and access to community college education and training. *The Annals of the American Academy of Political and Social Science* 586: 172-193.

Sheatsley, B. Paul. 1983. Questionnaire construction and item writing. *Handbook of Survey Research.* Orlando, FL: Academic Press: 195-230.

Sheffield, James, and Victor P Diejomach. 1972. *Non-formal Education in African Development.* New York: African American Institute.

Shils, Edward. 1983. *The Academic Ethic: The Report of a Study Group of the International Council on the Future of the University.* Chicago: University of Chicago Press.

Shrivastava, P., ed. 1996. *Academy of Management Review* 2, 1: 286-301.

Shulman, Herrnstadt Carol.1980. College and university endowments—or, singing the inflation blues. Washington: *AAHE Higher Education Research Currents.* Bethesda, MD: ERIC Document Reproduction Service, 181, 843.

Simon, H.A. 1960. The executive as decision maker and organizational design: Man-machine systems for decision making. *The Making The New Science of Management Decision.* New York: Harper and Row.

Sjoberg, Gideon, and Roger Neff. 1968. Selection of units and sources of data. *A Methodology for Social Research.* New York: Harper and Row: 129-134.

Skibbins, G.J. *Organizational Evolution.* New York: AMACOM, Endpaper.

Sloan, A.P., Jr. 1964. *The Management of General Motors. My Years with General Motors.* New York: Doubleday, Chapter 23.

Smith, Al. March 1986. Preserving and enhancing quality through effective program evaluation. *New Directions for Community Colleges* 53: 71-80.

Spaulding, Seth. 1977. What is Educational Planning? *Journal of Comparative Education.* 55.

Steck, H. 2003. Corporatization of the university: Seeking conceptual clarity. *The Annals of the American Academy of Political and Social Science* 585: 66-83.

Stevenston, H.W., C. Chen, and S. Lee. 1993. Mathematics achievement of Chinese, Japanese, and American children: Ten years later. *Science* 259, 5091: 53-58.

Stewart, T. Clifford. 1975. *The Role of the University. Strategies for Significant Survival.* San Francisco: Jossey-Bass Inc., Publishers: 18.

Sudman, Seymour. 1983. Applied sampling. *Handbook of Survey Research.* Orlando, FL: Academic Press: 145-194.

Sullivan, J.J. 1983. A critique of Theory Z. *Academy of Management Review* 8: 132-142.

_____. 1992. *Invasion of the Salarymen: The Japanese Business Presence in America.* Westport, CT: Praeger.

Sullivan J.J., and I. Nonaka. 1986. The application of organizational learning theory to Japanese and American management. *Journal of International Business Studies* 17, 3: 127-147.

Suzuki, N. 1984. Japanese MBAs: Frontrunners in the multinationalization of Japanese business. *The Journal of Management Development* 3, 4: 12-22.

_____. 1986. Mid-career crisis in Japanese business organizations. *The Journal of Management Development* 5, 5: 23-32.

Swiss, J.E. 1992. Adapting total quality management (TQM) to government. *Public Administrative Review* 52: 356-362.

Tachiki, D.S. 1991. Japanese management going transnational. *Journal for Quality and Participation* 14, 6: 96-107.

Tanaka, Greg. 2002. Higher education's self-reflexive turn: Toward an intercultural theory of student development. *The Journal of Higher Education,* March/April: 263-296.

Tanzi, V., and L. Schuknecht. 2000. *Public Spending in the 20th Century: A Global Perspective.* London: Cambridge University Press.

Taylor, F.W. 1911. Principles of Management. New York: Harper and Row.

Taylor, F.W. 1947. Principles of Scientific Management. New York: W.W. Norton.

Taylor, F. 1947. Scientific *Management*. New York: Harper and Row, 39-73.

Temple, J. Ronald. 1986. Weak programs: The place to cut. *New Directions for Community Colleges* 53: 65-70.

The Development of Higher Education in Africa: Report of the Conference on the Development of Higher Education in Africa. Tananarive: September 3-12, 1987, p. 14.

The Journal of Higher Education. 2002. January/February.

The State New. 1987. Educators must plan for 21st century, expert says. Friday, February 12: 14.

The University of Nairobi Act: Laws of Kenya. Nairobi: Government Printer, Chapter 210.

Thornton, James W., Jr. 1972. *The Community College, 3rd Ed.* New York: John Wiley and Sons, Inc.

Tokarczyk, M., and E. Fay, eds. 1993. *Working Class Women in the Academy: Laborers in the Knowledge Factory.* Amherst: University of Massachusetts Press.

Tsurumi, Y. 1982. *Managing Consumer and Industrial Marketing Systems in Japan.* Sloan Management Review 24, 1: 41-50.

Tung, R. 1984a. *Key to Japanese Economic Strength: Human Power.* Lexington, MA: Lexington Books.

Turabian, L. Kate. 1973. *A Manual for Writers: Of Term Papers, Theses, and Dissertations. 4th Ed.* Chicago: The University of Chicago Press.

Uhl, Norman P., ed. 1983. Using research for strategic planning. *New Directions for Instructional Research* No. 37. San Francisco: Jossey-Bass Inc., Publishers.

University of Nairobi Calendar. 1984/85: 18.

Van, Rooyen. 1978. *A Systems Approach to Budgeting in the Education Departments of Developing Countries: Lecture Discussion Paper No. 6.* Bethesda, MD: ERIC Document Reproduction Service, ED 180, 129.

Vaughan, D. 1996. *The Challenger Launch Decision: Risky Technology, Culture and Deviance at NASA.* Chicago: University of Chicago Press.

Vaughan, George B. 1984. Balancing open access and quality. *Change.*

_____. 1986. Part-time faculty: Nemesis at savior? *New Directions for Communities* 53: 23-32.

Vickers, G. 1961. Judgment the 6th Elbourne Memorial Lecture. *The Manager*, 31-39.

Vroom, V.H. 1974. A normative model of managerial decision making: A new look at managerial decision making. *Organizational Dynamics* 5: 66-80.

Vught, V. Frans. 1985. Negative incentive steering in a policy network. *Higher Education: The International Journal of Higher Education and Educational Planning.* Amsterdam: Elsevier Science Publishers, Vol. 14: 614.

Wagner, E. Thomas. 1986. Competing with the market place: The need to pay some faculty more. *New Directions for Community Colleges* 53: 87-92.

Warner, M. 1991. Japanese management education and training: A critical review. *Human Systems Management* 32, 2: 41-47.

Warwick, P. Donald, and Charles A. Lininger. 1975. *The Sample Survey: Theory and Practice.* New York: McGraw-Hill Book Company: 2 and 3.

Wattenberger, I. James 1983. New approaches to faculty compensation. *New Directions for Community Colleges* 53: 93-100.

Waugh, W.L. Jr. 2003. Issues in university governance: More "professional and less academic." *The Annals of the American Academy of Political and Social Science* 585: 84-86.

Weber, M. 1946. *From Max Weber: Essays in Sociology.* Translated by H.H. Gerth and C.W. Mills. Oxford University Press.

_____. 1947. *The Theory of Social and Economic Organization.* New York: Free Press: 328-340.

Webster's New Challenge Dictionary. 1979.

Weinberg, Eve. 1983. Data collection: Planning and management. *Handbook of Survey Research.* Orlando, FL: Academic Press: 329-358.

Weitz, A. Barton, and Robin Wensley. 1984. *Strategic Marketing: Planning, Implementation, and Control.* Boston: Kent Publishing Company: 2, 3.

Welzenbach, Lora F., ed. 1982. *College and University Business Administration.* Washington, D.C.: National Association of College and Univeristy Business Officers.

White, M. 1989. Learning and working in Japan. *Business Horizons* 32, 3: 41-47.

Wiley, David. 1977. *Africa: Establishing African Linkages, Past, Present, and Future.*

Wilson, J.Q. 1989. *Bureaucracy: What Government Agencies Do and Why They Do It.* New: York: Basic Books.

Wing, P. 1982. Emerging relationships between community colleges and state and local agencies. *New Directions for Community Colleges* 10: 51-75.

Wolin, S. 1960. *Politics and Vision.* Boston: Little Brown and Company.

Yarrington, Roger, ed. 1978. *Internationalizing Community Colleges.* Report of May 22-24, 1978, Assembly, Washington, D.C.

Yinger, J. Robert, and Christopher M. Clark. 1981. *Reflective Journal Writing: Theory and Practice.* East Lansing: The Institute for Research on Teaching: 1-31.

Zeiss, P. Anthony. 1986. Strategic management via institutional research. *New Directions for Community Colleges* 56: 35-48.

Zwerling, L. Steven, ed. The community college and its critics. *New Directions for Community Colleges*: 1-114.

Author Index

Subject Index

About the Author

Dr. Meshack M. Sagini distinctively passed the Cambridge Ordinary and Advanced level (diploma) examinations in 1966 and 1968, respectively. He also studied at the University of East Africa Dar-es-Salaam for two years, Middle East College in Beirut, Lebanon, for two years, Newbold College, England, for one year, and University of the West Indies for another year and received a B.Ed. (Honors) in History and a minor in Education in 1979. In 1982, he received a Masters degree in higher education management from Andrews University in Michigan. In 1987, he was awarded a Ph.D. in college and university administration from Michigan State University after submitting his doctoral dissertation on strategic planning and management. In 1997, Dr. Sagini completed a postdoctorate course in management and public policy from Oklahoma State University.

Professionally, Dr. Sagini is an educator with twenty-six years' experience in the teaching profession. Initially he worked as a teacher in elementary and high schools in Kenya during the late nineteen-sixties and early nineteen-seventies. He also served as a deputy high school principal for three years at Nyanchwa High School in Kisii, Kenya. In 1979/80 academic year, Dr. Sagini became a lecturer in the College of Education at the University College of the West Indies, Jamaica. At the same time, he intermittently worked as a sales manager for a Norwegian corporation (Norskbokforlaget) for eight summers (1976-83). Before the completion of his doctorate from Michigan State University, Dr. Sagini worked in the University as a Swahili language tutor for three years and as Graduate Administrative Assistant for one year. Between 1989 and 1991, he served as an assistant professor of Social Science and Organizational Psychology at Lansing Community College in Michigan. Since 1991, he has worked at Langston University as an Assistant and Associate Professor of History, Political Science, and Management Studies.

In 1999, Dr. Sagini actively participated in public policy research and analysis. He has written three books and several articles in professional journals. His first book, *The African and the African-American University: A Historical and Sociological Analysis,* was published in 1996. This book was written while

Dr. Sagini was an adjunct associate professor at the University of Oklahoma, Norman (1994 and 1995). The second book, *Organizational Behavior: The Challenges of the New Millennium,* was published in 2001. His third book is *Strategic Planning and Management in Public Organizations* (2005). He is also the Editor-in-chief of the *Journal of Scholarly and Scientific Perspectives: An International Journal of Scholarly and Scientific Research.*

Dr. Sagini has traveled extensively by visiting four continents (excluding Australasia and Oceania). He has been awarded a variety of honors, the best of which was given in the summer of 1997 by the American Political Science Association (APSA) for excellence in teaching. Second, Professor Sagini was selected for inclusion in the 8th edition of *Who Is Who Among America's 5% Outstanding Professors* in the country in 2004. He is a member of several professional organizations including the American Political Science Association, Oklahoma Political Science Association, Oklahoma League of Political Scientists, Mid-America Alliance for African Studies (MAAAS), Phi Beta Delta, Gale Group, LUISSO, African Studies Association, Association for International Development, African Professionals Association, and Langston University National Alumni Association. Currently, Professor Sagini is the President of MAAAS and Vice President of APA. Above all, Professor Sagini is an interdisciplinary scholar who writes proposals for funding, presents scholarly papers in professional organizations and teaches with power, interest, and excitement.